LIBERATING KOREA?

Arthur J. Paone

BELMAR PUBLICATIONS
504 – SEVENTEENTH AVENUE
SOUTH BELMAR, NJ 07719-3008
BelmarPub@aol.com

ISBN 0-9746366-0-6

Library of Congress Control Number: 2003097215

Dedicated to the memory of

VITO MARCANTONIO

(1902-1954)

Table of Contents

INTRODUCTION

Can a legitimate case be made for North Korea's mad scramble to produce nuclear bombs and a missile system capable of delivering them to the United States?

You should decide this for yourself. But before you do, learn about why the Koreans fear and distrust the US. It is history, and history is not often found on the front pages of our newspapers or on the evening news. So you may not know about the things I write about.

Imagine that you were born in a town in North Korea. Your uncle has been blind for most of his life – the result of an American bomb dropped on his village fifty or so years ago. A cousin is a strange recluse because she doesn't want people to look at her horribly disfigured face – the result of an American napalm attack during that Korean War. As a child she had been tending the fields with her mother when a US fighter swooped from the skies. You yourself have been brought up in their house because your parents were killed while riding to town one day in their ox-drawn cart — their bodies riddled by 50 caliber bullets from an American jet fighter. You don't live in the village you were born in because the Americans burned it down.

Because of that terrible war and the fear that the Americans might do it again, your country has had to maintain such a large army that it cannot afford much else. Your leaders for several years up to 2000 had been talking to the Americans about making some accommodation so your country would feel safe enough to reduce the burden of that large military establishment. The talks were going well. Your leader, Kim Jong Il, gave a lavish and warm welcome in 2000 to the American Secretary of State, Madeleine Albright, and everything was set to welcome the American President Clinton just before his term would expire at the end of 2000. But that did not happen because of the peculiar events following the Bush-Gore election. The country was negotiating consitutionally unchartered waters and the President did not want to out of the country at such a time. But North Korea, and the leaders of South Korea, felt that things were on track.

Then just a few months later in 2001 and with no warning a new President, George Bush, for no apparent reason slams the door in your country's face. On top of that he gratuitously insults and ridicules your leader. This Bush Administration then concocts an "Axis of Evil" linking your country, the Democratic People's Republic of Korea (DPRK), with some other imagined enemies of the US. You need to look at a map to see where the other members of this Axis are since you have rarely heard of them -- Iraq and Iran.

Finally, the Americans, step by step, set up one of the supposed allies in evil of yours, Iraq, for a turkey shoot. They invade that country even though it had made no hostile act against the Americans. The US of course is the most powerful nation on earth so it easily walks over the Iraqi defenders, using state of the art weaponry, and now occupies that ancient land. Treaties, promises, international law, the United Nations, the outrage of the rest of the world – none of that in the slightest deflected the Americans from their goal to change violently the government of another country.

Nothing could be clearer now to the DPRK, and probably to a dozen other countries, as to what course it has to take for survival: if North Korea does not want to be occupied by the Americans, it had better hurry up and develop a weapon that will keep the Americans away. If the Iraqis had the Weapons of Mass Destruction as the Bush Administration had claimed, they would not have been invaded. Just like with the Russians. The Americans had hated the Soviets but never invaded Russia because the Russians could drop the Bomb on American cities in retaliation. The same with China. But the Iraqi Government had mostly hot air for defense and they were quickly deflated.

Previously the tiny and impoverished Communist state of North Korea, left hanging by the collapse of its Soviet trading partners, had not wanted much. It asked only for a written promise from the United States that it would not attack the DPRK and for some financial aid to feed its people. But things are different now. No one can now trust the US. The American unilateral (not counting the British who went along for the ride to get back into their old colonial playpen) invasion of Iraq, enacting its new Doctrine of Pre-Emptive or First Strike, has given a geometric impetus to nuclear proliferation (Libya notwithstanding).

The message has sounded around the world – there is a new world order envisioned by the elite now ruling America. In that new world order only the actual ability to deliver a nuclear bomb to the United States will keep a disfavored country independent. Notwithstanding Washington and Downing Street's theatrical stream of misinformation, Hussein had been bluffing — he had no Weapons of Mass Destruction, much less any that he could deliver to America. But the North Koreans are not bluffing.

Few images better symbolize the harebrained mentality of the people now in control of our country than that picture of

Deputy Defense Secretary Paul Wolfowitz swaggering in the southern Philippines, surrounded by military bodyguards, but with a holster strapped to his shoulder containing his very own personal weapon (Associated Press Photo in <u>New York Times</u>, June 4, 2002). What intoxicating power! How many of us could live out so full the wildest of our childhood fantasies?

We have been trying to suppress agrarian guerillas in the southern Philippines since the day we took the islands from the Spanish in 1898. We called the peasant rebels Moros and then Huks, now they are being called some kind of "militant" or "terrorist" group, like the Abu Sayyaf. The endless American attempt to quelch whomever it is in the southern Phillipines who seem to have a mind of their own is even interwoven with the story of the legendary Colt .45 Automatic Pistol. That weapon with its massive blasting power had been specifically designed to be used against the Moro and Huk rebels in close combat. Now comes little Paulie packing a pistol. This time we will really put them down! I do not know, and I will not bother to spend the time to look it up, but I would bet that little Paulie never went through the rigors required to qualify as a Boy Scot, much less serve in the US Military. But now he is packing a pistol and advocating mayhem and violence around the world.

Over at the State Department there is the even more dangerous John R. Bolton, incongruously installed as the under secretary of state for arms control. The last person on earth you would want in such a sensitive position would be this zealot. Any foreign leader listening to this threatening bully would only accelerate his plans to develop nuclear weapons as a defense. In an interview with a <u>New York Times</u> reporter he supposedly indicated that the Bush Administration's policy on North Korea was best expressed by the title of a book written by a colleague at the American Enterprise Institute, "The End of North Korea."

On November 10, 2003 the embodiment of the Last Domino, Vietnamese Defense Minister, Pham Van Tra, was greeted on the steps of the Pentagon by the embodiment of the neo-Cold Warrior, Defense Secretary Donald H. Rumsfeld. No lessons were learned, however, as Rumsfeld continues re-enacting the role of yesterday's fierce warrior MacNamara, ignoring the wisdom of today's reflective MacNamara.

This is the crowd that Chairman Kim Jong Il has to contend with. He knows that he has been personally targeted by the President of the United States. George Bush, from his first days in office, has told anyone who would listen that he "loathed" Kim. How Mr. Bush could have developed this rather passionate feeling for a person he had never met and perhaps had never heard of until he read some briefing paper upon entering Office, is something of a mystery. Kim, however, wisely went into hiding after the Americans starting bombing Baghdad. The first bombing was a sneak-attack at night that needlessly blew up some poor soul's suburban home in Baghdad in an attempt to assassinate the Iraqi leadership. "Decapitating" an enemy, as they were calling it. The Americans were making up new rules for the game.

But do the **people** of the DPRK themselves, as opposed to their leaders, have anything to fear from the Americans? Indeed, George W. Bush's stated reason for his "loathing" of Kim Jong Il is the miserable lot of his people. So what of the little people of Korea, will they accept our generous and gratuitous offer to decapitate their leaders?

Americans do not get any definite images in their minds when they hear their leaders talking about liberating Korea again. We know that with the blood of our young men we saved at least part of Korea from the disease of Communism back in 1950. But exactly what happened and why is shrouded in the media distortions and government propaganda endemic during that period of hysterical anti-communism.

But to Koreans the images of that"liberation"are very vivid – and terrifying. Hundreds of thousands of Koreans, disfigured by American Napalm and phosphorous bombs, or living with missing limbs or blind or deaf because of American bombs and mines, have reminded their countrymen each day for the past 50 years what American"liberation"means.

By 1950 the Koreans had been squabbling among themselves for the 5 years since their release from the Japanese at the end of World War II. They were struggling to reorganize their society and move it from the feudal order of the past. After 40 years as a colony of Japan there was much that the Koreans had to work out among themselves. If left to themselves nature would have taken its course and the country would have grown into the shape and character that its people wanted.

They had no quarrel with the United States, thousands of miles away. Until the day our planes began the systematic destruction of their country, the Koreans had not killed or wounded a single American. There had been no Pearl Harbor, . . . no Bataan, . . . no Corregidor. No war had been declared against America. Yet we escalated this civil conflict among brothers into a brutal three year war, known to us as the Korean War, and brought the type of devastation to this small country that only a Great Power could bring.

During the Korean War the United States intentionally and without apology tried to kill every man, woman and child in North Korea, and, with less intention and some apology, did the same to our"allies"in South Korea. Korea became a playground for

American Air Power. New and bigger bombs were tested. Faster and more destructive fighter jets were developed. New techniques for destroying large dams, rice crops and cities were introduced. There was no North or South Korea to our Bombers, only "gooks" and targets. The deliberate burning of cities and killing of civilians in North Korea was called "strategic bombing;" while the inevitable burning of cities and the killing of civilians in South Korea was called "collateral damage." At a Senate Committee hearing on June 15, 1951, one year after the start of the conflict, the General who had commanded the American bomber fleet for the first six months testified that the devastation in Korea was already universal.

> *General Rosie O'Donnell:* "We have, to this date, in the
> Korean War, dropped **123,000 tons** of bombs; and in
> the entire [WWII] Mariannas campaign . . .
> throughout almost an entire year against Japan, **in
> which 57 major cities were flattened, we only
> expended 160,000 tons.**"
> *Chairman Connally.* "I am not concerned about **how many
> tons** there were . . . . You can talk about how many
> tons of missiles you dropped; **but I am
> concerned about the results** of the drops – what
> did you do?"
> *General O'Donnell:* "**The results** of the tonnage?"
> *Chairman Connally.* "Yes."
> *General O'Donnell.* "**I would say that the entire, almost the
> entire Korean Peninsula is just a terrible mess.
> Everything is destroyed. There is nothing
> standing worthy of the name.**"

General O'Donnell in 1951 thought that "everything" in Korea had already been destroyed with **123,000** tons of bombs. But the bombing nevertheless continued for another two years. Rubble was being ground into fine dust. Pilots were complaining about the boredom of bombing the same pile of ruins time and time again. By war's end in 1953, however, we would have dropped over an **additional 375,000** tons of bombs.

But that was way back in 1950. It was the Cold War. Can we say that it is different today? Are Kim Jong Il's fears that grew out of history well-grounded today? Would the Americans this time do the same thing or even use nuclear weapons against the Koreans?

I am afraid the answer has to be -- yes. The only reason we did not use atomic bombs in 1950 was a concern about the limited number of atomic bombs we had and the fear that the Soviets, for whose annihilation we were conserving the A-bombs, might retaliate with atomic bombs of their own. Now of course there are no more Soviets and America's arsenal of doomsday bombs is unlimited. So what would keep the US from nuking the Koreans?

From Kim Jong Il's view, it is one thing, and one thing only – the ability of North Korea to nuke the US or, maybe, one of its close allies, depending perhaps on the race of that ally.

■ From US Military Sources.

This book is a small attempt to explain why the Koreans legitimately fear and deeply distrust the Americans. The source material for my explanation will be American military records and publications. I will use mostly United States Military sources – either official military releases, testimony of military officers before Congress, official military biographies and reports and manuscripts produced by organizations and projects related to the US Military, like the United State Air Force History and Museums Program. For

LIBERATING KOREA?

the sake of transparency I set forth my sources in the text as I use them. The reader will forgive me for the voluminous use of quotations, the cumbersome citations by dates and the other open displays of sources that sometimes may get in the way of the narrative. I also use different typefaces and indentations to indicate different sources. I hope that the reader will be able to adjust to my unusual structure after a Chapter or two and then not even notice it. I want my evidence and conclusions to be instantly verifiable, as what happened is not easy to believe. Here are the exact words and deeds of the actors in that awful tragedy.

■　　　Diaries of the Generals.

The most interesting sources, I believe, are the diaries of the Generals. Many American Generals apparently have kept diaries of their war-time experiences. These diaries were not official documents nor were they officially sanctioned. In fact, they were frowned upon for obvious reasons. The motives for keeping these diaries must have varied. But one can tell that some of these authors, like General Orlando Ward, who commanded the 6th U.S. Infantry Division based in Pusan during the occupation from October of 1946 to December of 1948, wanted simply to keep track of his thoughts and to have a discourse with himself. On the other hand, a General like George Stratemeyer, Commander of the Far East Air Force during the first year of the Korean War, seems to be writing to posterity in his diary and consequently is less trustworthy. But still it is a diary and a lot more frank than the Official Releases he and his staff approved for the obfuscation of the American people.

The diary I rely upon primarily is that of General Stratemeyer. Stratemeyer's diary has been edited by William T. Y'Blood, carefully footnoted with very helpful explanations of

personalities and events, and published by the USAF in 1999. The
General had passed away 30 years earlier at the age of 79. Nearly
all the brackets [. . .] in the diary passages I reproduce were
inserted as explanations by the editor William T. Y'Blood. The rest
were added by me. (Stratemeyer, George E. , <u>The Three Wars of Lt.</u>
<u>Gen. George E. Stratemeyer: His Korean War Diary</u>. Ed. William R.
Y'Blood. Washington, DC: Air Force History and Museums
Program, 1999; US G.P.O. "Three' in the title refers to Stratemeyer's
personal battles with the Press (never enough credit to the Air
Force) and with the other military services (forever trying to horn
in on the Air Force's turf). These other wars take up more space in
his diary than the actual war in Korea.

Lieutenant General George E. Stratemeyer headed the Far
East Air Force during the first year of the Korean conflict (June,
1950 to May, 1951). He suffered a serious heart attack in May of
1951 and was replaced by Major General Earle E. Partridge. During
that first year General Partridge had led the US Fifth Air Force
operating under the Command of General Stratemeyer. Partridge's
deputy, who is mentioned frequently by those Generals, was Major
General Edward J. Timberlake, Vice Commander, Fifth Air Force.
The diary of General Partridge is less extensive than Stratemeyer's
as he was dealing more with the operational functions, but it
contains some important information. It has not been published,
though it deserves to be, and is available on microfillm from the
Air Force Historical Research Agency, Maxwell AFB (Roll No.
A1844, Call No. 168.7014-1). (www.maxwell.af.mil/au/afhra)

Since the heart of this work is General Stratemeyer's diary
and as he left Korea in May, 1951, most of my narrative deals with
the first year of the war. However, that is when most of the
movement and destruction occurred up and down the Korean
peninsula, with the war stalemated in the summer of 1951 at about

where it had started in June of 1950 and remained that way till final armistice on July 27, 1953.

- **Bolding**, *italics* and <u>underling</u> text.

I have emphasized certain words or phrases in the sources I quote, including the diaries, newspapers and books, by either making the text bold, underlining or by putting them into italics. I do this for clarity or to editorialize. Since I do it so often I have not noted that the emphasis was by me and not by the source. Therefore unless I note that it was that way in the original, the emphasis was added by me.

- THANKS FOR THE PICTURES . . . AND CAPTIONS!

Thanks to the privates, corporals, sergeants, lieutenants and captains in the US Army and to the airmen of the Air Force for the photographs they took in Korea. I have given the names of the Army photographers in most cases where they are identified on the photos I borrowed from the National Archives. The Air Force as a matter of practice did not identify the individual photographers. For the sake of authenticity I have almost always copied the captions as originally supplied by the Army or the Air Force with each photograph. I put the original caption in quotation marks. The reader needs to be a little careful about taking some of the captions without a grain of salt. After all, they were written in the heat of battle and many were intended as propaganda to bolster American domestic morale or slant the facts for some other reason.

■ **Tip of the Iceberg**.

I am always awed by the mass of material that has been preserved for history in the U. S. National Archives (cited as "N.A.") whenever I visit. But I am realistic enough to appreciate that not every decision or act has left a paper trail. In addition, the people who allowed their records to get to the National Archives were not always willing to let us see everthing. Much, I suspect, has been lost along the way.

MAPS

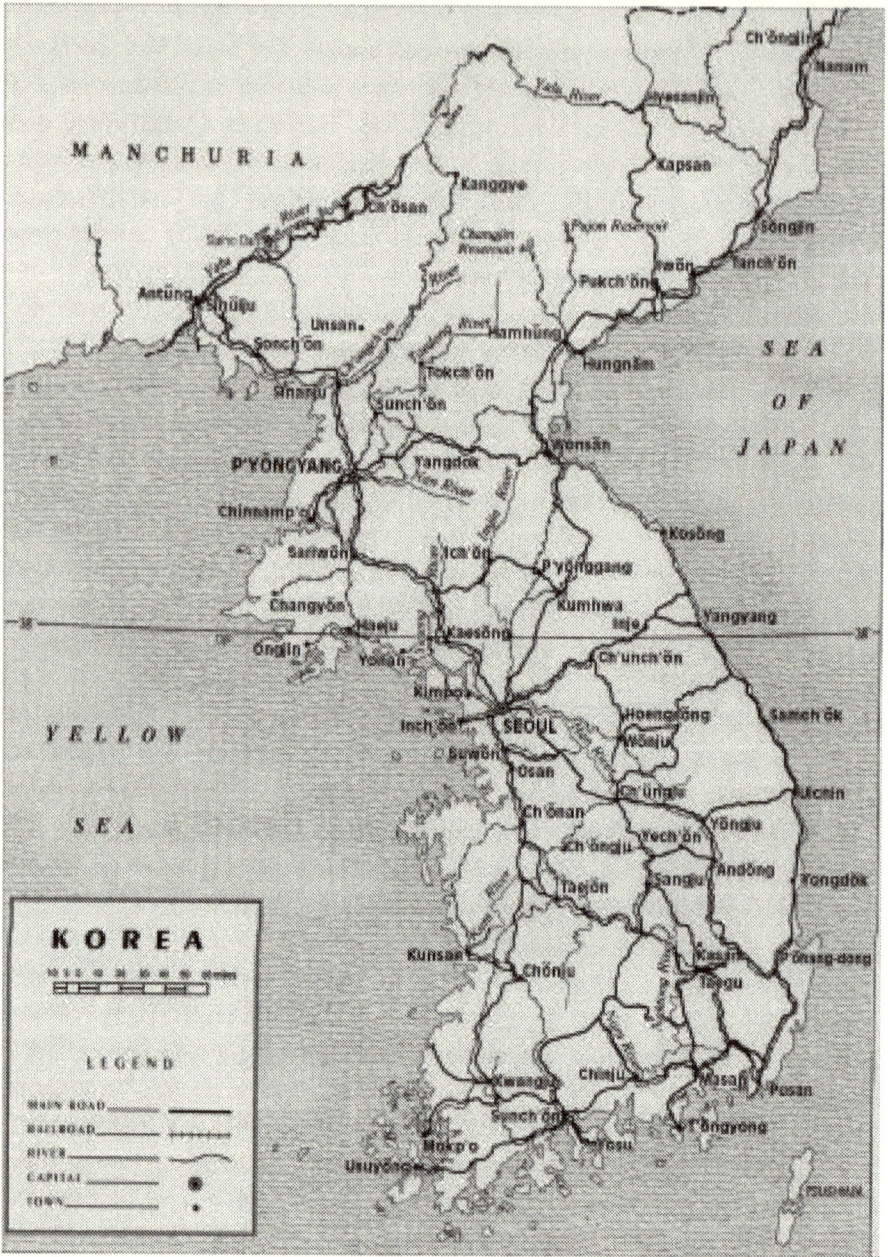

Korea 1950   (Y'Blood, *The Three Wars of Lt. Gen. George E. Stratemeyer*)

A

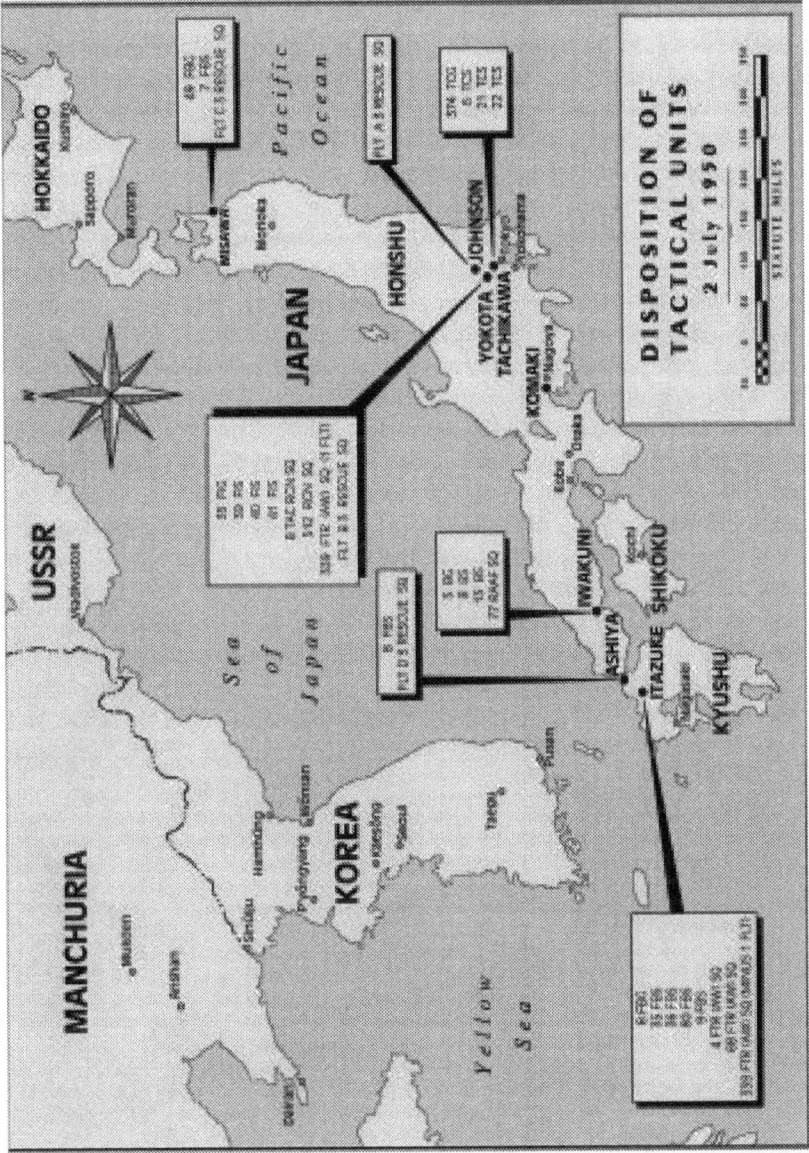

Disposition of UN Tactical Units, July 2, 1950 *(Y'Blood)*

B

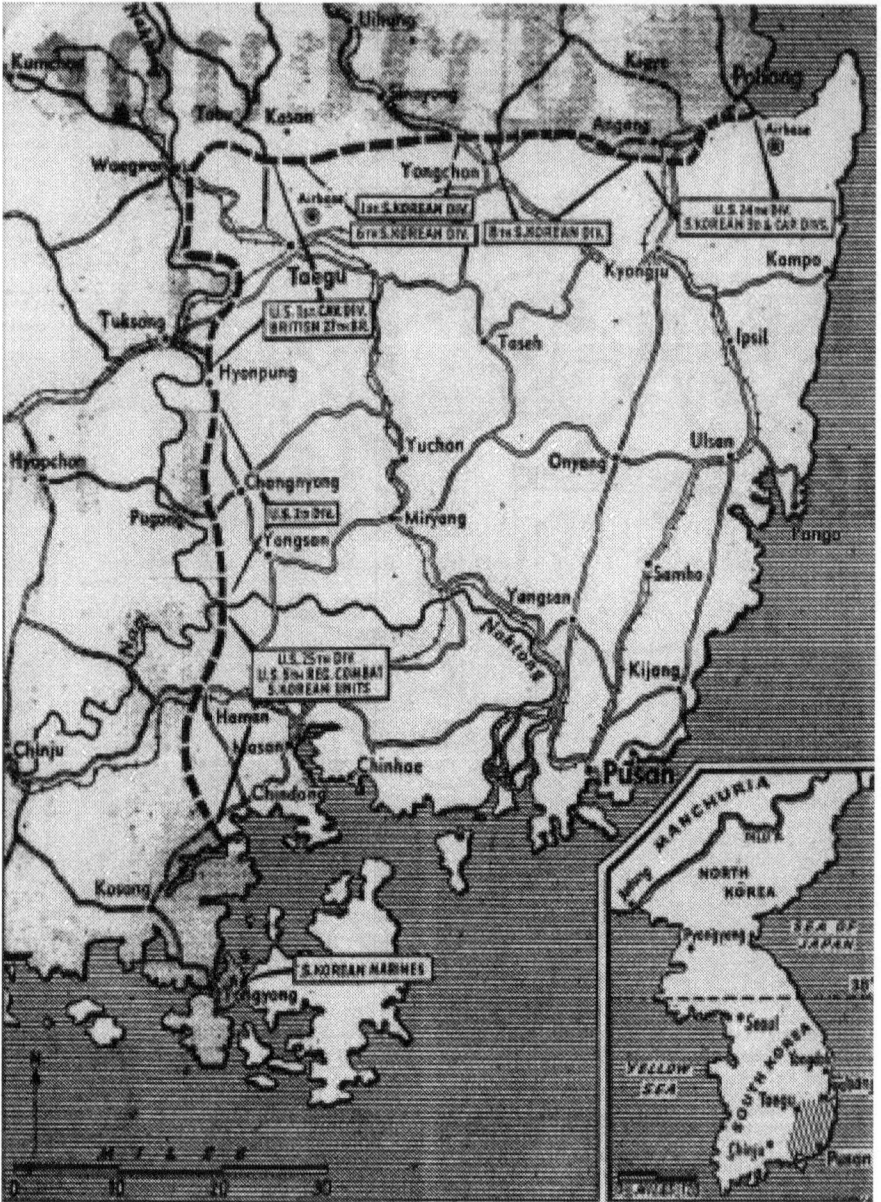

Pusan Perimeter September 13, 1950 (*New York Herald Tribune*)

C

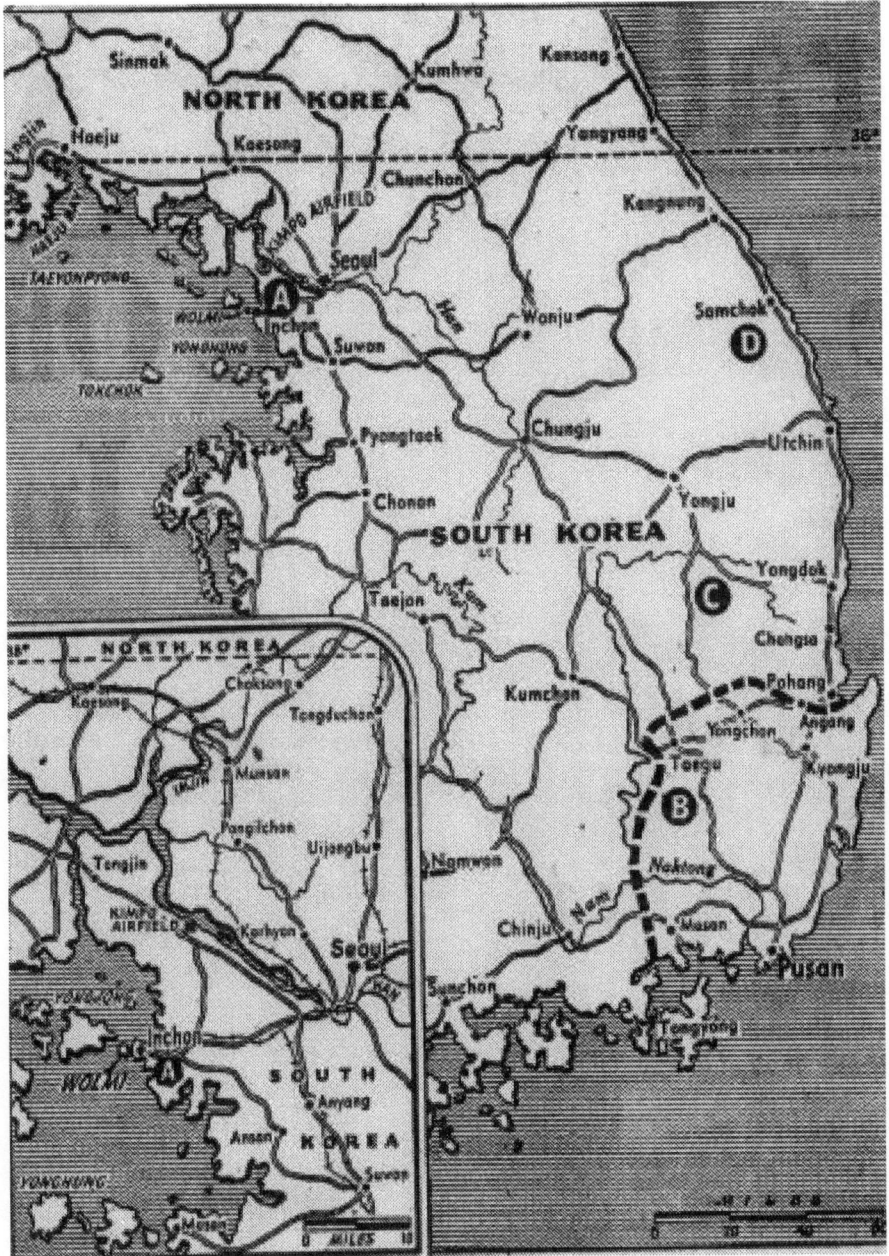

Pusan Perimeter September 16, 1950 *(Jack Luboff, New York Herald Tribune)*

D

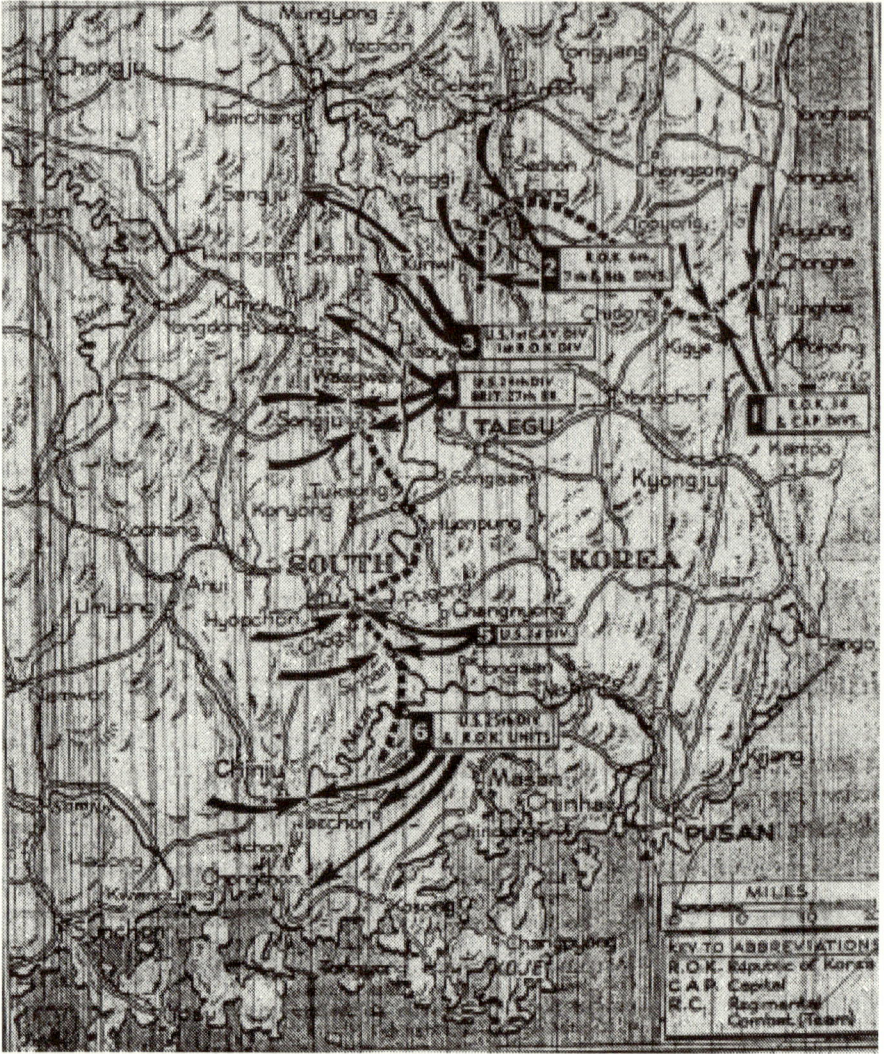

Pusan Perimeter September, 1950 (*New York Times*)

E

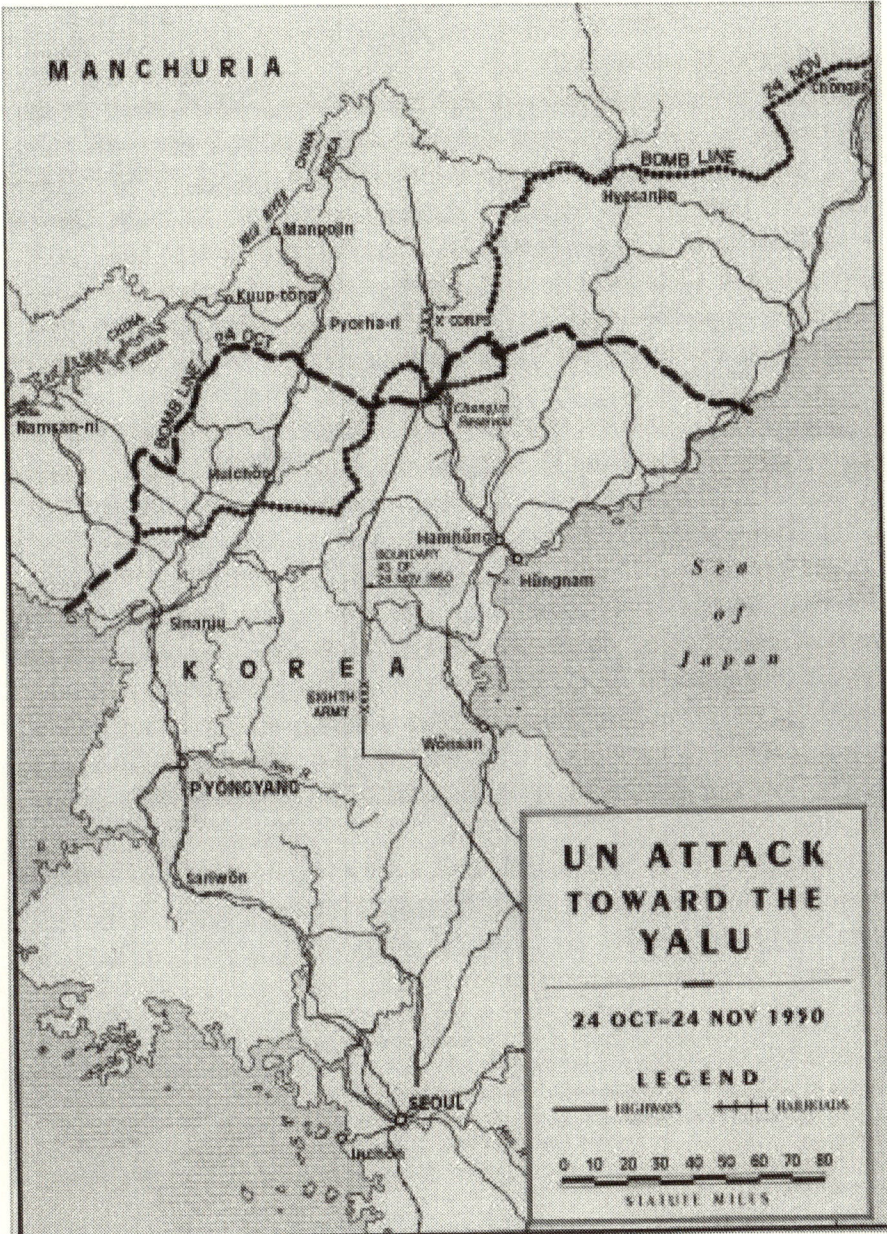

UN Attack Toward the Yalu   *(Y'Blood)*

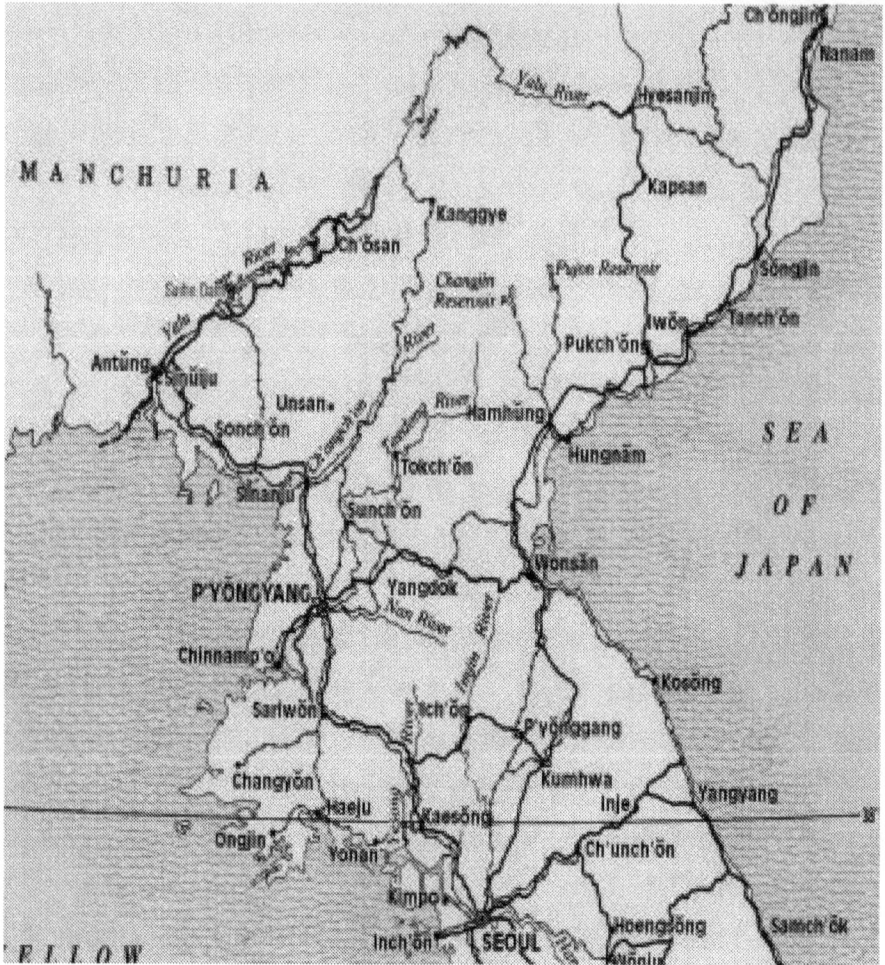

Northern Korea   *(Y'Blood)*

G

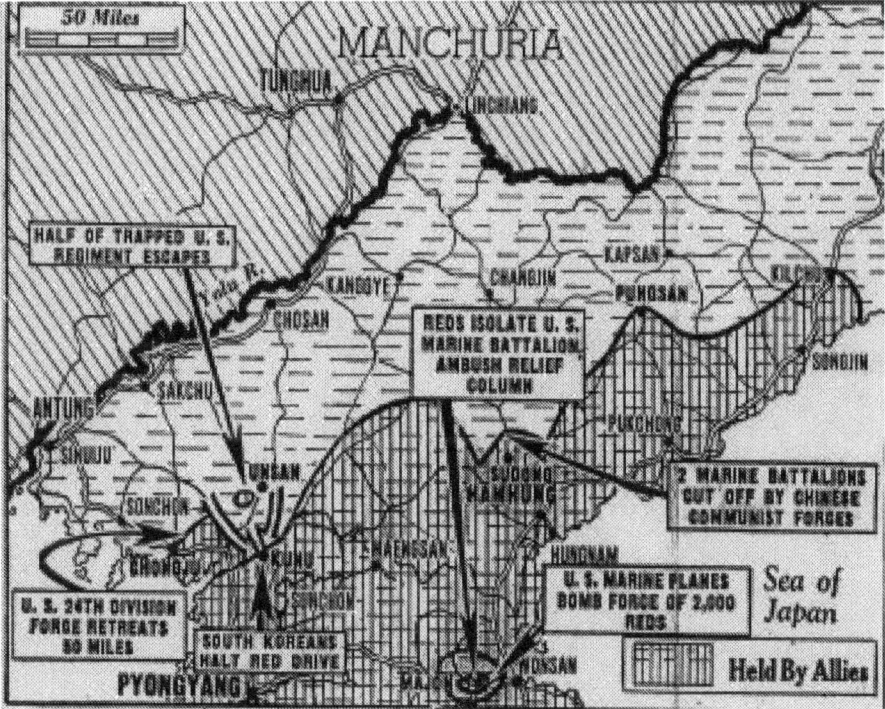

Retreat From the Yalu   (*Washinton Post*)

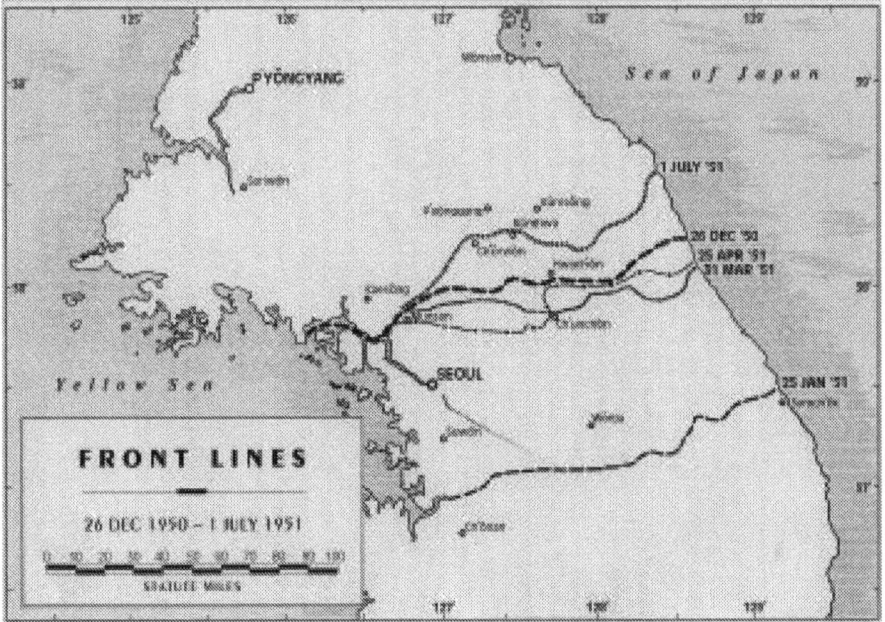

Stalemate   (*Y'Blood*)

H

CHAPTER I

CIVIL WAR IN KOREA

From Major General Earle Partridge's Sunday, 25 June 1950 [Tokyo time] diary entry:

> Returned to learn of invasion of South Korea by North Korea Army. ...374th [Troop Carrier Wing] and 8th [Fighter–Bomber Wing] were alerted to implement FAF [Fifth Air Force] Ops Plan #4. [Plan for evacuation of U.S. civilians and military personnel from Korea.] ....War officially declared by North Koreans 1100. Conference at my house about 1900. ... White [Lt. Col. John M. White, Jr. FEAF A–2] expressed view that U.S. would abandon South Korea to Reds. I disagree. This line of action is unthinkable and I await with interest the policy of the U.S. JCS.

Major General Earle Partridge's diary entry, Monday, 26 June 1950:

> General Almond [Major General Edward M. Almond, MacArthur's deputy chief of staff] called to relay information which he had just received from Colonel Wright [Col. W.H.S. Wright, acting chief of Korean Military Advisory Group, KMAG] in Korea. He stated that one of our Mustangs had jettisoned two tanks in the Seoul area and that one of these struck and killed six Koreans. The General was disturbed that our aircraft were avoiding combat rather than engaging and destroying the North Korean airplanes. He directed me to take the necessary action to insure that our AF patrols maintain an aggressive attitude in the accomplishment of their mission. (General Almond was especially caustic regarding the failure of one of our F-82 pilots to shoot down a Yak [North Korean fighter airplane] which flew over Inchon anchorage. The F-82 was 'bounced' but not shot at. Pilot of '82 ducked into the low cloud and when he came out seconds later, Yak had disappeared. . . .)

Major General Partridge was acting as the Commander of the Far East Air Force in the temporary absence of his Commander, Lieutenant General George Stratemeyer, who happened to be in Washington for meetings. Early the next morning, Tuesday, June 27th, General Partridge issued from his headquarters in Tokyo instructions to his pilots taking off from American bases in Japan to *"use aggressive action in the event that hostile aircraft interfere or attempt to interfere with FAF mission [of evacuation] or acts in an* unfriendly manner to South Korea forces or our own."

General Partridge, Tuesday, 27 June 1950:

A redline [very important message from senior official requiring prompt and special handling] from General Vandenberg [Hoyt S. Vandenberg, Chief of Staff, USAF] requested further data as to why our F-82 pilot avoided combat over Inchon yesterday. . . .

I was again called to the Dai Ichi Building [building in Tokyo where General Douglas MacArthur and the American occupation authorities were head-quartered] for a teleconference with Washington. Present were Generals MacArthur [Commander in Chief Far East, CINCFE], Almond, Hickey [Major General Doyle O. Hickey, Deputy Chief of Staff, Far East Command, FEC], Beiderlinden, Willoughby [Major General Charles Willoughby, headed FEC G-2, Intelligence], Wright and Eberle, and Admiral Joy [Vice Admiral C. Turner Joy, Commander Naval Forces, Far East].

The teleconference directed a major reversal of policy on the part of the US Government. CINCFE [General MacArthur] was directed to employ such naval and Air Forces as were at his disposal to bolster the SK [South Korean] forces and restore the territorial integrity of that nation. . . .

CINCFE turned to me and directed immediate action ... The general was almost jubilant at the end of the conference.

He outlined the far-reaching results which will be achieved if the air effort can be made effective tonight and tomorrow. He stressed again and again the necessity of hitting the North Korean forces in the next 36 hours with every resource at our disposal, carrying the action through the night if this is possible. He expressed the firm conviction that vigorous action by the FAF [Fifth Air Force – the unit under Partridge's command and stationed in Japan] would result in driving the North Korean forces back into their territory in disorder. . . .

According to General Partridge, the old General was "jubilant" that Washington had reversed its long and carefully crafted policy on Korea, which MacArthur himself had helped to shape, and decided instead for war on the mainland of Asia. MacArthur was 70 by this time and only a retirement from his Emperor-like status in the Far East had been looming ahead for him. Now, at long last, his realm was again the center of attention. Destiny was calling on him one more time.

MacArthur, like Partridge and a lot of other people, was surprised by the American reversal of policy. The Army had been trying from day one of the occupation of Korea in 1945 to get out. They considered Korea to be of no

strategic importance to the US and it was risky to have troops on such a vulnerable peninsula. If war with Russia started the troops on the peninsula would be slaughtered. The United States Air Force could neutralize Korea from
Japan and Okinawa and keep it from being used by the Russians. Mac Arthur was asked by the Joint Chiefs in 1947 for his opinion on Korea and he strongly advocated a pullout of the 45,000 occupation troops. In addition, he advised that no commitments be given to the Koreans, as their country would be indefensible in a war with Russia or China.

By late 1949 according to James F. Schnabel, an Army intelligence officer who served in the Far East and later wrote an official history of the Korean war, the American intelligence community assumed that there was going to be a civil war between North and South Korea by the next summer and that the North would conquer the South. In the intelligence briefing he received when he reported to duty in Tokyo, he was told this and "the point was not emphasized particularly and the fact seemed to be accepted as regrettable but inevitable."

The Russians had pulled out their occupation troops from North Korea in 1948 and the US was looking a little "colonial" in keeping its troops there. However, there was an element in Congress and in the State Department that wanted to keep any piece of real estate in the world away from the Communists. These groups' motives were varied – containment of Communism at any cost, twitching Russia's nose by creating a "test case for democracy" on the borders of Red Russia and Red China, or as Congressman Eaton (Charles A. Eaton, R. NJ), stated during the House Committee on Foreign Affairs hearing (June 16 - 21, 1949) on an economic aid bill for Korea:

> **We have 1 ½ billion brown people in the Orient.** They are for the first time conscious of their nationhood and their passion to be free. That is a revolution of tremendous world importance in itself.

There are two dominant forces in the world, the United States and Russia. Russia is making tremendous progress in the Orient. She has practically taken over China and proposes eventually to take over Japan. Now, how are we going to meet that?

Are we going to meet it with a mailed fist and an iron will or are we going to meet it with classifications and soft words? We might just as well spit in the face of a hurricane as to try that.
. . .

What is the decision of the U.S. Government? Are we going to stand up and notify Russia and the world that we are there in the Orient, we are going to stay there, and we **are not going to permit the Orient to come under the control of slavery** if it is possible to prevent it.

Congressman Eaton from New Jersey was a powerful man in Washington, the ranking or highest Republican on the Foreign Affairs Committee. He would be one of the House leaders invited to the White House by Truman during the first few days of the Korean conflict.

The Foreign Affairs Committee in June, 1949, was conducting hearings on the "Korean Aid Act of 1949," a bill introduced by the Administration proposing $150,000,000 in economic aid to Korea. Some Members of the Committee utilized the hearings to question the wisdon of the Administration's plans to withdraw the remaining 7,000 tactical troops from Korea.

James Webb, Under Secretary of State, was one of the Administration's main witnesses but he preferred to have George Kennan answer most of the questions "since I am very new at this business." He introduced Kennan as having just "been nominated by the President as Counselor of the Department, and who is our senior professional Foreign Service officer in the Department. He is the head of our Policy Planning staff. . . ."

Kennan, a prolific author to this day, was already famous for his hawkish writings -- painting the Soviets as senseless Oriental beasts who could not be reasoned with but only "contained." The logical result of containment, the use of the military to enforce it, though clearly understood and promoted by Kennan's enthusiatic boosters like James Forrestal (banker, Secretary of the Navy and then first Secretary of the combined Department of Defense), supposedly could not be foreseen by one of its most prominent wordsmiths. A year later when Kennan was disturbed that every-one else seemed to translate contaimnment into war, he resigned from the government. He continues to write non-apologies that he really didn't mean it that way.

Congressman Eaton asked them the following question:

> "Do you think we should stay in Korea
> and make that a clinic demonstration of **our
> principles of civilization?"**

There is a distinct undercurrent in the arguments of some Members of Congress. References to "Christian" and "Our Civili-zation" and "OurValues" come up repeatedly. Congressman Eaton would touch the same chord again, this time with even more curious language, on January 19, 1950 during debate on the House Floor for this same Bill:

> "The situation is tragic from our
> American point of view, because, if under the
> leadership and world program of the Russian
> Communists they are able to mass against **a
> handful of free, white folks here, such as we
> are**, with our traditions of democracy and self-
> government behind us, if they are able to amass a
> force of from a billion and a half to two billion of
> people against us . . . how are we going to main-

tain the civilization and the wonderful blessings
inherited by us from our fathers? . . . Korea [is] . . .
the last toe hold we have on the Asiatic Continent
. . ."

The Congressional Record shows that both Adam Clayton
Powell and his mentor Vito Marcantonio were in the Chamber that
day because they voted on the bill (against it). One would like to
have heard what they said to each other if they caught the New
Jersey Congressman's comments.

Back at the 1949 Committee hearings, Eaton's question about
keeping Korea for the sake of teaching "our values of civilization"
was answered by George Kennan on behalf of the Administration.
Kennan, a "blue blooded" diplomat who tacitly accepted Eaton's
value system, responded:

> **By armed force, no, sir,** because I do
> not think that is the answer, and I think there
> would be a real danger that if we were to do it we
> might make fools of ourselves and give the
> Korean Communists and the Russians a perfectly
> gratuitous little triumph . . .

> If one of the things we are afraid of is
> that Communist political sentiment might sweep
> down there, Communist penetration and Com-
> munist domination of the local political move-
> ments, that would happen with our troops there,
> and there is no worse position for our troops than
> to find themselves suddenly engulfed in a sea of
> adverse political sentiment.

> It is a question of defense by the
> southern Korean Government — what we call
> the legitimate Government of Korea, against
> Koreans from the North. I do not think our forces
> should be mixed in that. The Russians would love

to see that situation come about and they would
sit back there and laugh their heads off if we got
our forces engaged with any Koreans at all, and
there would be a strong temptation, then, on the
part of the people in southern Korea . . . to laugh
a little too, because they all, I think, like to see
occasionally thing happen to outsiders and the
forces of the big, white powers there. . . .

This was the set policy of the Truman Administration, and it
had been developed after careful study. The United States considered this tip of the mainland of Asia as the worst possible place to
have a showdown with Russia and it had no intention of allowing
itself to be dragged into a conflict on this indefensible peninsula.

Secretary Webb told the Congressmen that even having just
7,000 troops in Korea, the remaining occupational troops, down
from 45,000 at the beginning of the occupation in 1945, would
have a detrimental effect on the government and people of South
Korea in that it might create the false impression that the troops
would be there to fight, **"when they are not going to engage in a
Korean civil war."**

The Administration was requesting this $150,000,000 in
economic aid in addition to the arming and training of the South
Koreans for their self defense. As to objections that South Korea
was a police state under the authoritarian Sigmund Rhee whom
we had put in power, Mr. Kennan replied in effect that they were
all the same out there:

We realize that people are **not lily-
white anywhere** and throughout the **Far East
you are going to get a great deal of seaminess,**
a great deal of cruelty, a great deal of intolerance
and a great deal of inexperience in these groups. .
. .

If we can keep **these people** at least

independent and where they have possibilities for
a long term maturity of political institutions under
their own steam . . .

**I understand there is a possibility of
civil war in Korea. . . . I would not recommend
our getting our forces involved in there**. As I
say, I can think of nothing that would please the
Kremlin better than to see us get into a military
row **with a lot of Koreans**. . . .

State Department offcials were fully aware that
South Korea under Syngman Rhee was as undemocratice
a police state as existed at the time, but for Cold War
purposes they deliberately tried to mislead Congress into
thinking otherwise. Below at pages 38 - 39 I recite portions of a "Confidential Discussion," as it is titled in the
records, among the State Department's Far East experts
going on at that very time but not made public for decades
(Foreign Relations of the United States ("FRUS") 1950, Vol.
VIII, pp. 30-33).

At the same hearing the representatives of the Joint Chiefs of
Staff laboriously tried to explain to the Congressmen and Con-
gresswomen, some of whom thought that it would be nice to have
a "foothold" in Asia on the doorstep of Russia and China, why
Korea was of little importance to the United States and why the
United States should not get trapped into any fighting there.

Congresswoman Douglas (Helen Gahagan Douglas, D. Ca.)
asked:

"If the Army were to say, 'Well, it is
not safe to give up Korea and we are going to stay
for another year,' what would be the psychological
effect, not only in Korea, but throughout the rest
of that part of the world?"

Major General Charles L. Bolte, Director, Plans and Operations Division, Department of the Army, on behalf of the Military Establishment, answered:

> I am afraid that it would **create a delusion on the part of the Koreans**. Instead of their doing the building of their own forces, which we have been sponsoring, they might have an unfounded hope that the tactical units that we would have there, if we kept them there additionally, would become involved in case of an advance from North Korea, or even a Russian advance, and **we certainly would not want our tactical units involved in combat on the Korean Peninsula.**

Mrs. Douglas ironically would later lose her seat to Richard Nixon who attacked her as having voted with Vito Marcantonio on a number of issues. But she supported the Korean Aid Bill and later explained her position during the January, 1950 debate. She first quoted approvingly from President Truman's message to Congress on the bill:

> "'Korea [Truman said] has become a **testing ground** in which the validity and practical value of the **ideals and principles of democracy** . . . are being matched against the practices of communism. . .'"

And then she expressed her agreement with that concept:

> "The action of this House today, our decision to help the people of Korea in their fight for independence, or to **abandon them to slavery** will be our answer to the question of whether the Asian people can depend on our leadership."

Congressman Judd, (Walter H. Judd, R., Minn.), a Charter Member of the China Lobby, again at the hearings in 1949, wanted to know:

> "Are our naval and air forces in Japan
> going to be disturbed by the Russians getting a
> big base there at Pusan [South Korea]?"

General Bolte: "I think General MacArthur would be disturbed but he would prefer **not to be involved tactically on the Korean Peninsula.**"

Mr. Judd: "He would prefer to lose that base to the Russians rather than fight there himself?"

General Bolte: "Yes."

Later, *Congressman Lodge* (John Davis Lodge, R. Conn.)asked: "Why do we want to get out [of Korea]?"

Mr. Kennan:"Because it is **an exposed, unsound military position**, one that is doing no good, and we are anxious to get rid of positions of that sort."

The next day at the hearing some Congressmen kept on insisting that it would be dangerous to American interests in Japan to withdraw the remaining occupation troops from Korea. *Congressmen Vorys* (John M. Vorys, R. Ohio) observed:

> "I was told by a man who returned
> from Japan, Monday, who asked me what we
> were doing in Japan, that Japan was entirely
> indefensible from a military standpoint if the
> Communists took over the mainland. Would you
> care to comment on that statement or rumor?"

After a discussion"off the record,"*General Bolte* replied for the US Military:

"I would not agree with that. Very definitely we intend, in the last analysis, **if it came to a showdown, to hold on to Japan, Okinawa, and other islands in the Japanese archipelago.** . ."

Congresswoman Bolton (Frances P. Bolton, R. Ohio) inquired:

"The Army feels Japan is a very tenable spot, even if the airfields and so on in Korea become the property of the Soviets?"

After another discussion "off the record" General Bolte answered:

"That is so, Mrs. Bolton."

Mrs. Bolton persisted:"Where do you get your confidence?"

General Bolte responded:"I am familiar with our plans and we feel our bases are not only adequate but better."

Congresswoman Bolton:"The Communists can move down the coast to Sumatra and Ceylon and so forth? They can keep right on going without having to trouble themselves with inner China *[an embryonic Domino Theory?]*."

General Bolte:"We have arrangements with the Philippine Republic and have certain forces, air forces, in the Philippines by agreement. . . . We have other bases: Guam and Saipan, in the Pacific."

But Congressman John Lodge from Connecticut still could not understand how the military would say that it was not worth trying to keep the harbor of Pusan in South Korea, though his next question disclosed that he did not even know where it was.

Mr. Lodge:

> "General, as another Navy [?] man, I
> would be very much interested in having your
> comment as to the importance of the harbor of
> Pusan; whether you feel that the loss of that
> harbor, being, as I understand it, just a few [??]
> miles away from the island of Honshu [*Japan's
> main island is some 90 miles away*], would be
> serious to our position in Japan?"

General Bolte: "The only disadvantage in not holding on to the
Korean Peninsula is that it does not deny the use of the
Korean Peninsula to Soviet and Communist forces."

Mr. Lodge: "Do you mean there is no positive disadvantage in
our losing that port?"

General Bolte: "No, we are perfectly satisfied with what we
have."

Congressman Judd seemed to continue having a difficult time
in understanding, or accepting, that any part of Korea could not be
important militarily to the US: "We were told the other day that it
[Pusan] is the best natural harbor in all of Northeast Asia."

General Bolte: "It is a very fine natural harbor but our air bases
are well within range of any of those points, sufficiently to
deny them the use of it."

Nevertheless certain hawkish members of Congress were not
happy with the comments of the Generals from the Army, though
they had said they represented the Joint Chiefs of Staff. So Congressman Lodge asked for someone else to testify.

> "It just occurred to me, General, and
> this is in no way meant as a reflection on you, but

in order for this committee to pass in a responsible manner on this very important subject I thought it might be well to have naval testimony on this whole affair."

Accordingly and without protest the very next day Rear Admiral Edmund T. Wooldridge, Assistant Chief of Naval Operations, Department of the Navy, appeared on behalf of the Navy and Admiral Louis E. Denfeld, Chief of Naval Operations.

Congresswoman Bolton: "I understand there is a harbor in Korea."

Admiral Wooldridge: "Yes, there is. There is Pusan on the Southeast, and Inchon in the west central."

Mrs. Bolton: "Is it a good harbor?"

Admiral Wooldridge: "A relatively good harbor and relatively small."

Mrs. Bolton: "Would you be sorry to lose it?"

Admiral Wooldridge:

"If I may answer that indirectly, we would be sorry to see any harbor in the world go under Communist domination. But as far as the Navy having any desire to hold that for use in case of war is concerned, no, because it is too far advanced. It is projected too far into the enemy or potential enemy zone."

Mrs. Bolton: "Is the same thing true, General Hamilton, in the manner of an airfield in Korea?"

Brigadier General Paul M. Hamilton, Chief of Policy Division,

Directorate of Plans and Operations, Headquarters of the U.S. Air Force, Representing General Hoyt Vandenberg:

> "There is an airfield but there are no airfields which are considered to be of any tactical value. . . . **The air activity [of the US] in the case of hostilities in Korea, would more than likely be coming from bases further back,** and any enemy activity [would be coming] from out of Korea. **It is too hard to try and hold**. It is the same trouble the Navy has. The base is too advanced into enemy territory."

Later on *Congressman Judd* posed another question. Congressman Judd was a Christian Minister who had served in China in the tradition of a long line of Protestant missionaries from the United States. Judd had a wildly unrealistic conviction about our ability to control the outcome of the civil war in China between Mao and Chiang. His feelings were passionate about trying to keep the Communists from winning in China and he often heatedly sparred with Marcantonio over the issue. It is difficult for me to unravel the mixed motivations of the China Lobby -- but in my opinion they ranked in the order of financial, religious, and then political. His question was:

> "It has been testified that Pusan in our hands would not be of great value to us. Would it be of great value to the Russians and a detriment to us if it were in their hands?"

This was one of Congressman Judd's pet rhetorical techniques. Whenever someone would prove that the United States did not need a piece of territory for its own security, he would try to arrive at the opposite conclusion by suggesting that nevertheless it was just as important to keep it out of the hands of Russia. It was a very dangerous and belligerent zero-sum game. Truman later adopted it for Korea, Formosa and Vietnam.

Now, however, the representative of the Navy easily avoided the trap. *Admiral Wooldridge:*

> "I think possibly it would be **as un-tenable to them** as it would be to us because looking at the map you can see **it is within range of our air operations** from Okinawa and Japan."

The same issue was gone over again and again. Some of the armchair generals and admirals in Congress were reluctant to accept the reality that we should not or could not fight over every inch of ground in the world against Communism.

> *Mr. Fulton* (James G. Fulton, R. Pa.): "Is there any reason for having a forward strongpoint that would keep under airpower cover a certain area up in Russia, such as oilfields and industries?"

> *Admiral Wooldridge*: " I would say the degree of effort to hold a place there [Korea] militarily would be all out of proportion to the dividends that you would obtain from it."

> *General Hamilton:* "I subscribe entirely to that answer."

Again *Admiral Wooldridge* repeated the Joint Chiefs of Staff position on military action in Korea:

> "I do not believe we would want to have forces there which **might become involved in a Korean civil war.**"

One of the mightiest hawks and China Lobby enthusiasts in Congress was John Davis Lodge, Republican of Connecticut, who seems, from his following comments, to have envisioned himself also as a military strategist.

> *Mr. Lodge:*

"Let us assume that virtually the whole of China collapses, and that is followed by Indochina, Indonesia, Siam, Malava, and Burma *[another Early Domino-ist?]*. At that point I think you will agree that our position in Japan is threatened. Our position in the Philippines and Okinawa is seriously threatened. If we find ourselves in a war would there be no appreciable difference between having to make an amphibious landing on the continent from Japan, which would be our base, I assume, for combined operation, and having **a toehold in southern Korea**, which is, after all on the continent and which we could treat as a **beachhead**, from which to deploy our forces in a combined operation? That is a question addressed to all three of you gentlemen."

The response from the Military came from Brigadier General *Thomas S. Timberman*, Chief of Operations Group, Plans and Operations Division, Office of the Chief of Staff, Department of the Army:

"First: A base in Korea would not be a tenable base, as compared with that in the Japanese archipelago. Second: Any plans to reenter the [Asian] continent would no doubt bypass Korea."

Mr. Lodge: "Even if we held Korea?"

General Timberman: "Even though we held Korea, yes."

Mr. Lodge:

"Even if we held Korea, which is, as I understand it, 90 miles from the island of Honshu [*per Lodge it moved 90 miles since the day before*], is

it in the present plan – and if this is top secret do
not reply to it, please – it would not be the
present plan to **use southern Korea as a beachhead**, through which to place our troops and for
the Navy to keep pushing in more from Japan and
from the United States."

General Timberman: "From the Army point of view, **any reen-
try on the [Asian] continent would bypass and not use
Korea.**"

Mr. Lodge:"In other words, [*as if repetition and plain English
were not sufficient*] on the hypothesis that I have indicated
there would be virtually no strategic disadvantage to our
having no toehold at all on the continent of Asia?"

General Timberman:"It would be a very, very minor disadvantage."

However, the Members of Congress went on, as if their
denseness had no end, or just that they for some reason pretended
not to understand. This group of hawks did not like to hear what
they were hearing, but they were temporarily set back. The remaining 7,000 tactical troops were pulled out at the end of June, 1949.

Yet the very next year when Truman surprised everybody with
his complete turnaround, these hawks were the happiest crowd
around – notwithstanding that Truman's order crashed against
every well thought-out analysis. Events would only prove the
correctness of those analyses as we became engaged in a hopeless
conflict in Korea. And then with dumbfounding supidity we did
exactly the same thing in Vietnam.

The Military did not want to get entangled man-to-man in the
backyard of an enemy which grossly outnumbered us, and thousands of miles from our base. A common sense evaluation that the
politicians ignored to everyone's sorrow.

Mr. Fulton: "Why would it not be possible to continue to negotiate with them [the Rhee Government of South Korea] and keep a base there? For example, an air base or a navy base or something like that? . . ."

General Hamilton: "As far as the air forces are concerned, I do not think it is a question of why it will not be possible. I think it probably would be possible but there is no desire to incur the responsibility for it. There is no commensurate advantage."

Mr. Fulton: "Even though that extends the circumference of your air cover above Peiping and Mukden?"

General Hamilton: "Unless you wanted to go into the creation of very much larger air facilities than are there now, there is nothing to be gained by moving forward bases into the Korean Peninsula from where we could operate at the present moment."

Mr. Fulton: "Even though you could cover the whole way there?"

General Hamilton: "I know the con's heavily outweigh the pro's in any such undertaking."

Mr. Fulton: "I will have to take your word on that."

Each committee member seemed to want to feel and touch the same issue to be assured.

Mr. Smith (Lawrence H. Smith, R. Wis.): "I have asked you from a military standpoint how will this [proposed $150,000 economic] aid program [to Korea] increase our security...."

General Timberman: "The geography of Korea – that is, the land itself –is of no great importance strategically, to our military position in the Far East. . . ."

Mr. Smith: "It seems you have just admitted that **from a military standpoint it does not involve us?**"

General Timberman: "No, it does not."

Timberman tried at one point to summarize again one of the dangers of leaving <u>any</u> tactical troops in Korea:

> **"If we left troops in Korea we would be giving false hopes to those people because I do not think <u>anyone would suggest</u> we enter into combat with the northern Korean forces. . . "**

(The "anyone," whom General Timberman could not imagine existed, turned out to be the Commander-in-Chief, Harry S. Truman, just 12 months later.)

The following week Secretary of State Dean Acheson, who had been in Europe, appeared before the Committee and testified in support of the economic aid bill for Korea.

Secretary Acheson:

> "The Korean problem is one upon which we must act. . . . If you do not do it, you are absolutely certain that the whole situation in Korea will collapse and Korea will fall into the Communist area. If you do do this, there is **a chance** that it will not. We cannot tell you that Korea is going to stand up and under all pressures. We would not be honest at all if we told you that, but there is a good fighting chance that the Koreans can take care of themselves. I believe **we cannot possibly guarantee** the south-

ern Koreans their independence by American military power. **That is a very bad strategic position for us to be in.** It is a commitment which we should not undertake. . . .

This is the Secretary of State speaking on behalf of the President with respect to American Policy on Korea. It is a repetition of what his under secretaries had testified to and it was the policy as developed by the Government after years of study and incorporated into national policy papers.

These Committee hearings in June of 1949 were in "Executive" session and theoretically secret. The transcripts were not officially made available to the public until the mid-'70's. However the gist of his and the other witnesses's testimony was incorporated in majority and minority reports on the bill (House Report 962, Part 1, July 1, 1949, Part 2, July 26, 1949, 81st Cong. 1st Sess.) which in turn was repeated in the newspapers (for example, New York Times, July 2, 1949: "VOTE AID OR KOREA WILL FALL IN 3 MONTHS, ACHESON SAYS").

In 1949 Mao's forces pushed Chiang Kai-shek into the sea and were preparing to go after the last piece of Chinese territory, Formosa. Because the island of Formosa was so heavily armed Mao would need the assistance of an air force and navy, of which he had neither. So Mao had been gingerly approaching Stalin for air and naval assistance. Notwithstanding an American tabloid creed of faith, Stalin had not supported nor believed in the viability of Mao's revolution up to this point, and in fact had taken the practical path of national self-interest in making treaties and other arrangements with the existing Chinese Government under Mao's enemy, Chiang Kai-shek. In addition to their Formosa plans, the Chinese Communists also had their hands full in consolidating their control over the newly acquired land mass that had been laid waste by decades of civil war and incompetent and corrupt administration by Chiang Kai-shek.

Meanwhile in 1949, the leader of North Korea, Kim Il Sung,

was also anxious to finish the Korean revolution and consolidate all of Korea under his rule. Now that the Chinese Communist had taken all of China, except Formosa or Taiwan, he thought it was his turn. So he too approached Stalin with requests for military aid.

In response to Mao's requests, Stalin encouraged him to believe that he would get air assistance from Russia to take control of Formosa, in large measure to make up for the lack of Soviet support for Mao over the many years of civil war in China. Like Tito in Yugoslavia, Mao had fought and won his long civil war without much help from Stalin. Stalin therefore was being solicitous with the victorious Chinese leader. He did not need another independent and contrary Communist leader in the world along the lines of Tito.

However, as for Kim's entreaties for help in unifying Korea by force, Stalin firmly turned him down during their discussions in 1949. It was too dangerous in that the Americans might intervene. Stalin's foreign policy was dominated by extreme caution and the overriding principle of avoiding war with the Americans – whom he knew would not hesitate to use atom bombs to devastate Russia.(There is a detailed analysis based on the most recently disclosed Chinese and Russian documents of the Mao - Stalin - Kim relationship in Richard C. Thorton. Odd Man Out. Washington, D.C.: Brassey's, 2000)

But some months later the situation was apparently clarified for everybody. After January, 1950, Stalin, Mao and Kim Il Sung did not need any kind of intelligence service to determine exactly the American policy toward Korea. They did not need the warren of traitors and communists which right-wing politicians like Senator Joe McCarthy were claiming had infested the State Department. Because if they were not able to determine that policy from access to Congressional hearings or to the secret planning, discussions and policy papers issued by the Defense and State Departments and the National Security Agency, they could have found out the same thing by reading the newspapers.

Secretary of State Dean Acheson wanted to make sure that Stalin and Mao knew that we did not intend to intervene in Korea if there were a civil war there. Acheson at the time was trying, though primarily with words only, to entice Mao from Stalin by this and other strategies. Therefore he decided to go public in a big way so there would be no misunderstanding about American policy on Korea and Formosa – as if setting it in stone. Hence in a speech on January 12, 1950 to the National Press Club in Washington DC, he pretty much told the world that the US would maintain a hands-off approach to both Formosa and South Korea, no matter what happened in those localities.

Some historians theorize that Acheson was trying to separate Mao from Stalin, encouraging another Tito, by offering pieces of territory in Asia to China – the "wedge" theory. This theory was even openly speculated on at the time, as for example, in an article by the New York Times foreign correspondent, C.L. Sulzberger (March 3, 1950). Yet the most effective method of dealing with China at that time would have been to do what other countries of the world were doing and advocating, even our close British allies. That was to recognize the Communist regime as the legitimate government of China, give it the China seat in the UN and go about building normal trade relations with her. This would have been the right thing to do, but it was not done until two bloody wars later, millions of dead and wasted decades. In January of 1950 Truman and Acheson felt it would be politically dangerous if they went much beyond publicly offering to stay out of China's backyard. For the purpose of conveying this message, Acheson was not embarrassed to hijack temporarily the language of the Left:

> Let's come now to the matters which
> Asia has in common. . . . One of these factors is a
> **revulsion against the acceptance of misery and
> poverty** as the normal condition of life. Through-
> out all of this vast area, you have that **fundamen-
> tal revolutionary aspect in mind and belief.** The
> other common aspect that they have is the **revul-
> sion against foreign domination.** Whether that

foreign domination takes the form of colonialism or whether it takes the form of imperialism, they are through with it. They have had enough of it, and they want no more. . . .

The symbol of these concepts has become nationalism. National independence has become the symbol both of **freedom from foreign domination** and freedom from the tyranny of poverty and misery. . . .

Resignation is no longer the typical emotion of Asia. It has given way to hope, to a sense of effort, and in many cases, to **a real sense of anger**. . . . [M]uch of the bewilderment which has seized the minds of many of us about recent developments in China comes from a **failure to understand this basic revolutionary force** which is loose in Asia . . .

These sentences could have been spoken by the principal leftist political leader at that time, Congressman Vito Marcantonio of East Harlem. One could hear the Marcantonio tones in the speech. It was as if Marcantonio were pleading again with his colleagues in the House to comprehend the reality of the revolution going on in the East or cheering on his supporters from a stage in Madison Square Garden.

Much of Acheson's speech was in defense of the Truman Administration's policy on China against the China Lobby in Congress. The Administration had been under constant attack from right-wing Republicans, including periodic calls for Acheson's removal, for the "loss" of China to Communism. As if the utter corruption (for example, a good portion of American aid wound up invested in US real estate by Chiang and his cohorts), tyranny and incompetence of Chiang Kai-shek had nothing to do with Mao Zedong's military successes. Or as if the US had not already poured over $3,000,000,000 down the drain in support of Chiang.

In 1950 Acheson and Truman were too fearful of the Republican Right Wing and the China Lobby to do the sensible thing, that is, recognize the reality of Chinese Communist legitimacy and let them take the seat of China in the UN. But Acheson would at least try using words to disengage Mao from Stalin and this is where he found the language of the Left useful.

In light of America's subsequent slaughter of millions in Korea and its incomprehensible repetition in Vietnam just 10 or 15 years later -- all in a vain attempt to suppress indigenous national revolutions -- some of Acheson's language is chilling in its intentional deceit.

> **Our real interest is in those people as people**. . . .It is important to take this attitude not as a mere negative reaction to communism but as **the most positive affirmation of the most affirmative truth** that we hold, which is the **dignity and right of every nation, of every people**, and of every individual to **develop in their own way**, making their own mistakes, reaching their own triumphs but acting under their own responsibility. . . .

The speech is generally interpreted as a desperate attempt to keep Mao from joining up with Stalin – an abortive, short-lived and faint-hearted US attempt to drive a wedge between China and Russia. Acheson may not have known it at the time, but it was much too late. The billions of dollars and years of military support we had given Chiang Kai-shek had convinced Mao to "lean" toward Stalin. Mao had already concluded that Stalin was much more likely help in his goals of gaining Formosa and reconstructing China. In addition, there was the reality that Russia, China's neighbor, had troops remaining in Manchuria and Mongolia after WWII. Russia further had long-time interests in railroads and ports in China which rights were recently confirmed in treaties with the just-expelled Government of Chiang Kai-shek. In retrospect, of course, to have expected China to turn its back on Russia at this point and take up with the US was foolhardy.

Acheson was a serious admirer of all things English, an Anglophile in education, speech, manner and dress. The lofty proclamation of sympathetic understanding for the revolutionary spirit in Asia in his National Press Club speech can compare only with the often proclaimed lofty aims of the British in trying to civilize the people of India during the decades they bled it dry. Imperialism on its face is an ugly thing. So it requires a fine development, to a Churchillian art form, of the language of self-righteous hypocrisy to mask it.

The Americans had just finished a messy military occupation in Korea where tens of thousands of people had been killed because they were suspected of seeking radical change in their feudal society. Then we turned the country over to a near-insane fanatic'. One by one Rhee killed off his opponents, old and young, Right and Left. The leftist leader Lyuh, who had headed the short-lived People's Republic in 1945 after the surrender of Japan, was assassinated in 1947. Even Rhee's ancient right-wing comrade from decades of exile, Kim Koo, was assassinated in July, 1949. When a Koo ally asked for an independent investigation of the killing, he was arrested by Rhee's military police who were now routinely making mass arrests without warrants. When a major Korean newspaper also suggested an investigation of Koo's killing, it was closed down and its chief editor arrested (New York Times, July 1 - 3, 1949). Apparently without the slightest qualms Rhee would later order the execution of tens of thousands of these political prisoners at the start of the Korean War.

The deceit at the top of the American Government was pervasive, even among the deceivers. We now learn "officially," 50 years later, that Truman had been hiding a number of foreign policy decisions even from Acheson. It turns out that Truman at this time was secretly giving his approval to a CIA plan to destabilize the leftist government of Guatemala. This was being done primarily for the financial benefit of the United Fruit Company, which was having struggles with labor, – a course of action resulting in decades of violence in Guatemala and the deaths of hundreds of thousands (U.S. Department of State, Office of the Historian: "Foreign Relations, Guatemala, 1952-1954," July 7, 2003 <http://www.state.gov/r/pa/ho/frus/ike/guat/20195.htm>; Stephen Kinzer gave excepts of these recently declassified Guatemala papers in New York Times, July 6, 2003). Dean Acheson, unlike our Collin Powell, was a real Secretary of State so his being kept out of the loop by Truman says something about Truman that is somewhat inconsistent with his straigtforward, "Honest Abe" image.

Also at the same time America was shipping arms and other support to the French to suppress the nationalists in Indo-China and to keep what was left of the French colonial empire. Even in 1950 there was no mystery about the causes for the fighting in Vietnam or the futility of it. Headlines in newspapers were already categorizing the French attempt to suppress Ho Chi Minh as hopeless: "VIET NAM FIGHTING IS ENDLESS, COSTLY," (Tillman Durdin, New York Times, March 3, 1950). Though it must be noted that the editors of the Times at the same time were urging Truman to help the French against the "communists" in Vietnam as part of the overall policy of "containment."

Ho Chi Minh himself seems to have been taken in by the American duplicity as he would actually write letters directly to President Truman requesting help in his people's quest for liberty against the French, in the spirit of the American Revolution.

The part of the National Press Club speech that day, however, which has received the most attention was where Acheson announced what areas of the Pacific America considered vital to its security. "They are essential parts of the defensive perimeter of the Pacific, and they must and will be held." Then he drew a line, something easy to comprehend and which would eliminate any tragic misunderstandings:

> This defensive perimeter runs along
> the Aleutians to Japan and then goes to the
> Ryukyus [Okinawa]. . . . [and then] to the Philip-

pine Islands. . .

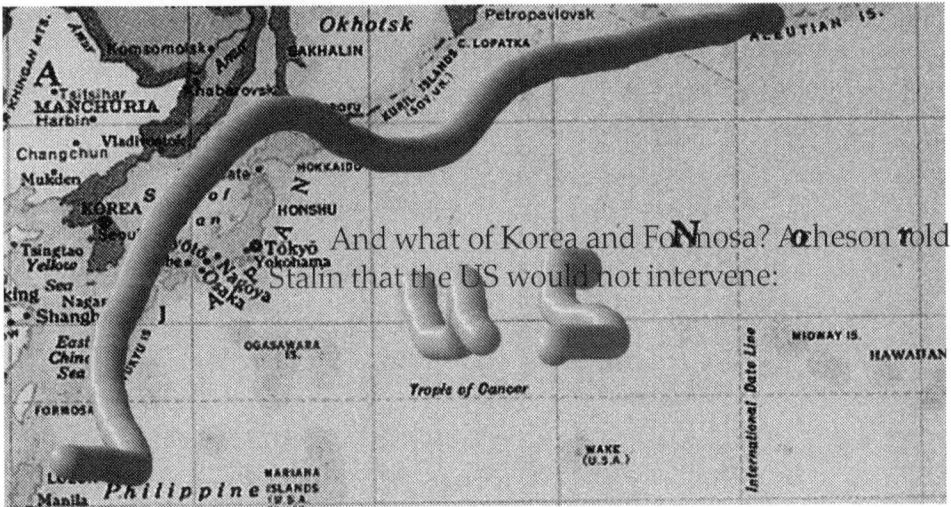

And what of Korea and Formosa? Acheson told M Stalin that the US would not intervene:

And what of Korea and Formosa? Acheson told Mao and Stalin that the US would not intervene:

> So far as the military security of other areas in the Pacific is concerned, **it must be clear that no person can guarantee these areas against military attack. . . .**

To anyone living in the Pacific area it certainly was vitally important what this Atomic Superpower considered its bailiwick. One would not want to cross that line intentionally. Therefore the Asians had to be grateful to this American who had made things simple. He had just drawn a clear line on a map that even the blind, deaf and dumb could comprehend. If you lived in Korea, the message was loud and clear, almost deafening, as Rhee's violent reaction the next day made evident — the Americans had just said publicly that Korea was not of vital concern to them, that the Koreans were on their own militarily.

That precisely reflected the Administration's testimony to

Congress six months earlier – the US was seeking to help Korea with limited economic and military aid, but we had no intention of getting involved in a civil war "with a lot of Koreans." The doctrine was enshrined in a National Security Paper supposedly known only to senior officials for their guidance. The Russian troops had been withdrawn from occupation of North Korea in 1948; the United States troops in South Korea had followed in 1949. Now the Koreans would have to settle their affairs among themselves. Likewise for Formosa.

Those areas, Acheson said, would have to look to thier own efforts and the "international community" if they were attacked, not to the United States. We could not stretch ourselves all over the world, we had to draw a line somewhere, and this was it. Directing someone to the "international community" or the UN at that time was like sending a thirsty man to the desert. Since its founding just after WWII, the UN had done nothing militarily and was toothless in that regard, particularly since all five members of the Security Council had the veto power to prevent unwanted action by the UN-- the compromise device employed by its creators to assure its birth. In reality, the United States and the Soviet Union were the only powers that could "guaranty" security. If the US said it could not, then you were on your own.

Acheson had already put in place the mechanism for the US to stay out of the Korean conflict everyone expected without losing any "face." In December, 1949 he had instructed Ambassador John Muccio to have President Rhee, in the case of a major military attack across the 38th Parallel, to appeal to the *United Nations* -- **not** the United States. The UN, Acheson instructed Muccio, had already "anticipated the possibility of a major military conflict in Korea" and had all the appropriate bodies in place to deal with it. (See Confidential Memo No. 83, Acheson to Muccio, December 14, 1949: FRUS, 1949, Vol. VII, p. 1108).

It was soon after this speech that Stalin began to change his advice to Kim Il Sung. He no longer would veto Kim's passion to reunite Korea and he agreed to give him arms and military advisors. But Stalin remained cautious. He warned Kim that if his plans for a swift conquest of the South did not work out and he ran into trouble, that he could expect no help from Russian troops. Russia had no intention of risking war with the United States. If Kim needed additional manpower down the line, he would have to turn to China.

Therefore Stalin based his tentative approval to Kim's plans upon Kim's getting Mao to agree to them as well. Mao, wanting Stalin's help in taking Formosa, and indebted to the Koreans for the thousands of ethnic Korean soldiers who had fought with the Communists in China's civil war, could not very well say no to Kim. When Kim later visited Mao and described to him Stalin's enthusiastic approval for Kim's plans, Mao could only nod a reluctant approval. Even then he told Kim that China was in no position to be of any material help (Thornton, Odd Man Out).

Kim assured Mao that he did not need any more help than what Stalin was providing. Contemporary participants have told us that Mao was never shown Kim's battle plans, which had been drawn up by the Russian military advisors, nor the date of the attack. Mao was still piling up men and equipment for an invasion of Formosa when Kim attacked South Korea and ultimately put a halt to Mao's own plans.

Congress, shortly after Acheson's January, 1950, National Press Club speech, got on board by at first rejecting and then grudgingly approving some economic aid to Korea. The Congressional debate which the Russians, Koreans and Chinese could have read in the US Press, confirmed that the Americans did not think that Korea, though important symbolically, did not warrant any military action.

The Truman Administration had sent over to Congress in the Spring of 1949 an "urgent" request for $150,000,000 for Korean economic aid – much of which involved the purchase of American products like cotton, fertilizer and oil and then paying American shippers to transport them to Korea. It requested action as soon as possible as the Government of Korea would not last 3 more months without the economic assistance from the United States. The House Committee held the June hearings quoted above and approved the request in a hotly divided vote in July, 1949. But the House itself took no action on this "urgent" matter until the following January. That in itself would tell any observer that Korea was not vital to the United States.

When the 1949 Aid Bill was finally debated in Congress the week following Acheson's National Press Club speech, much of the testimony from the "Executive" hearings was repeated or paraphrased by the debating Members of Congress. Then the House defeated the Bill, by one vote (192-191).

Congressman Christian A. Herter, R. Mass., summarized a portion of the testimony:

> "Testimony will be given here . . . that Korea is militarily untenable, that under none of our defense plans as such could we consider trying to hold Korea in the event of aggressive action north of the thirty-eighth parallel by either Communist trained Korean troops or by Russian troops."

Congressman Vorys repeated arguments he had made in Committee:

> "In this legislation there is no direct benefit to our military security; our troops are out; the Soviets can come into south Korea whenever they wish.... Why, therefore, do we go   forward with this program which does not involve our military security, which does not help solve our own economic problems and will not solve Korea's economic problems . . ."

Mr. Chiperfield (Robert B. Chiperfield, R. Ill):

"This proposed action would be putting money down a rat hole. If the island of Formosa, located over 100 miles from the mainland of China, cannot be defended against aggression as contended by Secretary of State Dean Acheson, how much less could South Korea be defended being the tail end of the peninsula, with guerrilla activities in North Korea and Communist control in Manchuria?

As we pointed out in our minority report:

"Korea is hopelessly outflanked by the adjacent land mass of China, and the peninsula has no connecting link with any friendly continental power. Every ton of supplies contemplated to be furnished under the terms of this legislation must be transported vast distances. . . ."

The testimony before our committee disclosed that Korea was not considered as vital to our security program.

Congressman Lemke (William Lemke, R., N.D.):

Are we going to withdraw? Are we going to throw another nation to communistic Russia? That is the whole question. Or are we going to call a halt and take a stand for the people who still believe in peace and not in aggression. . .
.

We were told by the highest officials in Korea that if we would let them alone they could reunite their country that we so cruelly divided and that belonged to them. **Of course there is civil war between these two factions.** The Communists go over in nightly raids of the South

Koreans; but the South Koreans have 22,000,000 people and the North have only 9,000,000. The South Koreans can take care of themselves unless Russia steps in.

Congressman Burnside (D., West Virginia):

Korea is the **only Christian country** in Asia. *[Actually it was essentially a Confucian and Buddhist society, and had been that for at least a thousand years. The missionaries had been more successful there than elsewhere in the East, particularly during the Japanese occupation. Still only about 10% of the populaion was Christian; though Sigmund Rhee and many of the wealthy class were missionary-educated and were at least nominal Christians].* **All the Christians here** certainly should think about endeavoring to the best of their ability to maintain the only Christian country in Asia.

Congressman Jackson (Donald L. Jackson, R. Calif):

South Korea is hopelessly outflanked on the west by the adjacent land mass of China, and that the entire line along the thirty-eighth parallel is open to full-scale and unrestricted warfare at any time.

South Korea lies 7,000 miles west of San Francisco. . . . Vladivostok 500 miles to the north. It is quite obvious that in any economic or political challenge to supply contesting forces in the north and the south, that we would be at a decided disadvantage as represented by the difference between 500 and 7,000 miles.

The third of the arrows [on the map], and perhaps the one most important from the

Soviet standpoint, is the one which indicates the direction of and the distance to the Russian industrial area east of the Urals. **It is inconceivable to many of us that the Communists would countenance the maintenance of such a threat to their productive capacity.** . . . but if anything is likely or certain in this world today it would appear to be the eventual engulfment of South Korea by the rampant forces of communism. . . .

> **South Korea is no Japan, no Okinawa, no Philippines. Not one word of military testimony is on the record indicating the essential nature of the peninsula** in the plans for the national defense. To the contrary, it has been stated time and again that from the military standpoint South Korea is **indefensible and tactically isolated.** . . .

On this first go-around in the House the Bill as noted was actually defeated by the margin of one vote. <u>Newsweek</u> described Dr. John Myun Chang, South Korea's ambassador to the US, as stumbling out of the House gallery after the vote "pale and shaken." <u>Newsweek</u> went on to repeat the Hawk Party Line:

> "What it meant to him was that the part of Korea he represented was now to be surrendered to the Communists of Northern Korea. It might well mean **slavery or slaughter** for his people, even his friends and family."

The same article also ridiculed Vito Marcantonio for celebrating the defeat of the bill with Adam Clayton Powell. "We did it," <u>Newsweek</u> quotes what Marcantonio supposedly said to Powell in the Speaker's lobby, "our two votes killed the bill."

But it was only the first time the Truman Administration was defeated in a request for money which it claimed was essential in the fight against Communist expansion. Truman and Acheson could not afford to allow the enemies of their grand strategy of "containment" to have any victory, however small and insignificant. It immediately got to work and with a promise of about $10,000,000 for Chiang Kai-shek added to the Korean Bill, it got the one-issue China Lobby Members to vote for the Bill on a second vote taken on February 9, 1950. It now passed, 240 - 134.

During debate on this second go-around Congressman Vito Marcantonio seemed to be echoing Acheson's National Press Club speech, or was it the other way around?

We have spent more than $3,000,000,000 since VJ-day to save Chiang Kai-shek when Chiang Kai-shek was on the mainland of China. . . . Now it is proposed that, with $10,000,000 at most, we may save Chiang Kai-shek on the island of Formosa. It seems to me that **we fail to realize the real causes for our failure**. We failed to save Chiang Kai-shek because the people of China, people everywhere in Asia, are **throwing off the shackles of foreign control,** exploitation, and tyranny, and are establishing for themselves, through **their own native revolutions,** if you please, their own governments. **I say that this Congress has failed to recognize fundamental principles; that the people of China are entitled to their revolution** just as much as the people of the United States were entitled to their revolution back in 1776.

What has been the result? The people of China have established their revolution and are now consolidating it. We are not going to halt it. We are not going to stop it either with hydrogen bombs or with the $10,000,000 to Chiang Kai-shek on the island of Formosa. The corrupt, tyrannical government of Chiang Kai-shek is something of the past. It is finished. It has been done in by the people of China. **We in the United States must not forget what history has taught us, that never has the defense of tyranny and corruption anywhere in the world been in the interest of the people of the United States.** We here are continuing the defense of tyranny and corruption by going to the aid of Chiang Kai-shek. In doing so we continue to ally ourselves with a crooked Fascist dictator against 400,000,000 Chinese people, their nation, and their friends all over Asia.

What I have said about China is equally applicable to [Korea]. **We have heard talk about the defense of democracy in Korea.** We are told that this $60,000,000 must be used for the rulers of South Korea in the defense of democracy. First of all, what is the situation with respect to the people of Korea? I wish the Members of this House, before voting on this so called Korean aid bill, would read both volumes I and II of report of the United Nations Commission on Korea. ... [Y]ou can well recognize that **you cannot just go into a country, draw a line, and divide the country in two**; the United Nations recognized it, and they recognized that what the people of North and South Korea wanted was independence and a unified nation.

Marcantonio then recounted the stories from the newspapers about Sigmund Rhee's authoritarian rule, the wholesale arrests of opponents, both Right and Left, calling them all communists, the overflowing jails, the arrests of even right-wing opposition leaders in the Assembly, the assassination of political and social leaders, the constant turmoil in South Korea. Marcantonio continued:

> So that the story of South Korea is a repetition of Chiang Kai-shek's tyranny in China. It is the story of tyranny, it is the story of corruption, it is the story of suppressing the national aspirations of the people for a united and independent country.
>
> We tried to help this tyranny in China. We failed. We are now repeating the same interference in Korea. We are going to fail there too. . . .

What Marcantonio was saying in Congress about the situation in Korea was exactly what the experts in the State Department were discussing among themselves in private.

The following comments are taken from a confidentail policy discussion held at the State Department among the officials responsible for our political policy in Korea (Confidential Memorandum of Conversation by the Officer in Charge of Korean Affairs (Bond), dated March 15, 1950, FRUS, 1950, Vol. VII. pp. 30-33):

> "Dr. Bunce: . . . was most anxious to discuss . . . the difficulty which the American Mission in Korea was encountering in dealing effectively with President Rhee and his personal entourage. . . . **The Mission was seriously concerned with the increasing tendency on the part of President Rhee toward a personal authoritarian type of government back by police support.**"

Bunce then described Rhee's "somewhat equivocal" (was this diplomatic language for corrupt?) conduct in the sale of 100,000 tons of rice to Japan. Further, Bunce was concererned that Rhee "had continued to by-pass the provisions of the Constitution. . . ." He also thought that if things conintued as they were "that the coming elections in Korea would be dominated by the police and youth groups."

W. Walton Butterworth, in charge of the Far East desk, declared that in Korea there was "no such thing as 'normal democratic processes.'"

Everyone at the meeting agreed, however, about the "necessity of reatively optimistic statements **for Congressional consumption** in connection with consideration of Korea aid bills, [and] . . ."**the time had not yet come when all of the circumstances** of the situation, as they were being discussed at this meeting, **should be made available to Congress**."

One of the participants, Edward W. Doherty in the Office of Northeast Asian Affairs, even thought that "if the present trend continued very long, the time might come when the lesser of two evils would be to cut loose [from Korea] and run the risk of incurring such [propaganda loss of face] consequences."

Yet just four months later, on June 25th when the civil war in Korea finally breaks out in full, Truman ignores all the careful planning and military realities and decides to go in. Truman was proud of being a simple man, with simple and straightforward answers. And he was convinced that a sign of leadership was the ability to make decisions quickly, and then stick to them. Consequently it seems safe to describe as window dressing his supposed consultations at Blair House, the temporary White House, during the days following the outbreak of hostilities. He had already decided to go to war immediately when he heard of the fighting.

Years afterward in a November 16, 1959 interview Truman discussed his *modus operandi* in making decisions:

> "In the long run, the jump decision that I made in the beginning was usually the right one. . . .[You] immediately make a decision when things are put up to you, and you don't want to tell anybody that you've made the decision. . . . in the long run, if you're heart's right and you know the history and the background of these things it'll be right. . . You'll find nine times in ten the decision off the cuff, in the long run, is the correct one. . . . **When Dean Acheson called me** in Independence and told me that the North Koreans had invaded South Korea and asked me what to do, **I said, Get the United Nations agreement that we're going to prevent that from happening.**"

Under Secretary of State James Webb met Truman the day of Truman's return to Washington, cutting short a visit to his family in Independence, Mo. on news of the Korean fighting:

> As soon as the doors of the car were closed . . . the President immediately stated that . . . this was a challenge that we must meet. I think his words were something like this: **'By God, I'm**

going to let them have it.' . . . . I intervened and said"Mr. President we have done a great deal of work with all concerned . . . and I think you should hear these carefully worked out recommendations before making up your mind as to any action to be taken.'The President in effect said,'**Well O.K., of course, but you know how I feel.'**

The buck certainly stopped with him, though millions would soon wish that he had passed it on. Unfortunately the issues confronting the President of the United States were complicated and needed a delicate and subtle hand. Harry Truman's gut anti-communism broke out immediately upon the death of Franklin Roosevelt. FDR had been carefully nurturing a post-war world order based on cooperation with the Soviet Union. Truman put a swift end to all of that.

Page 4:
Photo of General Douglas MacArthur, Hanada Air Base, Tokyo, Japan.
US Army Signal Corps   Photographer Kaye 19 October 1948

Page 36:
Photo of Vito Marcantonio that appears in I Vote My Conscience, Ed. Annette T. Rubinstein and Associates, The Vito Marcantonio Memorial, 1956, reprinted by the Calandra Institute, 2002. Also in Vito Marcantonio, Gerald Meyer, State University of New York Press, 1989.

Page 40:
Photo of President Harry S. Truman by the US Army Signal Corps, AFB in Hawaii, on his trip to see General MacArthur at Wake Island during the Korean War.   13 October 1950

CHAPTER II

THE AMERICANS ARE COMING!

From the diary entry of General Partridge, Tuesday, 27 June 1950:

> During the course of the evening, General Almond
> called to give me a very rough time indeed regarding
> the failure of the AF to drop a single bomb in Korea
> yesterday. During the course of the teleconference, I had
> been so incautious as to predict that we would have a
> B–26 [light bomber] mission operating against the
> North Korean forces before dark. This mission did
> come off but smaller than had [been] anticipated
> because most of the B–26 aircraft were engaged in
> escort activities. The small force of five airplanes which
> finally took off were aborted due to bad weather; in
> addition to that, the strikes that were scheduled to
> continue through the night were scattered because of
> the bad weather.
>
> General Almond took a dim view of the entire
> proceeding and said so in no uncertain terms, particu-
> larly when he discovered that the forecast for this
> morning's weather was bad. He repeated again and
> again that in order to save the South Korean forces
> and their government from collapse, it is mandatory
> that we take some visible action in support. **He
> wanted bombs put on the ground in that narrow
> corridor between the 38th [parallel] and Seoul,
> employing any means and <u>without any accuracy</u>.**
> . . .

Partridge did the best he could. On the morning of the 28th

he sent out from airports in Japan two flights of 12 light bombers, B-26's, to sweep along the 38th parallel for the purpose of strafing and rocketing "targets of opportunity." In the afternoon four heavier bombers, B-29 "Superfortresses," the World War II work-horses which each carried a bomb load of 20,000 pounds, were launched in pairs of two. One pair roamed

"the road and rail lines between Seoul and Kapyong and the other [pair] covered similar arteries between Seoul and Uijongbu [both of course in South Korea]. Each bomber crew **toggled out bombs against anything that looked to be worth a bomb**. It was a strange employment for the strategic bombers [which are designed to fly at high altitudes and drop bombs

against large targets], but General MacArthur had called for a maximum show of force" (Robert Futrell, USAF Military Historian, The USAF in Korea).

According to another USAF publication, Steadfast and Courageous: FEAF Bomber Command and the Air War in Korea: "Some thirty tons of bombs were dropped in this fashion."

More in accordance with their design and mission, though stretching their fuel capacity, several sorties of F-80's and F-82 fighter aircraft flew from Japan to the battlefront to strafe what they thought were the North Korean lines. Both the B-26 light bombers and the F-80 and F-82 jet fighters were to make an "extreme effort" to hit "moving traffic" among other targets of opportunity in the area between the 38th Parallel and the front lines, now well south of Seoul.

The next day, the 29th, Partridge was able to launch eight Superfortresses, in 1950 their "heavy" designation was changed to "medium" because of the introduction of the even heavier class of B-36 bombers. The eight B-29's now broke off into two sets of four, one set dropping bombs on Kimpo airfield outside Seoul which the South Koreans had so recently abandoned. The other four each dropped its 20,000 pounds of bombs on the main railroad station in Seoul, only a few days before, the Capital of South Korea.

The unlucky inhabitants of Seoul, as well as the city itself, suddenly had their status changed, by no act of their own, from "friendly" to "enemy." Not a good thing when the air was dominated by angry American planes whose pilots were being pressed to "hit anything." Kimpo and Seoul were repeatedly bombed by the US almost every day for the next 3 months.

General Stratemeyer, Saturday, 15 July 1950:

> Directive issued and received from General MacArthur through General Almond to hit Kimpo airport and the marshalling yards at Seoul today, using B-29's...."

Stratemeyer, Monday, 17 July 1950:

> [Sending General Mac Arthur] a set of pictures showing the destructive effect of the FEAF Bomber Command strike yesterday on Seoul — 1,504 x five hundred pound bombs were dropped — or 376 tons.

On the 30th of June nearly all the B-29's that were now ready for combat were loaded up with fragmentation bombs to attack the Air Force's first target actually in North Korea, the airfield at Wonsan. However, at the last minute the bombers were redirected to give emergency assistance to the battlefront in South Korea – they were ordered to give tactical support to the collapsing South Korean Army. The B-29's, designed to fly best at altitudes over 20,000 feet, flew from Kadena in Okinawa (a 10 hour round trip) and struck "what appeared to be troop formations on the approaches to the bridges, with no real knowledge of the results" (USAF, Steadfast).

Stratemeyer, Tuesday, 4 July 1950:

> Received word that inadvertently, portion of the South Korean line was strafed by my planes inflicting some damage to that portion of the line.

Unfortunately this urgency to hit something, just anything, and the fact that the Air Force was unprepared for conflict of this sort resulted in the early few days of the war in killing almost as many South Korean soldiers as North Korean ones. "Friendly fire" terrorized both friend and foe alike. Bombers were sent out with no more instructions than to hit whatever targets looked good. Fighters strafed anything moving on the roads. Tons of bombs were dropped with no clue as to where they were going. A show had to be put on.

This indiscriminate bombing was made worse by the simple fact that all the bombing was being done in South Korea, the area we were supposed to be rescuing. Truman's advisers were not unaware of the political risks. Clark Clifford, a close adviser who had earlier left the Administration to return to private law practice, wrote a short note on June 29, 1950 to Truman in which he said:

"I am concerned about the present order which limits our aid to that area south of the 38th parallel. I understand the reason for such order but I am distressed that, in bombing towns and cities in South Korea, **we are bombing friendly people and friendly areas.**"

Everything was being done by the seat of the pants. The wheel was being reinvented as there were no plans for American involvement in a civil war in Korea. MacArthur and the Generals at the teleconference with Washington during the first few days of the invasion were not the only ones surprised by Truman's decision to go to war. The Air Force, like the rest of the Military, had no plans for a war in Korea. The idea of fighting in Korea had been so completely rejected as unsound by US military planners that the only plans ever made for Korea were for evacuation of American Nationals in case of a conflict. So everything else after Truman's orders to go to war had to be created from scratch.

It wasn't just that the South Koreans had not been equipped with modern weapons nor properly trained. The American soldiers themselves, who had been on almost civilian occupation duty in Japan and were so suddenly thrown into the battle to stop the advancing North Koreans, were totally unprepared, physically and mentally, to go into combat. In addition, they were not properly equipped. For example, **their 2.36--inch rocket launchers,** the World War II bazookas, would not penetrate the new **heavy T34** Russian tanks being used by the North Koreans. Heavy artillery and tanks up to the task were not even stationed in Japan. The North Korean soldiers, on the other hand, spearheading the drive were mostly seasoned veterans from the wars in China – many thousands of exiled Korean guerillas had fought with the Chinese almost simultaneously against the occupying Japanese and against the Nationalists of Chiang Kai-shek.

So when the unprepared and under-equipped Americans were fed piecemeal into the battle, it only resulted in a slaughter and a rout — and the ones being slaughtered were the Americans and some South Korean units. The bulk of the South Korean Army and all of the South Korean police were busy fleeing south or killing political prisoners on the orders of the faster fleeing Sigmund Rhee. While the police would not stand and fight the northerners, they had enough time and ammunition to open the jails and execute the men and women who were about to be freed by the northerners – executions that they would later blame on the

Communists.

Stratemeyer, 25 June 1950:

      Enroute back to Tokyo after two weeks' temporary duty to Washington, D.C. and landed at Hickam [AFB in Honolulu] when the news reached me that North Korea had declared war on South Korea . . . . to take not only South Korea but the rest of the world by surprise. Field intelligence had broken down somewhere and FEC had no forewarned knowledge of the massing of the estimated 200,000 troops nor their intent to cross the Parallel. Upon receipt of news of the <u>civil war</u>, I changed my plans to return direct to Tokyo via Wake instead of Okinawa.

"Lt. General George Stratemeyer, r, being welcomed back to Haneda Air Base just south of Tokyo by Maj. General Earle Partridge, L, who had acted as Commander of the FEAF in the temporary absence of Stratemeyer. Also in attendance, center l to r, Maj. Gen. Victor Bertrandias and Brigadier Gen Edward White." June 27, 1950 OPI, DOD

Lt. General Stratemeyer had no hesitancy in calling this a <u>civil war</u> among the Koreans. During the testimony before the Foreign Affairs Committee in 1949, quoted above, a number of witnesses confidently predicted not only a civil war within 1 to 3 years of the US occupation troop withdrawal in 1949, but also that the Communists in North Korea would sweep through South Korea. That was exactly what happened. Why anyone was surprised is a mystery to this day.

Civil war among Asians, thousands of miles away, was not something the United States was equipped to handle. The quagmire here and later in Vietnam was what settled Military Doctrine had long advised against. Civil war meant the US soldier often could not tell friend from foe, with the inevitable unhappy consequences. The cities being fought in were as likely to be that of our "allies" as our foes, with the same cities changing allegiance several times. The "enemy" could disguise itself so easily and infiltrate our lines. The end result was that Americans destroyed as much of South Korea as we did North Korea and killed almost as many south of the 38th parallel, whom we were "liberating," as north of it, who by the whim of that latitudinal marker magically had become our "enemies." For the same reason one often heard that many American soldiers called both south and north Koreans "gooks." POW Dean commented on that in particular, and wished he had done more about stopping that when he could have. Similarly the stories of Americans killing civilians thought to be "guerillas" or harboring guerillas were depressingly far too numerous.

Yet here we were, sending ultimately 35,000 young American men to their deaths because Truman wanted to prove that he could be as tough against the Communists as his Republican hecklers. The Washington Post, the day before the outbreak of hostilities, carried a U.P. story reporting that

> Eastern States Republicans today . . . cheered Senator Joseph R. McCarthy (R. Wis.) for his free-swinging campaign against the State Department. . . . Republicans from 17 states and the District of Columbia . . . apparently gave McCarthy a green light for his campaign to prove the State Department is infested with Communists.

Not surprisingly Truman's decision to go to war received widespread acclaim in the United States, almost universal in the Press. For years Truman had been bashing Communism and the imagined threat of Russian imperialism. He had generated a few false war scares at the most effective times for either passage of some legislation or to improve his Party's election chances. He had given official approval to the Red witch-hunt when he unleashed the specter of disloyalty in high places with his Loyalty Review Board. He, with the help of that truly peculiar monster, J. Edgar Hoover, had out right-winged the right-wing in the quest for communists, traitors and homosexuals in the State Department and the other agencies of our Government. Even Congressmen were not immune to the witch-hunt, judging by the secret and extensive surveillance by the FBI of dissenting political figures, including Congressman Vito Marcantonio.

But by 1950 the "anti-communist" train was getting away from Truman. He needed to get back into the conductor's seat. Instead of being viewed as the tough boss-man fighting the cancerous spread of Communism in America and the world, as he was hoping to be thanks to his energetic "loyalty" review programs, his enemies were making him a target for being "soft" on Communists. The Korean War was the ideal vehicle, therefore, for Truman and his allies to get back up to the head of the line. It pushed the right button, at the right time. Finally, many were saying, that demon Stalin was going to get his due.

Truman's gambit seemed at first to work. When his aggressive message announcing that he had authorized MacArthur to use the Air Force and the Navy against the North Koreans was read to Congress, many of his erstwhile most bitter critics rose to their feet to join in the cheering. "ALMOST UNANIMOUS APPROVAL IS VOICED IN CONGRESS BY BOTH SIDES – HOUSE CHEERS" (New York Times, June 28, 1950). "A BLOW FOR PEACE" (New York Herald Tribune, June 28, 1950). "SAVING KOREA" (Washington Post, June 27, 1950).

In Congress the leaders of each House read the President's statement that he had ordered MacArthur in Tokyo to use what

Navy and Air Force he had available to him in the Far East Command to halt the invasion, though the use of troops were not yet authroized. It was greeted with enthusiasm and relief – and war cries. "I rise to congratulate the administration upon the entry of abdominal fortitude in the far-eastern policy," declared Representative Hugh D. Scott, Jr., Republican of Pennsylvania."I am glad to see that guts have finally received their proper recognition. . . ."

The New York Times reported:

> Senator William F. Knowland, Republican of California, who has been a frequent critic of Administration Far Eastern policy, was the first to take the floor in support of the President's announcement. . . . He was followed by Senator Leverett Saltonstall, Republican of Massachusetts. . . . Senator H. Alexander Smith, Republican of New Jersey, said the action was in line with the responsibilities of the United States to carry out our obligation. . . . Senator Henry Cabot Lodge Jr., Republican of Massachusetts, expressed the hope that President Truman 'will not shrink from using the Army if the best military judgment indicates that that is the effective course to take . . .' (June 28, 1950).

The policy reversal lead to some chortling by Republicans: "U.S. FAR EAST POLICY REVERSED BY TRUMAN'S ORDER FOR ACTION: Stand of Herbert Hoover, MacArthur, Taft and Other Republican Senators Seen as Upheld (New York Herald Tribune, June 28, 1950). But Truman's "bold" move had "sterilized" his Republic critics, at least for the time being.

The newspapers, however, did point out that not everybody got up and cheered. "The most outspoken objection to the Chief Executive's course was expressed by Representative Vito Marcantonio, American Labor Party of New York, who charged that Mr. Truman had usurped the powers of Congress by declaring war against North Korea. . . ." (Harold B. Hinton, <u>New York Times</u>, June 28, 1950)

From the Congressional Record we find that after the President's message was read and House Members began, one after another, almost to shout approval for the President's aggressiveness, Vito Marcantonio immediately spoiled the party when he stood up and grimly gave his own impromptu appraisal of the President's gutsy performance.

The words I am using do not adequately describe **the disastrous consequences this course will have** on the people of the United States unless checked by the people themselves.

I refer specifically to these words the majority leader read from the President's statement: *"In these circumstances I have ordered United States air and sea forces to give the Korean Government troops cover and support."*

Then again the President is quoted: *"Accordingly I have ordered the Seventh Fleet to prevent any attack on Formosa."*

This means the utilization of Americans in our Armed Forces in **two civil wars,** one that is taking place in Korea and one that is well nigh completed in China. **For all purposes, we were at war with the government and people of Korea,** and we might as well face it, the moment these words were enunciated.

I would be remiss to the things in which I believe if I did not stand up here and state my opinion on this matter. After all, Mr. Chairman, you live only once, and it is best to live one's life with one's conscience than to temporize or accept with silence those things which one believes to be against the interests of one's people and one's nation. . . .

I know we are going to have and we have been having a lot of war drum beating. The beating of the war drums has been such that they may drown out reason. But I think it is time, before it is too late, that we pause and take inventory of what has happened in Asia.

We have been warned time and time again and all signs in Asia have been pointed to what? That the people of Asia, the people of China, have been seeking national liberation. . . .

I remember the words I said here on February 7 about Korea. I stated in the well of this House that the defense of tyranny was never in the best interests of the people of the United States. I pointed out the similarity between the rottenness that existed in the Chiang Kai-shek government and that existing in the South Korean Government – the imprisonment of 40,000 people; the harsh exploitation of the people, the feeling of unrest, and the contempt for the rulers of South Korea on the part of the general masses

LIBERATING KOREA?

of the people. **It was a government imposed on the people of Korea by force of arms, a police state**; and I stated at that time that that Government could not long endure, that it would be wiped out by the will of the people of Korea.

I also said at that time that **you cannot take a nation and draw a line through it and divide it and split into two countries a nation which is an ethnic unity, a people united culturally and racially over centuries.** But we tried to do it. . . . The tyrannical rulers of South Korea continued to deny this legitimate aspiration of the people, ruthlessly suppressed every endeavor on the part of the people to achieve this objective and thus created an irrepressible conflict.

Here now we are sending American aviators to lay down their lives, sending American sailors to lay down their lives, **and who knows how soon it will be before our infantry will be sent to lay down their lives to defend, aid and abet tyranny** and perpetrate aggression against the Korean people who strive for a united and independent nation.

Now you may want this action. I do not. I know that the American people will not want this action **when they think it over**, and I know that they will thrust through this terrible dark cloud of war that has been descending on them. **Oh, yes, you can indulge in attacks on communism.** You can keep on making impassioned pleas for the destruction of communism, but I tell you that **the issue in China, in Asia, in Korea and in Viet Nam is the**

right of these peoples to self-determination, to a government of their own, to independence and national unity.

Remember one thing: A bomb was dropped on Hiroshima. It had terrible consequences, but it did not frighten the people of China and it did not frighten the people of Korea. For again, **these people despite the terror of the atom bomb have refused to abandon their efforts for national liberation. They will no more abandon this objective than the American people did during our Revolution**. . . .

War is not inevitable; there are alternatives, but this declaration on the part of President Truman is an acceptance of the doctrine of the inevitability of war. I stand here and challenge that doctrine. I say that the ingenuity of Americans and people all over the world challenge this doctrine.

These words of dissent pushed some parts of the House into an angry mood and Members began verbally attacking Marcantonio.

Congressman Abraham A. Ribicoff, D. Conn.:

If we were to follow his [Marcantonio] advice this Nation would gradually surrender nation after nation to Soviet imperialism. The Gentleman from New York says that the action of the President will lead to disaster. I contend that any other action by the President of the United States would lead to disaster. . . . **[Marcantonio] talks as if this were an action by Korean patri-**

ots; this is action by pawns of Soviet imperialism.
. . . 'Peace through strength' should be the slogan
of the United States. We should not continue to
back away time and time again because Russia
seeks to make a move. . . ."

Congressman Hays of Ohio:

> The gentleman from New York
> [Marcantonio] either with deliberate intent or
> through ignorance, sees fit to defend upon this
> floor time and time again the naked acts of ag-
> gression against various free governments of this
> world which are directed and dictated from
> Moscow. . . .
>
> He talks today about the nations of
> Asia determining for themselves which sort of
> government they are going to have. **I wonder
> who he thinks he is kidding? You know and I
> know that the march of Red communism
> across China was not dictated by the Chinese
> people, it was dictated by the Kremlin, it was
> financed by the Kremlin,** and the armies which
> march across China were armed by the Kremlin.
> This invasion from North Korea against South
> Korea is not the will of the Korean people. It is
> directed by a bunch of gangsters who have been
> sent in from Russia or Manchuria . . . If we sit idly
> by and allow them to do it, they will **subject the
> free nations of the world one by one to a state
> of slavery. . . ."**

But the next speaker, the conservative Republican from Pennsylvania, James G. Fulton, who knew Marcantonio from years of
tangling with him from the other side of the aisle, to his everlasting
credit, tried to call a halt to these personal attacks on Marcantonio:

In the House today this is a time of high feeling and critical decision, and we people who want to see the right course taken by the United States must feel sure that those who disagree with us have the right to speak.

Instead of criticizing and instead of aiming bellicose words at one man in this House, we ought to be reassured that the advocates of a certain point of view have the right to stand up here and say it. . . . Each of us, if we are fair in this House, must restrain ourselves from name calling, must settle ourselves down and say to the gentleman from New York [Marcantonio] **'You keep on speaking because no matter whether we disagree with you, you certainly speak honestly,' and I might even say this afternoon under the temper of certain portions of this House, 'and bravely. . . .'**

The name-calling may have stopped in the House, but the Press picked it up. On June 30th the New York Times editors had this to say under the headline: "VITO PASSES THE TEST:"

The Communist attack on Southern Korea has provided another one of those tests to which Moscow subjects it's followers . . . **the hard core of the faithful** remains undisturbed, and prominent among them is the present Representative in Congress of the 18th District – Vito Marcantonio. **He attacked President Truman from the floor of the House, then took his stand with convicted Communists in Madison Square Garden** and denounced American aid to Korea as 'Operation Desperation by Wall Street and the imperialists.'

Marcantonio has passed Moscow's

test. He has shown that **he will defend Russia against the United States, against the interests of true peace and justice**, against the facts and the dictates of common sense. He has earned the confidence of the Politburo and lost any last shred of respect which his fellow-countrymen might have felt for him. **He has always been a nuisance**; now he has passed beyond that stage. The sooner he is deprived of his Congressional soapbox, the better.

The <u>Washington Post</u> on June 29th under the editorial headline: "COMPANY THEY KEEP" tried to ridicule Marcantonio by saying that he and the very conservative <u>Chicago Tribune</u> were now bedfellows with the Communists in their similar claim that the President had 'usurped the powers of Congress by declaring war without its consent.'

The following month when Marcantonio was the lone vote against a military assistance bill (361-1), the <u>Daily Mirror</u> (New York) under the editorial tag: "STILL THE SAME STOOGE" stated about Marcantonio: " The best stooge Stalin ever had in the U.S. Congress has come through again in familiar fashion. . . ."

Marcantonio did not just debate the issues on the floor of the House. He took to the streets with his ideas as well — he would organize meetings and attempt to persuade in every way he could. Two days after the House debate he is one of the speakers at a Madison Square Garden rally, along with Paul Robeson, the opera singer and civil rights crusader who just had his passport lifted by the State Department; Gus Hall, the recently convicted leader of the US Communist Party and Ring Lardner, one of the "Hollywood Ten" convicted of contempt of Congress for refusal to "name names" at a hearing of the House Unamerican Activities Committee and soon to go to jail.

Starting the story with: PROTEST RALLY AT GARDEN HITS U.S. KOREAN AID: 9,000 HEAR MARCANTONIO, ROBESON, CONVICTED

RED TERM IT A WAR PLOT," the New York Herald Tribune quotes Paul
Robeson as saying that the American intervention "is the culmina-
tion of a wicked and shameful policy which our government has
ruthlessly pursued with respect to Colonial peoples" (June 29,
1950).

These were formative times for America -- how would she
utilize this unique historic opportunity as the greatest power on
earth. Truman was setting the mold -- running over and crushing
the Marcantonio voices in America who were seeking alternatives.
A back-page article in the Washington Post of Wednesday, June 28,
1950, contained this seemingly ordinary story about a place most
people never heard of :

> "INDO-CHINA LOOKS UPON U.S. ACTION
> IN KOREA AS PATTERN IN EVENT OF RED INVASION
> THERE."
>
> Hanoi, Indo-China. June 27 (AP). **United States
> action in the Korean crisis is looked upon in
> Indo China as a pattern of future American
> action in the event this country is invaded by
> Chinese Communist. . . ."**

Whoever this reporter was quoting, certainly got that right.
Though as it turned out, there was no Chinese Communist invasion of Vietnam, just an American one.

CHAPTER III

SITTING DUCKS

Korea in 1950 had several major cities, some large towns, but people lived mostly in villages that their families had lived in for many hundreds of years. The Koreans had accepted the concept of Buddha from China before the time of Christ and reshaped it as they made Buddhism the basis of their culture. During the Chosen Dynasty in the 14th Century they likewise accepted the teaching of Confucius from China and reshaped it as well as it became the official Korean way of life for the duration of the Chosen Dynasty into the 20th Century. Under the influence of Confucianism the family dominated life, and the patriarch lead the family. Villages were composed of extended families related to each other and presided over by the patriarch of the head family.

The faculty members of several Korean universities who teach housing and interior design have written a very instructive book called <u>Hanoak: Traditional Korean Homes</u>. There are eight names listed as authors, Choi, Jae-Soon; Chun, Jin-Hee; Hong, Hyung-Ock; Kang, Soon-Joo; Kim, Dae-Nyun; Min, Chan-Hong; Oh, Hye-Kyung; and Park, Young-Soon. It was published in 1999 by the publishing house of Hollym International Corp. with locations in Elizabeth, NJ and Seoul, Korea. They have a web site that includes a listing of their books on Korea in English (httpl//www.hollym.com). <u>Hanoak</u> is easy to read and follow, partly due I am sure to the fine translations by Maija Rhee Devine. I have taken from this book much of the information I use here in this part of the Chapter on Korean culture and the structure of their homes, including some excellent photographs taken by Suh, Jai-Sik.

According to <u>Hanoak,</u> a census of 1933 listed about 7,800 tribal villages with 30 or more families; 3,000 with 50 or more, 1,200 with 70 or more and 400 with 100 or more families. The design of the villages was based on the Confucian concept of family and leadership by the head family. So the major house belonged to the patriarch of the head family, immediate relatives had choice sites nearby, and so on. As noted, villages expanded by the number of related families attached to them. This is an important fact to understand if we are to comprehend the depth of the pain and damage caused to this society by uprooting even one of these ancestral villages.

Nagganupsong, a traditional village. *"Typical layout of a cluster of thatched roof houses whose roof lines harmonize with the shapes of the surrounding hills."*   <u>Hanoak</u>, Photo by Suh, Jai-sik

As expected, the size and quality of homes depended on the class of the family, though the Government in the Chosen Dynasty had various regulations to guard against ostentatious and lavish structures in accordance with Confucian principles. For our purposes it is only necessary to note that the materials used were primarily wood, straw, mud and, in the finer homes, tiles. The commoner lived in a home with wooden floors, mud walls and a thatch roof. The upper classes had walls of logs or carved wood and roofs of tile.

All the living accommodations reflected the philosophy of Confucius, with more space and prominence always given to the head family in a town or village, and to the patriarch of that leading family and to the eldest son. Among the commoners the same Confucian family principles were followed but of course with less material and space. But the authority and order was the same, with respect shown to elders and to ancestors.

"The exterior view . . . of a kiyok or bent or L-shaped house."
Photo by Suh, Jai-sik in <u>Hanoak</u>.

"A beautifully constructed and decorated upper class house."

According to Confucian principles, the men and the women kept separate quarters in those houses where people could afford to do so, usually only in upper class houses. In the women's quarters were the kitchens and gardens. In the men's quarters were the studies. The first son often had his study right next to the father's study.

"The courtyard of the women's quarters of the Chunghyo-dong. Landscaped in the middle with trees and flowers, the courtyard elicited a sense of comfort and security. The kitchen, where women folk spent most of their time." Hanoak. Photo by Suh, Jai-Sik.

Variations in temperature accounted for much of the differences in type of construction. In the farther north with the colder winters and heavier snow, much thought had to be given to sturdy walls and roofs not only for insulation but also to withstand the weight of the snow. The roofs may have been thatched and the walls made of mud or logs, but they were layered and constructed in the northern area to emphasize warmth and in the southern areas to take advantage of the breezes. In the towns and cities the homes were clustered close together as they grew over the hundreds of years.

*"The exterior view . . . of a tubangjip (log house) typical of Ullung island.
The sturdy log walls withstood heavy snow falls. Secondary wudegi walls were
constructed all around the house to prevent blockage of passageways between
buildings by snow accumulation."*   <u>Hanoak</u>.   *Photo by Suh, Jai-Sik.*

The best pictures of Korean cities, towns and villages before
the destruction of the Korean War would have been the reconnaissance photos taken by US planes. One reads the daily mission
reports in the National Archives of the reconnaissance flights and
realizes that we took the perfect before-and-after pictures, as the
photographers had first to photograph the targets for the pilots
and then photograph after the bombing to let the pilots know if
enough damage had been done. For some reason I found only a
number of the "after" photographs among the Air Force photos
given to the National Archives. Somewhere along the line the
"before" photos lost their way or I just did not look in the right
places.

The mission reports from the reconnaissance flights make
interesting reading. The photo interpreters seemed happiest when
they did not see a soul on a targeted city street, or saw them
crouching in the shadows of doorways -- meaning that the citizens

were fearful enough of the sound of the oncoming reconnaissance plane that they had run for cover. On the other hand, you can detect annoyance when they remark on people "nonchalantly" walking in the streets or riding a vehicle in the face of the approaching enemy plane which they would not have known was coming just to take pictures.

However, I did find some photographs from the 1920's and 1930's in Volume I and Volume II of an historical pictorial series generously lent to me by the librarian in the Korean Cultural Service located on the 6th floor at 460 Park Avenue, New York.

The photographs in the rest of this Chapter, therefore, come from these Volumes in that library. The identification of the cities or buildings and any quotations I use are taken from the English portion of the descriptions accompanying the photographs in these Volumes. These were the scenes in the 1920's and 1930's of the towns, presumably even more developed by 1950, that we leveled during the Korean War. *Remember the names.*

CHINNAMPO, *City View*

Association of Financial Unions bulding, Hamgyŏngnamdo province.

함경남도 금융조합 연합회

Hamhŭng products Exposition Hall.

함흥 중심가에 자리한 함흥물산 진열관

Hamhŭng district court.

HAMHUNG. Financial Unions Bldg; Esposition Hall; District Court.

LIBERATING KOREA?

평양 공소원 지방 재판소

District court of Appeal, P'yŏngyang.

평양 공회당 당시에는 꽤 멋있는 건물이었다.

Public Citizens Hall.

P'yŏngyang Railroad Hotel managed by Railroad Office.

평양 철도 호텔 철도국에서 경영한 호텔 하나. 익인 고관들과 친일파가 주로 이용

PYONGYANG. *District Court of Appeals.*
Public Citizens Hall.
Railroad Hotel.

District court, Shinūiju.

독립군을 괴롭힌 일경 본부. 애국지사와

새로 지은 신의주 경찰서 건물.

Newly built police station.

받았었다. 그들과 친일파만이 을 세웠으나 외과 의원 일제는 중요 도시에 도립 시설이 잘 갖춰진 것으로 알려졌던 도

Courts and Police station in Shinuiju (Sinuiju).

70   LIBERATING KOREA?

Panoramic view of Ch'ŏngjin ②   청진항 전경② 아름다운 이 도시를 일제는 마음대로 유린했다

City scenes of CHONGIN.

Hoeryŏng
会寧

Walled border city. Far behind runs the Tuman River.

"HOERYONG. Walled border city. Far behind runs the Tuman River."

KUNSAN

시가지 남쪽에서 바라본 목포항   Mokp'o streets commanding a view of Mokp'o port.

MOKPO

WONSAN Railroad Station.

전주 남문

South Gate, Chŏnju.

South Gate, Chonju

Chonju Street in Kunsan, 1920's.

Chonju in the 1920's.

(Above) Kaechon Elementary School building with students and teachers lined up in front. (Left page) The school's Pongmyong Pavilion. Both built 300 years ago.

SITTING DUCKS

CHAPTER IV

COOKING KOREANS

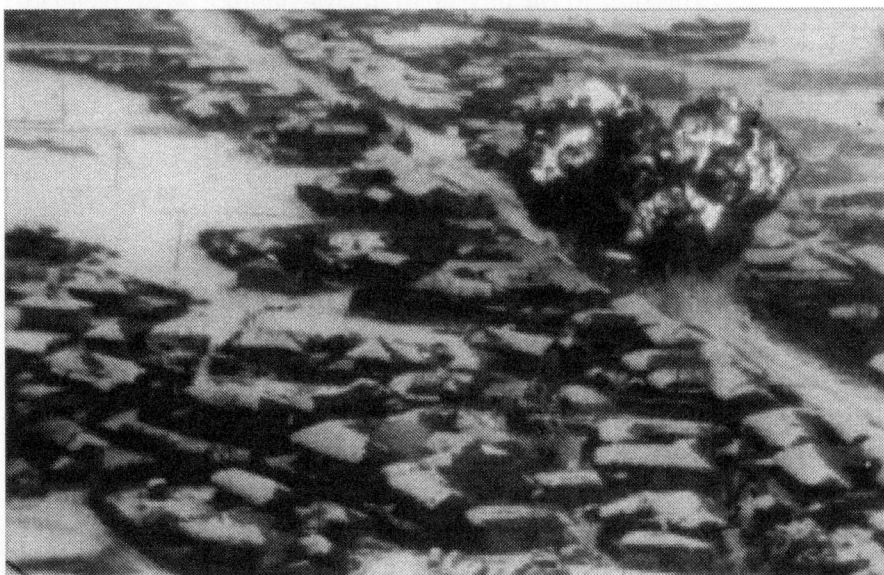

Stratemeyer, Friday, 7 July 1950:

> Complimented by General Almond, Chief of Staff, GHQ, FEC, on our news release as of today which started out — "Far East Air Forces has now completed 1,100 sorties. . . .
>
> General Dean called from Korea and gave me four targets over which he wanted air support. Apparently as has been shown by test, our bazookas can not penetrate the Soviet Tank. . . . General Dean's targets were all mostly on arteries — rail, ferry crossing and the road between P'yongta'ek and Osan. . . .[Location of first contact between American troops and the North Korean forces, about 49 miles south of Seoul.]
>
> Weather unfavorable; two F-80's lost; missions directed against factories in the North, bridges, convoys, and troop movements. F-82 on an 'intruder mission' in the Inch'on area [the South Korean port city near Seoul] dropped one napalm bomb; results believed by pilot to be good. . . .

An "intruder mission" is a flight behind enemy lines often at night intended to harass the enemy. This is Stratemeyer's first mention of napalm, but the next day he refers to the first use of napalm by 2 F-51's.

Stratemeyer, Saturday, 8 July 1950:

> The first use of napalm brought about these results (I have been urging its use now for about a

week): 2 F–51s on a bombing and strafing mission report using 1 x 6 napalm and destroyed: 4 small tanks, 5 trucks with 35 ft. trailers. Four vehicles exploded – other equipment damaged by 50 cal. fire.

Stratemeyer continued to press his forces to use napalm.

Stratemeyer, Wednesday, 19 July 1950:

Asked my Operations for a report on napalm usage.

According to USAF historian Robert Futrell, General Stratemeyer from early in the Korean conflict insisted on the wide use of napalm. He had seen the effectiveness of napalm in World War II and wanted it used. But in the beginning of the war the requirement that the pilots fly low to drop the tanks of napalm caused problems because of faulty fusing and mixtures. In addition, the preparation of the napalm mixture and its attachment to the planes added heavy burdens to the already overworked ground crews. Hence the crews and pilots resisted its use.

However, after some experimentation, the fighter-bombers became adept at utilizing napalm and it became a popular weapon among pilots. The 8th Fighter-Bomber Group called napalm "the most effective weapon yet introduced." A 110-gallon napalm bomb would spread over an area about 275 feet long and 80 feet wide, according to Futrell, and burning with a 1500 degree flash, would normally devastate the area.

"Napalm was also considered as an effective weapon against dug-in troops, vehicles, and **village targets**" (Futrell). Village targets, from what we have seen above, were ideal burning objects. The tank dropped in the middle of a village would spread a hellish fire 275 feet by 80 feet and would swiftly spread from one thatch and wood house to the next – quickly consuming the entire village before anyone could escape, particularly if the napalm were dropped on the village at night. Later in the conflict huge 4,000-pound cannisters filled with napalm were being utilized by the Air Force.

"LIQUID FIRE - This dramatic picture shows how enemy supply buiod-up areas and warhouses look after a strike by Fifth Air Force B-26 'Invader' bombers of the 452nd Bomb Wing (light). When aerial reconnaissance showed that a landing along the river near Hanchon in North Korea contained stockpiles of supplies, B-26's laden with napalm, rockets and .50 caliber ammunition, were soon off to the attack. Brisk winds fanned the flames into every nook of these thatch-topped huts, and prevented thousands of tons of supplies from reaching enemy Communist forces."
May 1951   USAF Photo

The follwoing is another caption written by the USAF for one of its napalm photos:

"Enemy Supply Dump Inactivated — The strategy employed by bombadiers of the 452nd Light Bomb Wing when one of their B-26s placed a napalm bomb dead center in this enemy supply dump in Korea was based on getting an assist from 'mother nature'. Fierce winds sweeping over the flat terrain soon had the entire concentration blazing. Fighters and light bombers of the US Far East Air Forces have given the napalm treatment to thousands of tons of vital enemy supplies and equipment far to the rear area, in a program of interdiction to prevent their being put to use on the front lines. January 1951"

A napalm bomb is one type of "incendiary" bomb. The idea is not just to cause fire, but to have a burning substance spread around, attach to as much as possible and be nearly impossible to put out before the substance itself disintegrates. Gilbert Dreyfus explains that "napalm" is a jelly substance obtained from the salts of aluminum, palmitic or other fatty acids, and naphthenic acids. The substance is added to tanks of gasoline.

"These acids give a viscous consistency to gasoline so that an incendiary jelly results," that is, a flaming blob that splashes on people and things and cannot be extinguished. The most frequently used container for napalm was one containing nearly 500 liters of gasoline, jellied by an addition of napalm varying from six to thirteen percent.

"Napalm acts not only by burning but has an equally devastating effect which consists of a complicated process whereby shock, absorption of oxygen from the air, smoke and noxious gases become lethal" (Dreyfus). Many of those killed by a napalm bomb are killed by carbon monoxide poisoning. *Taking shelter during a napalm attack is useless, as the shelters have their oxygen sucked out by the napalm and asphyxiation results.* Hence the two main causes of death by napalm is by fire and by asphyxiation.

Indeed the Air Force soon perfected the technique of having napalm attacks preceded by strafing by fighter pilots or bombing with general purpose bombs. This was intended to chase people into shelters which would then become their tombs when the napalm was dropped. The Official Releases from MacArthur's Headquarters that described bombing raids would often mention this order of attack. This was the reason for it.

The napalm burns on a human are distinguishable from ordinary burns "by the fact that they are covered with viscous black magma resembling tar. The depth of the burn is always considerable" (Dreyfus). Shock and infection are some of the other causes of death. And in napalm burns, "a final element is of great importance: this is the gravity of facial burning. Eye burns can lead to loss of one or both eyes. Nasal and ear passages involved develop extended suppuration and necrosis which abscess with unbearable pain to the patient. The face becomes hideous with psychological trauma of formidable proportions." The best chance for survival is evacuation immediately and comprehensive treatment in a medical facility at the level of a "general hospital."

"A dead center hit is scored with a deadly napalm tank on an enemy supply concentration near Wonsan in Korea. Crew members of one of the B-26 Invader light bombers of the Fifth Air Force's 452nd Light Bomb Wing registered this bulls-eye on a recent interdiction flight...." March 1951 Official US Air Force Photo

Needless to say, most victims of napalm bombing in Korea were not "immediately evacuated" and treated at a "general hospital" level.

There are no reports that the North Koreans or the Chinese who entered the war later when the Americans reached the border with China ever used incendiary or napalm bombs. This may be because they did not have any. But in any event they could not deliver them as the Americans controlled the air for the most part from day one. Usually the American bombers could fly with no fear of encountering enemy planes, though this changed somewhat later in the war when Chinese, and Russian, it was later learned, pilots manning MIG-15's challenged the Americans in the area just south of the Yalu that became known as "MIG Alley." But for most of the war and over most of Korea the US bombers were free to roam and had the luxury of utilizing the most efficient techniques of destruction.

The FAS Military Analysis Network describes a napalm bomb as a mixture of benzene (21%), gasoline (33%), and polystyrene (46%). Neither gasoline nor benzene can be extinguished with water, gasoline floats on water and is of course dangerous if inhaled or swallowed. Polystyrene "is the white, tough plastic that is used to make cups, plates . . . It dissolves easily in acetone and benzene, but not in gasoline. . . . Heated polystyrene softens at about 185 F. . . . In air, polystyrene melts and burns with a yellow, sooty flame."

Another napalm Air Force photo caption reads:

*"**Most Feared Weapon** — Prisoner interrogation has determined that napalm bombs are the most feared of all weapons used by the US Far East Air Forces in Korea. Shown is the blast from one of these fire bombs as it begins to envelop a building used as a military barracks by the Communists. The jellied gasoline covers the building and is forced through open windows and doors by the blast. In the upper left of the picture can be seen flames from the first of two napalm tanks dropped by B-26 light bombers on a village used by the enemy in Korea to shelter troops and store supplies." USAF January 1951*

"FIERY INFERNO" "Thatch-topped huts harboring supplies of food, lubricants and ammunition aided the destructive power of napalm, as the entire enemy supply concentration is turned into a fiery mass. Crew members of the Fifth Air Force's 452nd Light Bomb Group made this interdiction strike on a Communist supply storage area near Wonsan in North Korea." April 12, 1951   Official US Air Force Photo

"WOODED INFERNO. A fiery inferno envelopes enemy troop concentrations in this wooded area as Fifth Air Force B-26 Invaders loose their load of napalm (jellied gasoline) bombs on these positions in close support of United Nations troops."

May 29, 1951   Official US Air Force Photo

LIBERATING KOREA?

CHAPTER V

GOD HELP US! THE AMERICANS ARE COMING!

The North Korean Army quickly rolled over the South Korean defenses at the 38th parallel on June 25th. Kim Il Sung, the North Korean leader, had been a famous Korean nationalist who fought as a guerilla against the Japanese occupiers of his homeland. He had operated out of Manchuria until he had to flee because the Japanese Army was getting close to capturing him. He went to Siberia where he found Communist Russia ready to support him and his cause. He was trained by the Soviets and joined their Army.

When the Soviets declared war against Japan and marched into Manchuria and Korea, they had wisely brought Kim Il Sung and other ethnic Koreans like him back to Korea. Siberia had served for 40 years as a safe haven for Korean nationalists escaping the Japanese colonialists. Thousands of Koreans were born in Siberia and therefore served as a natural connection between the Soviet Union and Korea. That is one of the reasons the Soviets had an easy time of it during their occupation of North Korea.

The core of Kim's troops were Korean veterans like himself from the Soviet Army and, to a greater extent, ethnic Korean veterans of the Chinese Communist Armies who had fought first the Japanese and then the Chinese Nationalists. He had 135,000 men in 8 full divisions, each including a regiment of artillery; 2 divisions at half strength; 2 separate regiments; an armored brigade with 120 Soviet T34 medium tanks; and 5 border constabulary brigades (United States Military Institute, <u>American Military History, The Korean War</u>).

The South Korean Army (ROK) had 95,000 men, M-1 rifles, and 89 105-mm howitzers, but no tanks. More significantly, while some of its officers had experience with the Japanese Army, very few of its soldiers had seen combat. The Army had received limited training by a 500 man American Advisory Group which in turn had a low priority in Washington.

The idea was to deny Korea to the Communists but with as little expense and risk as possible. The Americans had caused the division of Korea in 1945 primarily to irritate the Russians, who of course had an immense historical and physical interest in this country on its very border. When the Truman Administration was considering procedures for the surrender of Japan, many decisions had to be made about which Ally would accept the surrender in any particular location, and then get the troops there. The US was the only nation with the ability to make the arrangements. Already there were forces in the US Government who had targeted one of our allies, the Soviet Union, as a potential enemy and began treating it that way. So, while we were on the one hand helping our British and French allies, and even the Dutch, reintroduce their troops back into their old colonies before the natives got used to the idea of being their own masters, on the other hand we were also trying to box in the Russians.

There seems to have been many hands in the mix of decisions that were made on the surrender. But I came across an interesting "TOP SECRET" memo dated August 11, 1945 from the erstwhile and future banker, Edwin W. Pauley, now special Ambassador for President Truman for "Reparations" (indemnity from Japan and Germany, both in money and in territory). The Top Secret memo, written as Japan was surrendering, was addressed to "The President and The Secretary of State." It read:

> Conclusions I have reached thru discussions on Reparations and otherwise (I repeat otherwise) lead me to the belief that our forces **should occupy quickly as much** of the industrial areas of Korea and Manchuria **as we can**, starting at the southerly tip and progressing northward. I am assuming all of this will be done at no risk of American lives after organized hostilities have ceased, and **occupancy to continue only until satisfactory agreements** have been reached between the nations concerned **with respect to** reparations and **territorial rights** or other concessions.

(A copy of this memo is in the "H.L. Wolbers Papers," U.S. Army Military History Institute, Carlisle Barracks, Pa).

The huge industrial facilities and dams developed by the Japanese in Manchuria seemed to be Pauley's primary focus. In the typed memo the words "Korea and" are written in by hand just before the typed word "Manchuria." Was this an afterthought, reflecting Korea's low priority status even with the most greedy of Truman's advisors? Or was it just a typo? Was this banker's recommendation political or economic -- that is, based on the emerging "containment"concept or merely taking assets for Americans?

Pauley suggests that we grab and hold onto as much territory as possible, not only for monetary reparations, but until we are satisfied that "territorial"rights to this real estate have been properly determined. This raises a number of questions. What"territorial rights" had to be determined? Manchuria belonged to China historically and Korea belonged to the Koreans. What was there to decide? Moreover, as for Korea, FDR and later Truman had promised "liberation" and independence to this colony of Japan. Again, why did Pauley, and whomever else in the Government is represented by the ideas in this memo, think that territorial decisions or concessions were involved?

Now in the rush of things, the Americans would try to snatch as much land as possible on the borders of Russia -- and hold on to it for "concessions." Not a good signal to the Russians. And a very bad omen for FDR's and Vito Marcantonio's vision of post war cooperation between the US and the Soviet Union.

These instructions apparently found there way to the men in the joint military-civilian task force who were making up the plans for the surrender. Among that group was the future Kennedy-Johnson Secretary of State, the brilliant Colonel Dean Rusk, a fervent Christian and anti-communist from the South, who was to become a protege of Dean Acheson. According to Rusk he actually drew that fateful line along the 38th parallel -- complying with instructions to "occupy quickly as much"of Korea as possible, even though no American troops were nereby.

But while the nascent "containment" hawks in Washington were delighted that Stalin, by agreeing to the proposed Order No. 1 to be issued by MacArthur, had allowed them to keep part of Korea out of his hands, they were unwilling to invest much else in it. The bottom line was that Korea was of no military value to the US. This was an economic and strategic policy subsequently enshrined in a National Security Paper – documents used as guiding principles for all governmental agencies.

In addition, while the Americans wanted to aggravate the Russians and try to make fools of them on their own doorstep, they did not want anyone getting them into a war. This later led to a constant tussle with Sigmund Rhee who just would not behave like the compliant figurehead Hodge had hoped he would be. The missionary-educated Sigmund Rhee, who had been out of the country for decades and was already in his seventies, and his coalition of wealthy landlords, industrialists and other Japanese collaborators, frightened the Americans with their constant talk of invading North Korea and uniting the country by force. Consequently the weapons given to Rhee -- M-1's, vehicles, artillery, and the like, were purely of a defensive nature. No air force, no navy, no tanks. When John Muccio, the Ambassador to South Korea, tried to lobby in Washington for some airplanes for Rhee, he was referred to the National Security Paper. Get that changed, he was told, and you will get your planes.

The Korean groups that were armed with these weapons (the constabulary or army; the Japanese-trained police force; and the anti-communist youth groups recruited from refugees from the communist zone) were enough to enable Rhee and his allies to set up what was essentially a police state, but they were no match for the northerners. So when the attack came, the veteran and well-armed northerners marched freely down the peninsula.

In addition to being better armed and trained, there was another essential reason why the North Korean Army marched so freely down the country. As they moved into South Korea **they were greeted by a friendly population of relatives.** POW General Dean later gave witness to the fact that the northerners were being readily accepted by the population in the south, even with enthusiasm.

In turn the northerners were not laying waste the countryside as they moved down; they were not looting and raping or indiscriminately slaughtering their brothers; they were not burning down the towns and villages. It was not the practice of the North Korean Army to open up its way by laying down a path of devastation. No planes from the North firebombed the cities in the South. No armada of aircraft and warships from the North bombarded the cities into a wilderness. As the battle between the northerners and the southerners ensued, it was clear that neither side had the plans nor the firepower nor the desire to burn down every one of their own cities, towns and villages when they confrounted each other.

At this point if they had been left alone — as most observers had thought they would be, as American policy in its own National Security papers had assumed they would be, and as people like Congressman Vito Marcantonio had pleaded — the country would have been unified in a few weeks with an infinitesimal amount of bloodshed and destruction compared to what was to happen. Instead, Truman's surprising intervention inevitably led to transforming the Korean Peninsula into a wasteland – as a result of the massive tonnage of explosives, napalm, phosphorous and other incendiary bombs that the Americans unloaded onto the entire peninsula for the next three years.

With the most powerful nation in the world now in the war, what would have been a neighborhood disturbance resulting in scratches to the brawlers, evolved into a nightmare. In the beginning it was the retreat by the South Koreans and the Americans *down* the peninsula to the final defensive beachhead at the port of Pusan, that regrettably required the destruction of **South Korean** towns, villages and cities so as to deny them to the advancing enemy. Later it would be the American advance *up* the peninsula that regrettably required firepower to blast away the enemy in front of them. Never mind that the blasting would not only kill enemy troops, but also the population caught in the middle and would destroy their homes, factories, stores, farms, animals, sewer systems, water systems, electrical systems, and everything else it took to live.

What little difference there was in the American military approach to our "allies" south of the latitudinal line of the 38th parallel and to our "enemies" just north of it is illustrated by one of *General Stratemeyer's diary entries, Wednesday, 19 July 1950*:

Had a conference with General MacArthur at 1815 hours and talked from the following notes: . . . Bombing will be visual if possible; by radar if not. The weather over the immediate battlefront [which at that time was well into South Korea] is predicted 'poor' for tomorrow (20 July); however, one bomb group medium will be given targets in the area between the 37th and 38th Parallels [that is, over South Korean cities and towns] and will attack if possible. I propose for air strikes tomorrow (20 July) to use one bomb group medium on the airfield and supply dump of bombs and fuel at (#1) P'yongang, (#3) Onjon-ni, (#5) Mirim-ni. **Visual if possible; by radar if not,** and one bomb group medium on the airfield and supply of bombs and fuel at ———— [in original]. Our reconnaissance pictures show that there are great supplies of fuel, bombs and other types of supplies just adjacent to these airdromes. **Because of weather, we might have to do radar bombing; however, these airdromes are in North Korea and if all bombs do not hit target area, it <u>should be of no concern</u>.**

Nearly all the bombs dropped on Korea in those days would be what we now call "dumb bombs" – bombs without any guidance, just aimed from the plane, taking wind and velocity and height and weather and visibility into consideration. (There were experiments with guidance systems, such as the Razon and Tarzon bombs, but these primative versions of guided missiles were even more inaccurate than radar bombing.) Even with the best of weather and in daytime with visual bombing, dumb bombs would be anywhere from 10 to 800 feet off their mark – two and a half football fields away. If you were bombing the Verrazano Bridge from 16,000 feet, a number of your bombs would have to hit and wipe out Bay Ridge and Bensonhurst in Brooklyn and a good deal of Staten Island near the Bridge. Taking out the Brooklyn Bridge would wipe out half of Manhattan. That was with visual bombing. With radar – the off-target rate would be even higher.

Nevertheless, there still was a significant difference between *visual* bombing and *radar* bombing. If the bombs are to hit the airfields and supply dumps only, and not the rest of the adjacent city or town, then it obviously would be better to fly lower and actually see the targets.

(*F-51 Mustang dropping napalm bomb on N.K. industrial site. USAF August, 1951.*)

On the other hand, if you do not care if the bombs miss their target, then you can fly high over the clouds, using radar and hope that most of your bombs hit the target. The higher the bombers flew, and the B-29's usually flew at a range of 16,000 to 30,000 feet, the less accuracy there was. Likewise in poor weather with everything hidden by clouds or at night, accuracy suffered. The less accurate the bombing, the more destruction to the civilian population and their homes. If the civilians were in the south, that was regrettable but an inevitable consequence of war; but if they were in the north, then, as Stratemeyer notes, "it should be of no concern."

"BOMBS AWAY - *Regardless of the type of enemy   target lying in this rugged, mountainous terrain of Korea, very little will remain after the falling bombs have done their work. . . ."*

USAF Photo   February 1951.

From the damage done ultimately to South Korean cities, however, it would seem that in the end Stratemeyer's attempt at making a distinction between North Korean civilians and South Korean civilians did not help the South Koreans very much.

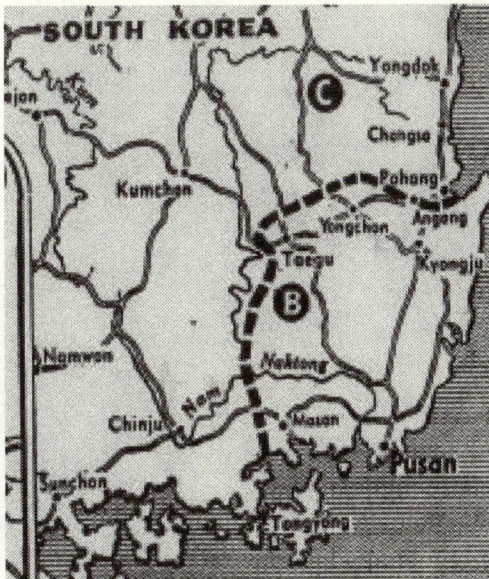

(Map: Jack Luboff, <u>New York Herald Tribune</u>, September 16, 1950)

By August 3rd the Americans were quickly building up their forces and ground weapons – marines were pouring into Pusan, they now had 3.3-inch"super-bazookas"that could penetrate the T34 tanks and had the equal or better Sherman and 45-ton Pershing tanks. But they were still in retreat. They were now leaving their positions on the banks of the narrow Kum River and consolidating to what they hoped would be a strong natural barrier on the south side of the broader Naktong River. The ultimate defense perimeter for the Americans and South Koreans had shrunken down to a **150 mile semi-circle around the port of Pusan** on the southeast tip of Korea. As the Americans withdrew **they destroyed the towns and villages they were abandoning.** These towns and its inhabitant, of course, were in South Korea.

The Army photographers and its caption writers did their best to soften the images. But in fact we were driving Korean families from their ancestral homes and villages -- developed over a thousand years. Then we burned them down. The Russians would later charge in the UN, to the derision of the US Delegate, that those villagers who refused to evacuate were executed. We have no records of that. Photographs, though, seem indisputable. These are soldiers in the line enforcing the evacuation.

8A/FEC-50-6239   12 Aug 50

"WAR IN KOREA:
"SOUTH KOREANS EVACUATE THEIR
HOMES, AS THE 25TH INF DIV TAKES
OVER THEIR TOWN. . . ."

Photo by PFC Weider (SJK)
US Army

Each of the following three photos carries the same caption from the US Army.

"A South Korean village burns as a result of an ammunition dump explosion in the Shinjumik section, Korea, where US troops are supporting the 1st ROK Div in action against the North Korean invaders."

US Army
3 Photos by Sgt. Stewart
26 Aug 50

Everybody walked . . . . except the Generals.

Refugees fleeing from combat area, near Taegu, Korea."

Photo by Capt. Scheiber US Army   20 Aug 1950

August, 1950

US Army
Photos of
Refugees
during the
American
and ROK
retreat.

"General J. Lawton Colins,
Chief of Staff, U.S. Army;
Lt. Gen. Walton H. Walker,
CG Ground Forces in Korea;
and Maj. Gen William
Kean, Jr., CO 25th Inf. Div.
leave the 25th Inf. Div.
command post at Masan in
a jeep."

US Army, Buckle
23 August 1950

GOD HELP US!

On August 1ˢᵗ MacArthur's Command issued *Official Release 180* which read in part:

> *Fifth Air Force and R.A.A.F. [Australian] fighters, flying about 259 sorties close to the battle line, hit vehicles, buildings and railroad rolling stock at Namwon, Hwanggan, Yosu, Sunchon, Hadong, Yongdong, Kochang, Chirye, Chonju, Yechon and Andong [again, friendly South Korean towns]....*

From the August 3, 1950 <u>Washington Post</u>:

> **"The defense perimeter . . . was marked by flaming towns and villages, from Chinju on the south to Yongdok on the east** coast 80 miles north of Pusan. . . . Latest to fall was flaming **Kumchon**, 35 miles northwest of Taegu, South Korean provisional capital [which is] 60 miles northwest of Pusan. . . .

The <u>Washington Post</u> article of August 3, 1950 continued:

> Correspondent O.H.P. King, with ground forces in the area, said air strikes **set Chinju ablaze and fired the neighboring village of Sachon** in a five-hour raid. . . . The withdrawal was 'orderly and planned.' . . . Aircraft continued to give heavy, close support to the ground forces. They flew more than 500 tactical sorties Wednesday with their major effort thrown into the Chinju sector. The southern coastal towns of Mokpo and Yosu were hard hit with naval gunfire as well as aerial rockets and cannon fire. British and South Korean naval craft shelled Mokpo. American destroyers hit Yosu.

Before the American retreat, Yosu, Mokpo, Chinju, Sachon, Yongdok and Kumchon, with their neighboring towns and villages, were functioning South Korean communities. Some dating back a thousand years. Now they were "military targets" subject to carpet bombing because the advancing enemy might use them.

Official Release 176 from MacArthur's Headquarters issued the day before announced:

> *Yosu, on the southern tip of Korea, was*

attacked on Monday by F-82 twin Mustang fighter pilots, who strafed marshalling yards and set fire to warehouses and storage dumps with rocket and machine-gun fire. . . . The light B-26 Invaders used rockets to set fire to warehouses north of the Kum River

and supply trucks moving on the road south of Seoul.

The <u>Washington Post</u> reported on the 2nd of August:

> NAVAL FORCES POUND YONGDOK — An American observation pilot cruising over the Yongdok [South Korea] front Tuesday reported that North Koreans had fallen back to positions 1500 yards north of the ruined port. Troop concentrations within range of shore fire took a heavy toll of North Korean troops.
>
> Yongdok has been pounded repeatedly by allied naval forces cruising close offshore for deadly, high velocity bombardment runs.

On the 4th the <u>Washington Post</u> further reported:

> In the only other major ground action Thursday, South Korean troops of the Third Division re-occupied the battered east coast port of Yongdok, 80 miles north of Pusan, to reestablish it as the eastern anchor of the defenders.
>
> Yongdok has been heavily shelled by United States and British cruisers and destroyers. The warships sent six and eight-inch shells into the North Korean Fourth Division as it pulled back. . . .

The most detailed public accounts available in English of

the Americans destroying a South Korean city as they abandon it in a retreat are two articles by reporters who flew over Kumchon while it was being destroyed, perhaps in the same observation plane. One reporter, W. H. Lawrence, wrote for the <u>New York Times</u>, while the other, Hal Boyle, writing for the Associated Press, had his article published in the <u>Washington Post</u>, both on August 3, 1950.

Lawrence's article is headlined: "KUMCHON ABLAZE, AIR VIEW REVEALS – Writer Flying Along the Front Sees Earth Scorched as U.S. Troops Narrow Perimeter." Lawrence reported:

> Kumchon is in flames below us, aban-doned by United States forces withdrawing in the direction of the Naktong River line. The Eight Army pulled out of Kumchon and a number of Korean villages today, not as a result of enemy pressure but to take up new positions on a new defense line. . . **The Americans are pursuing a scorched earth policy** as they withdraw, **leveling villages** to the ground so that the enemy cannot take advantage of houses or other buildings to camouflage his tanks, supplies and vehicles from the attacking United State Air Force in the day-light hours. . . .
>
> When the First Cavalry Division quit Kumchon it did a thorough destruction job. As we flew over the city . . . we could see a score or more fires burning. . . . Dense clouds of smoke rolled up, blotting out for minutes at a time the bright blood-red sun, about to set behind the city.

Lawrence explained that there was no contact between the retreating G.I.'s and the advancing North Koreans. The Army was pulling back its northern and western lines to behind the Naktong River where they would dig in and wait for reinforcements from the Marines then landing at Pusan. He relates how the plane he was in then flew south and west of Taegu, still held by the Americans and South Koreans, for a quick run behind the enemy lines. "Below us, Hyopchon, which the Americans lost two days ago, was aflame and American fighters were active in the general area."

The reporter tells his readers that during this flight over destruction and devastation he was able to listen with earphones to some of the conversations between American pilots and ground control officers. He

> "got a momentary but impressive account of **the field day that the Air Force was enjoying** against the enemy on a bright sunshiny day."

From some of that conversation:

> *Pilot* to ground control: 'There's a town on that Y in the road which we'll have to hit again. . . .'

> *Pilot* to ground control: 'We got those gooks (a G.I. nickname for North Koreans) [Lawrence's explanation] crossing the river. I'd guess there were fifty to 100 of them crossing from north to south headed toward Chirye.'

Hal Boyle, writing for the Associated Press, had a somewhat different take on the same scene of desolation. His headline in the Washington Post was: "KUMCHON IS A HADES AS YANKS WITHDRAW"

> Leaping towers of orange flame are burning out the heart of ancient Kumchon to-night as . . . American troops pull out. . . . [I]t is like having a bleacher seat in hell to see it from a plane circling at 500 feet. The entire western

waterfront is burning – about 500 yards or more of solid flame and billowing black smoke.

The red and orange tongues lick skyward at least 100 feet. In the northeast quarter of the city another area erupts like a vast furnace door suddenly opened. . . .

There is dust, discomfort, danger and death below. But if an artist could paint the scene from this height he could make war look beautiful – if you thought only in terms of color and not of wasted effort and broken bodies. . . .

The American withdrawal is a fighting one. They are mad because gook guerillas even dared to raid their command post before dawn.

On the hillside, phosphorous artillery shells burst like gigantic powder puffs. Three nearby villages have joined in the concert of flame. Through the thickening smoke a blood-red sun shines a bloody farewell to a bloody day. . . . It shines like a beacon to Dante's Hades – a red sun lighting a red victory. . . .

Kumchon is only another of the many cities that have fallen to the Communists in the last few days [and therefore destroyed by the Americans]. . . . From Kumchon in an 80-mile arc sweeping southward to Chinju on the south coast the battle line could be followed **by a string of flaming villages**.

Stratemeyer, 3 August 1950:

> "One F–51 believed hit by small arms ground

fire; crashed near Kumchon."

The American withdrawal to the east banks of the Naktong River was considered a success as it was done without the North Koreans realizing what was happening. There was little contact between the forces and so losses were light for the Americans and South Koreans. In addition, only burnt out rubble was left for the North Koreans.

> "United States fighter planes strafed the west banks of the Naktong River today, scattering Communist soldiers who were moving toward that United States defense line with carts. . . . Eight Navy Corsairs **bombed and rocketed villages west of the river. They left them in flames**"(Washington Post, August 5, 1950).

> "Although the retreat has again shrunk the defense perimeter, . . . the invaders got [only] further **acres of scorched South Korean territory**, and plans and intelligence officers regard the withdrawal as a successful and profitable maneuver" (New York Times, August 4, 1950).

Stratemeyer, Friday, 4 August 1950:

> Headquarters' Advance [the 5th Air Force headquarters in Korea with Generals Partridge and Timberlake] evacuating Taegu for Pusan."

As it turned out Partridge decided to keep part of his staff at Taegu and the 8th Army Headquarters under General Walker also stayed at Taegu until September. Rhee and his government and US Ambassador Muccio likewise remained at Taegu. The city of Taegu, about 65 miles from Pusan, on the perimeter defense line around Pusan, never fell to the enemy. The North Koreans by this time were becoming exhausted and the pounding by the US Air Force on their very long supply line was having an effect. While the American and South Korean troops on the ground could not feel it yet, the turning point had been reached.

But this was no comfort to the population of Korea, particularly South Korea. During the next month a defensive holding action along the 150 mile long Pusan perimeter resulted in the destruction of even more friendly towns.

Official Release 358 issued September 1st:

> *Fighters and light bombers flew all day, then others in their groups took over operations and flew all last night.*
>
> *One flight of F-80's rocketed and strafed military installations in a town near Pohang [South Korea] last night, setting fire to warehouses and other buildings occupied by the Communists. The town was Yonggadong. Fourteen separate fires were counted by the pilots as they left. . . .*
>
> *Light invader bombers late yesterday attacked North Korean headquarters in Kumchon, about twenty-seven miles northwest of Taegu.*
>
> *It was a high altitude mission [meaning, more likely to be inaccurate] but the bombs made a good pattern on the target," said First Lieut. . . .*

On September the 1st the <u>New York Times</u> reported that "the enemy had captured the town of Kigye — now also a mass of ruins –and had been driving on Pohang. . . ." On the 2nd one of its reporters recounted the fate of another South Korean town from which the Americans had retreated:

> From a ridge to the east of Haman, air force and marine fighters could be seen swarming on Haman first with rockets, then with bombs

and finally strafing the foe inside. At one period there were eleven Corsairs over Haman taking turns inflicting punishment on the enemy inside the town. Huge clouds of white and black smoke billowed up from the burning town. . . .

When there was any lull in the air cover United States artillery opened up with round after round into the town itself.

The Washington Post on September 6th reported:

"Sixteen miles to the northeast of Kyongju, fallen Pohang was reported afire from a American B-26 bomb raid. The Reds Tuesday night seized Pohang, second only to Pusan as a port of supply. . . . Pilots reported Pohang was in flames."

On the 7th it told of the end of another South Korean town:

"Twenty-three miles southwest of Taegu, the town of Changnyong was described by Associated Press correspondent Don Huth as a fire-gutted battleground."

Pohang, already being described as afire as a result of the American retreat, was fated to see the Americans a month later coming the other way.

And so it went, town after town – the Americans destroying Korean towns south of the 38th parallel that we said we had come to save from slavery.

CHAPTER VI

CAUGHT "BEHIND ENEMY LINES"

Most of the area and its population of 20,000,000 we claimed to be rescuing from the poisoning menace of communism were now "behind enemy lines" or "behind the bomb line." It was not healthy to be behind those lines as any target considered to be of military value to the enemy was fair game for strafing with 50 mm machine guns and rockets or bombing with GP (general purpose explosives) or napalm – day or night. The Bomb Line was the temporary line drawn by the military commanders between friendly and enemy forces for the purposes of bombing. Everything on the enemy side of the Bomb Line could be bombed, but on the friendly side of the Bomb Line only targets that had been identified and approved or under the direction of a controller could be bombed. At first the targets that might be of military use to the enemy behind the Bomb Line included all roads and bridges, ports and airports, warehouses, factories of every sort, power plants, large stores of rice and other foods. Then it began to include any structure which the enemy "could" use to hide troops, weapons, etc. Hence the list soon included schools, hospitals, churches. Eventually just any house or building behind enemy lines and anything moving behind enemy lines was fair game.

Even the long, narrow, pain-drenched lines of refugees were included as legitimate military targets. Retired Air Force Major Alton A. Pendleton piloted a F-80 jet fighter with the 49th Fighter Wing stationed at Taegu (K-2 – airfields got "K" numbers for identification) during the Korean War. In his 1998 autobiography, Three O'Clock High, he reports that because "enemy soldiers would get inside a refugee column and move down the road in broad daylight" the fighters had standing **"orders to strike the entire column. The pilots did not like it, but most of us followed orders"** (Chapter I: "MIG ALLEY," 21 August 2003 http:// www.onr.com/user/dtg/Chapter 1.htm).

The pilots carried rockets and 50 caliber "API" (armor piercing incendiary) bullets for strafing and they would dutifully mow down the refugees — men, women and children — though Major Pendleton noted that some of the pilots "silently objected to this and put their ordnance to the side of the refugee column." Since everyone knew that these objecting pilots, if they wanted to, could hit a single individual while flying at 500 mph, their fellow pilots would "tease" them on these occasions for being such bad shots (Pendleton, Chapter I).

Official Release 188 (August 2, 1950) from MacArthur Head-quarters in Tokyo:

*Fifth Air Force B-29's flew an increased number of night in-truder missions aimed at North Korean troop and supply move-ments being carried out under the cover of darkness. Night flying B-26's bombed and **strafed bridges and highways in the Seoul area and south**. A marshalling yard at **Ansong** was bombed and **vehicular targets were hit at Seoul, Yosu and Taejon**. Possible damage was inflicted on a bridge in the Seoul area.*

*Daylight B-26 missions were flown to **Mokpo** where the **dock area** was bombed and **left burning**, as well as to **Seoul** and **Taejon**. The light bombers attacked four hangars at Taejon now believed to be serving as repair shops.*

*Fifth Air Force F-80 jets and F-51's were joined by Royal Aus-tralian Air Force Mustangs in flying more than 400 armed recon-naissance and close support sorties **behind the North Korean lines.***

*The fighters kept up a **constant stream of attacks**, including some night operations aimed at troop concentrations, vehicles and other military objectives.*

*Assigned target areas ranged from **Yongdok and Yonghae** on the east coast to **Mokpo** in the southwest. At the latter city F-80's brought their rockets to bear on the marshalling yard , railroad station and **a factory** causing fires and extensive damage.*

*F-80's also claimed a **power plant** at **Kunsan**. . . . Fifth Air Force F-51's fired a **power station** and supply dump at **Chinju** and a **power plant** at **Yongdok**. Bridges were bombed or rocketed at **Yonghae**, **Kochang** and **Chinju**, and the marshalling yards at **Sunchon** were strafed and bombed. **Dock installation at Yosu were strafed and left burning**. . . .*

Each of these cities and towns we were destroying was in an area we had in 1945 casually carved out of the peninsula, called a "democracy" in 1948 by the name of South Korea and finally in June of 1950 declared worthy of shedding American blood to save from communist "slavery."

The south Korean port city of Mokpo was now in enemy hands, so it was being systematically obliterated. Here is a scenic view of Mokpo in the 1920's, which now must have seemed like the "good old days" to the inhabitants of Mokpo even though they had then been under hash Japanese colonial rule.

Suffering the same fate from the liberating Americans was Mokpo's sister port city Kunsan. Again, this city had been better off under the Japanese, at least it was allowed to exist. From the Korean Cultural Service Library we can find scenic views of a peaceful Kunsan in the 20's. Under Japanese rule, but at least not in flames.

Mokpo's streets commanding a view of Mokpo's port.

The targets in these towns and cities of necessity were located next door to where people lived – people who had only days before been living in freedom under the "democratic" government of our ally, South Korea. Now we were blowing up their factories and power plants.

Since daylight travel was especially hazardous to the North Koreans, most of their movement was at night. US aircraft, therefore, would strafe the roads during the night, in addition to the daylight flights. As the resourceful northerners were using foot power, carts and oxen to drive the Americans off the peninsula, "anything" that moved on the roads was a legitimate "military" target. Jets screaming down from the skis could not be expected to make any fine distinctions between a northern in uniform or a southern civilian. The figure in the field could be sowing seeds for wheat, or he could be a guerilla sowing the seeds of revolution. Since oxen could be used for pulling a cart full of troops, as well as a cart full of hay – they could be blasted.

With most of Korea behind enemy lines and the United States Air Force free to roam the entire peninsula without fear of the non-existent North Korean Air Force, every human and animal moving in Korea outside the 150 mile safety zone of the Pusan perimeter was in jeopardy from the American planes. Not surprisingly, Pusan was inundated, according to American press releases, with refugees fleeing communism and seeking democracy and freedom – and incidentally safety from the endless and terrifying attacks of American planes.

From the diary entry of *General Earle Partridge, 16 December 1950*:

> During recent days we have been carrying out attacks beyond the bomb line on any activities which might have military significance. For example, **we have been attacking all males** who are **carrying arms** or who are moving about in a manner which indicates that they are **potential enemy**.

One has to ask whether a pilot going 500 miles an hour could tell the difference between a male and a female, a boy and a man. Moreover, how could the pilot determine at that flashing speed that the individual was carrying something that might be a weapon – or a walking stick, or a rake? Or how does a streaming fighter determine in a second's time that the person is "moving in a manner" that indicates he is a "potential enemy?"

"Refugees fleeing from Combat area, near Taegu." 20 Aug 50 US Army.   Capt Scheiber.

What the honest General, I believe, was trying to tell posterity, without saying so, was that they were shooting at and trying to kill anything that moved on the other side of the Bomb Line.

Partridge continued:

"We are attacking any transportation and carts, animals capable of acting as beasts of burden. . . . ."

Partridge also mentions in his diary that he had learned through *"friendly sources"* that some of the victims were South Koreans or that they were *"entirely innocent."* But there was nothing he could do about that. *"This is a matter of extreme regret, but I do not know how to direct selective attacks without giving the enemy sanctuary over a wide area."* The inevitable military consequence of the political decision to intervene in a civil war.

In this December 16, 1950 passage of his diary he describes one such incident. It was an attack near Yonan in South Korean territory west of Kaesong.

It was reported by an ECA [Economic Coopera-tion Agency — an American government agency giving aid to the South Koreans] official that several of our aircraft worked over some South Koreans who were collecting peat. Extensive damage was done, many people and animals killed, and 30,000 bags of peat destroyed.

These facts, which he knew had to be a common occurrence in South Korea, however, did not create any dilemma or even hesitation on his part. It was war and he had his orders. He did not like it, but his conscience was clear.

"This Air Force was operating within its instructions. The . . . attack was made outside of the bomb line."

Bridges and roads were being constantly bombarded to make them unusable to the advancing northerners, but somehow the northerners kept coming. One of their key assets in furthering their swift advance was the local South Korean population. According to General William F. Dean, the local population in the south quite readily agreed to form endless work gangs for the northerners to repair the roads and bridges that were being demolished by the Americans. General Dean, awarded the Congressional Medal of Honor and an impeccable source, made that important observation while an involuntary eyewitness "behind enemy lines" for three years as a North Korean captive (General Dean's Story).

These thousands of workers, who happen to have lived south of the 38th parallel and therefore theoretically were the ones we had come to save from slavery, of necessity became primary targets for the American planes.

The planes, however, could not be everywhere all the time. In addition, at the distant sound of their jets or engines, the South Korean workers would drop their shovels and flee into the woods, leaving only the old and slow-footed of the workers for the F-51's and F-80's with their machine guns and napalm. This too was annoying to the Americans until they devised a method of dealing with these industrious and hardworking South Korean crews. The answer was the "delayed action" bomb.

The fuse on a bomb could be adjusted to trigger an explosion at a predetermined detonation time – from one to 144 hours. In addition, the B-29 armaments specialists could rig the fuse so that any attempt by the North Koreans to defuse one of these unexploded bombs waiting to do their damage would trigger the bomb's explosion (Lt. Col. George A. Larson, U.S. Air Force (ret.), Military.com). Early in the conflict, therefore, the United State Air Force began mixing into its bomb loads a number of bombs with delayed action fuses. Roads would be bombed and cratered. After the planes had safely gone, the South Korean work crews would come out to repair the damage. Then an hour later, or 12 hours later or the next day or days later, the crew would be blown to pieces by the time-bomb.

Official Release 554, 15 October 1950:

> *"Twenty-six B-29's attacked seventy-eight different targets with generally excellent results. . . . Delayed-action bombs will further hinder any use of the rail and highway system."*

US Navy historians marveled at the persistence and ingenuity of the Korean men and women, those who happen to be north of the 38th parallel as well as those south of it, who would repeatedly rebuild bridges as fast as the Americans could destroy them. James A. Field, Jr. in Chapter 10 of the Department of the Navy's History of United States Naval Operations: Korea, originally published in 1962, tells a story about these workers and about the use of delayed-action bombs in an attempt to defeat them.

On March 2, 1951 a vital and vulnerable link in a rail line was discovered. A bridge was sighted in North Korea eight miles southwest of the town of Kilchu. The rail line was hidden for long stretches in tunnels burrowed through the hills but there was a stretch that passed over a deep gully on a single track line on top of a six-span bridge, 650 feet long and 60 feet high. This 650 foot span over a deep gully was a perfect target. "The tunnels," according to Field's account, "made it difficult to bypass; its height made it difficult to repair."

The bridge was attacked by Navy Corsairs on March 2nd but

they were only able to damage one of the approaches. Navy Lieutenant Commander Harold G. Carlson, leading his Corsairs from the *Princeton* in two attacks, ultimately succeeded on March 7th in dropping one of the six spans, damaging a second and shifting two more out of line. The Admiral in command of the Task Force christened the valley in honor of Commander Carlson, thereafter to be known in Naval history as "Carlson's Valley."

But what followed is where the story gets its fame. On the 14th of March the Americans were surprised by an examination of routine reconnaissance photos to discover that workers had made "rough but effective repairs in the form of wooden cribbing [framework], built up [60 feet] to replace the missing spans."

So a 4th Strike was made the next day, knocking down all the new construction and dropping another span. Yet within two days pilots saw large piles of wooden ties assembled in the gully in readiness for rebuilding. "The extraordinary persistence of this engineering effort, paralleled at all important broken bridges, . . . demonstrated the availability of repair crews and materials. . . ."

Admiral Ofsite was getting tired of sending his Corsairs to destroy the same bridge so he appealed to the Air Force. On March 15th

> "Admiral Ofsite recommended . . . that Bomber Command be asked to inhibit repair activity by seeding the gully with long-delay bombs. . . . On the 24th a B-29 was sent out with a bomb load fused for long and varying delays, and three days later the effort was repeated."

Even with these unpleasant surprises for the men and women working on the bridge, "the enemy continued to press the work with great determination. . . . By the 30th, cribbing of the four central spans and the northern approach had been completed, transverse members had been installed, and only the rails were lacking." Admiral Ofstie then sent off Strikes 5 and 6 which destroyed everything, "leaving only the concrete piers."

The Koreans finally abandoned reconstruction of that 60 foot high bridge — but they were not discouraged. Later photos revealed to the Americans, according to Field's official Naval History account, that the labor force had begun to construct a four mile circuitous bypass, including eight new short and low bridges. So the Navy's Corsairs began attacking these new bridges. However, after repeated attacks followed by repeated rebuilding, it was the Navy that gave up. "The new simplicity of repair made the site no longer an attractive one" for the Corsairs. Admiral Ofsite's Task Force then turned their attention southward to the area of Songjin and through the months of April, May and June "the same sequence of destruction, cribbing, destruction, and bypassing would take place" (Field, <u>History of United States Naval Operations: Korea</u>, Chapter 10, Part 2, 1962, Department of the Navy – Naval Historical Center, Washington, D.C. edited 2000 for Online Publication, July 4, 2003 <http://www.history.navy.mil/books/field/ch10b.htm>).

.... the fighters had standing "**orders to strike the entire column. The pilots did not like it, but most of us followed orders**"

LIBERATING KOREA?

CHAPTER VII

SEOUL— BEYOND THE BOMB LINE

Seoul, Korea's largest city with an estimated population in 1950 of 1,400,000 and until weeks earlier the capital of the country we had come to save, had quickly fallen "behind enemy lines." It was Korea's major city, had important industries, highways, bridges, power plants and other forms of modern infrastructure. Consequently it and its surrounding towns and villages became a major bombing target. Daily attacks were scheduled from the first day of the war and grew in intensity until the assault at Inchon on September 15th.

Stratemeyer, Saturday, 15 July 1950:

> "Directive issued and received from General MacArthur through General Almond to hit Kimpo airport and the marshalling yards at Seoul today, using B-29's...."

Stratemeyer, Monday, 17 July 1950:

> "Signed a letter to General MacArthur ... with a set of pictures showing the destructive effect of the FEAF Bomber Command strike yesterday on Seoul — 1,504 x five hundred pound bombs were dropped — or 376 tons."

Stratemeyer, Thursday, 3 August 1950:

> Called to General MacArthur's office at 1900 hours. Those present were: (other than CINCFE and myself) Almond, Wright, and Weyland. We discussed with him a signal [message] which he had received from General Walker telling him that a pilot had reported several convoys going south toward Seoul and three trains moving south toward Seoul. In the discussion, CINCFE reiterated that **he wanted a line cut across Korea, north of Seoul, to stop all communications moving south.** Of course, I was delighted to receive that direction as we had preached that doctrine since the B-29s arrived.

Stratemeyer already had prepared his list of targets for an "interdiction" line which ran along a belt between the 37th and 38th parallels (note by the editor, Y'Blood, to Stratemeyer's August 3 entry, citing Futrell). The goal was that nothing was to pass through that interdiction line. Communication targets in that belt were to be targeted and bombed heavily and repeatedly. This "interdiction" line, this "no man's" land which was to be laid waste, again was in South Korea and occupied by the people we had come to save.

Stratemeyer, Friday, 11 August 1950:

Sent following memo to O'Donnell:

The Bomber Command has been plugging away at the west railroad bridge at Seoul from 28 June to date, and it still stands. . . . Apparently 500, 1000 and 2000 pound bombs are ineffective. There are larger bombs available for the destruction of this target at Okinawa. . . . I still want it taken out and urge that it be a continuing target for the FEAF Bomber Command until it is destroyed.

The bridge was finally destroyed on August 20th after nine B-29's dropped 54 more tons of bombs on it in one day and 37 Corsairs and Skyraiders from the Navy had a go at it.

The question occurs as to what happened to all the tons of bombs that had been **missing the bridge for two months**? Tons of bombs were being rained on Seoul almost daily, yet major targets remained intact.

The Far East Air Force Reconnaissance Branch's Report No. 56 dated July 24, 1950 reported that "NO DAMAGE" was done by previous bombing raids to the railroad yard at Taejong. It is described as "2,100' long, 11 tracks wide." That would seem like a pretty big target -- but the bombs repeatedly missed. Similar reports were made for targets in Seoul and other cities. The erring bombs presumbaly landed on unintended areas near the targets. Nearly all the targets were within the cities being attacked, their power plants, their factories, their roads and railroad yards. If the bombs were missing those targets, what were they hitting?

Yet it was not just bridges and roads in and around Seoul that were bombed. Every conceivable object that might be of assistance to the occupying North Koreans was bombed. Clearly it was impossible to avoid inflicting immense damage upon the residents of Seoul – both on their lives and on their means of living.

The FEAF's Reconnaisance Branch was responsible for daily photographing of potential targets as well as damage results after a bombing raid on specified targets. Its reports in the National Archives (Record Group 341) contain a mass of detail (though no photographs).

Numerous targets were listed by the longitude and latitude coordinates in the Seoul area almost every day from late June to its recapture in late September. The same target numbers and coordinates are listed day after day until the damage report was satisfactory. For example, the Ryuzan Railroad shops and yards, Target No. 43, with coorinates 37:31:45 N, 126:57:45E, is listed as having "No damage" from the photos taken on July 3, 1950. The same Target No. 43 is listed again from photos of July 11 but no damage report given. However for July 24th the Ryuzan shops and yards are reported with "extensive damage to shops" and "all tracks leaving yard on North end cut at or near choke point." But it also states that "repairs under way." Finally the July 26 report for Target No. 43, the Ryuzan yard, reads: "severly damaged."

Electricity resources for the enemy now in Seoul, and incidentally for the 1,400,000 residents as well, were high priority targets. Two thermal electric power plants in the Seoul vicinity with coorinates of 37:33:00 N, 126:54:00E and 36:18:45N, 127:26:30E (Target Nos. R6.92 and R6.159) are listed on July 23 and July 20th respectively.

Another goal was to eliminate communication for the enemy in Seoul, and of course for eveyone else. Photographs of bomb damage to Target No. R6.122 with coordinates 37:31:15N, 126:58:15E, are reported on periodically, including July 23, July 24, July 26, August 5th and August 21st. Target No. R6.122 is described in the July 24th report as a "Radio transmitter station" consisting of "four towers, 1,800' between outside towers. One probable transmitter building. Three minor buildings."

It appears that what the photo interpreters could not identify was nevertheless classified as a legitimate milltary target by merely labeling it as "unidentified." For instance, Mission Review Report No. 56 dated July 24, 1950, lists the usual suspects as targets in and around the Seoul area – airfields, power plants, electric company buildings, machine manufacturing plants, bridges, railroad tracts, railroad yards, transformer stations, "possible" military barracks, "probable" ammunitions storage areas, shipyards, port areas. But it also lists at least 12 sites, described only by their latitude and longitude coordinates, as "Unidentified industry." It appears that **any** building, anywhere in the City, where people could work, any place where anything could be manufactured -- baby carriages to bombs -- was attacked. Nothing escaped. The result was predictable.

So many were killed that children became parents overnight to their little sisters and brothers. These photos were taken after only the first "liberation" of Seoul by the US.

"South Korean children attend worship services in damaged church near Seoul. . . ."
US Army Photo by Cpl Ronald L. Hancock 29 Oct 50

"Korean Women and children search the rubble of Seoul for anything that can be used or burned as fuel."
US Army Photo by Capt. F.L. Scheiber   1 Nov 50

"Small Church near Seoul, damaged during heavy fighting by US troops against the North Korean Forces in that area...." US Army Photo By Cpl Ronald L. Hancock 29 Oct 50

Actually, this was from bombing damage as there was very little ground fighting when the Americans retook Seoul.

There had been 1,400,000 people in Seoul. Those who were left still had to eat and keep themselves warm. Begging and scavenging became the norm for the survivors.

"A group of South Korean children, left homeless by the destruction of Seoul, wander through the City streets in search for food." US Army Cpl. R. Hancock 29 Oct 50

Though this type of bombing and strafing went on through August and into September, the people of the Seoul area had seen nothing yet. MacArthur's brilliant amphibious landing with 260 ships well behind enemy lines at Inchon, the port just northwest of Seoul, set the stage for an as yet unseen demonstration of destructive power throughout all of South Korea.

Stratemeyer, 15 September 1950:

> "*0630 hours Marines debark Inchon.*
>
> "*0900 hours general offensive, EUSAK*" [Eighth United States Army in Korea, then under General Walton Walker].

Official Release 442 from MacArthur's Headquarters, *Friday, 15 September, 1950*:

> *American and British cruisers and destroyers plus carrier aircraft brought the war home the past two days to the Communist-held Inchon-Seoul area. The bombardment of the area under the direction of Rear Admiral John M. Higgins, U.S. Navy, was the preliminary blow. . . .*
>
> *A furious forty-five minute bombardment by cruisers and destroyers . . . at the crack of dawn this morning carried on until the Marine amphibious group cracked the beach. . . .*
>
> *For two days preceding the landing the cruiser, aircraft carrier and destroyer forces had been pummeling practically every section of the Inchon area. . . .*

The bombardment was so successful that the landing met little resistance according to General MacArthur who observed the landing from a ship offshore. The only enemy reaction noted by reporters were "principally of small arms fire."

The next day when the newly liberated residents of Inchon, a city of 250,000 people before the American liberation, returned to their city, they found "two-thirds of the buildings destroyed and many friends and relatives dead. The city still was smoldering from the impact of the bombardment" (New York Herald Tribune, September 17, 1950). Reporters interviewed Korean Rear Admiral Sohn Wun Il, Chief of the tiny South Korean sea force. He estimated that those two-thirds of Inchon "was destroyed mostly by shelling." The Tribune's report gave the official explanation of why so much of the rescued town had to be destroyed in order to rescue it:

> "American and British naval forces
> tried to concentrate on Red gun positions but the
> guns were all over the hilly peninsula on which
> the city is built."

Korean Admiral Sohn's marine brigade was mopping up in Inchon and had the job of "distinguishing friend from foe," no easy task in a civil war. He told reporters that the residents of the city had unfortunately just returned yesterday from an earlier evacuation and walked right into the American and British bombardment, so that "many were killed." Yet, Rhee's Admiral insisted "the people seem happy. . . . They are glad to see the Communists driven out" (New York Herald Tribune, September 17, 1950).

A writer for the Associated Press had more to say on Admiral Sohn Wun Il's comment that "the people seem happy" for the American liberation of their now "blackened and badly torn" city:

> The people certainly do not look
> happy. If they are glad the war has finally passed
> them by, they do not show it. . . . Today they were

going about the sad business of trying to live in the midst of great devastation, to bury their dead, get a bowl of rice to eat. . . .

The people were not so much as glancing at the [US] marines and sailors pouring through. . . . A woman sitting on the edge of a stone pier, motionless as the stones themselves, stared out across the harbor. It was littered with junks and half-sunken small craft. Perhaps one of them had been hers. Her eyes never shifted and her head never moved.

A Korean boy – he looked about 14 years old – made his way painfully down the street, holding his right leg stiff and straight. A blood-stained bandage was wrapped round his knee. . . .

A truckload of prisoners passed. The captives wore white clothing, not uniforms [meaning civilians?]. They stood in the truck, packed tight and holding their hands over their heads… (New York Times, September 17, 1950).

This was the first large city recaptured by the Americans. The intrepid but fervently anti-communist reporter Marguerite Higgins was on the scene with the Marines. She reported that the North Korean Army during their 10 week occupation "appears to have been well behaved as individuals" (New York Herald Tribune, September 18, 1950). Nor had there been any of the mass executions that Rhee's government was inflicting on its people and then falsely reporting to the world and headlined in US newspapers as having been done by the Communists. Indeed, the former Inchon mayor's reinstatement by Major General Oliver P. Smith, commanding the First Marine Division, proved the contrary. This Rhee government official, Pyo Yng Moon, had been arrested by the northerners when they captured the city months earlier. Yet he was found safe and sound, having been "released last Friday after the Marines landed" (AP, Washington Post, September 20, 1950).

From *Official Release 451*, 17 September 1950:

> *"With the liberation of Inchon from Communist rule now accomplished, elements of ROK forces have been charged with the preservation of its internal law and order and with the restoration of its constituted civil government."*

Rhee's police now began another of its many roundups of persons suspected of collaborating with the northerners. Estimates of civilians executed by Rhee after the recapture of South Korean cities range all over the map as no serious attempt was made to keep track. The Americans, Australians and British were not conducting the executions, but, except for one exceptional group of Australians, they were looking the other way.

The Americans marched through Inchon and on to Seoul, 25 miles to the east, preceded every step of the way as usual by a continuous and rolling destructive bombardment.

> Carrier-based Navy planes concen-
> trated their 315 strikes in the Inchon-Seoul-
> Kimpo area in close support of the advancing
> marine forces. Navy dive bombers dropped 246
> tons of incendiary and fragmentation bombs, 120
> jellied gasoline bombs and fired almost 1,000 five-
> inch rockets (New York Herald Tribune, Septem-
> ber 17, 1950).

The Navy reported the next day on the armaments used in what it actually called its "precision" bombing of Inchon by planes from its carrier force.

> *"In three days . . . the planes dropped 246 tons*
> *of incendiary and fragmentation bombs, 120 napalm*
> *bombs and 979 rockets."*

The US newspapers merely repeated this characterization of the bombing as "precision" bombing (for example, New York Times, September 17, 1950, p. 3). One would think that it was obvious that the term "precision bombing" in 1950 was an oxymoron, certainly if 246 tons of napalm and incendiary bombs were dropped with the result that two-thirds of a city was wiped out.

The Americans went on in a few days to take over Seoul with little resistance and behind a rolling mass of explosives and na-palm.

> "Thousands of Leathernecks spanned
> the [Han] River on their way to liberate the
> former South Korean capital city. . . [T]he guns of
> United Nations cruisers loosed a terrific aerial

bombardment which wiped out the 200 Reds [on the other side of the river] prior to the morning crossing. Low-flying planes covered the Marines as they reached the east bank and began pushing toward Seoul" (Washington Post, September 20, 1950).

As it turned out, this "liberation" was short-lived. Some months later the Americans and the Rhee government again had to evacuate Seoul, this time to the advancing Chinese. But shortly thereafter the American and South Korean armies took it back again.

James Field, writing for the US Naval Historical Center, commented about this repeated "liberation" of Seoul:

"Seoul . . . on the 15th [March, 1951] was reoccupied without a fight. But two conquests and two liberations had taken a frightful toll, and hardly a tenth of the city's original population still skulked amid the ruins."

"Makeshift houses like the ones pictured here are used by the families in Seoul, Korea, who were left homeless during heavy fighting between US Troops and the North Korean Forces in that City."

US Army Photo
by Cpl. Ronald L. Hancock 31 Oct 50

CHAPTER VIII

CLEARING A SAFE PATH ... THROUGH SOUTH KOREA

On September 15, 1950 the Americans launched a general offensive along the Pusan line at the southern tip of Korea to coincide with the amphibious invasion at Inchon. The northerners had essentially expended themselves by this time and the Americans probably could have broken out of the Pusan perimeter without the assault at Inchon. But that assault seemed to have caught the northerners unprepared, with no reserves, and threatened to entrap their army which was well south around Pusan. They had not deployed any serious forces in their rear nor near the area of Seoul-Inchon. The North Koreans therefore began immediately to pull out some of their troops on the Pusan perimeter to go north again – either to battle the invaders or at least to escape any envelopment. But there were still battles and resistance in many sectors along the Pusan perimeter.

As at Inchon, the path for the advancing American Eighth Army now breaking out of the Pusan perimeter was leveled with as much firepower as the unchallenged US Air Force and the US Naval forces could unleash. Again, all of the destruction was visited on the people in South Korea whom we had come to save from slavery.

> "The Communist line of retreat was following the route of conquest it took during July and August. The road back led over 'Heartbreak Highway.' The paved roadway runs 90 miles south of Seoul across the Kum River to the devastated town of Taejon, then turns eastward for 53 miles to cross the Naktong River at Waegwan and enter Taegu" (Washington Post, September 20, 1950).

Futrell, in his Official United States Air Force History, tells of the use of delayed action bombs and napalm bombs during this advance:

> Roads to the northeast of Seoul were mined by B-29's with delayed action bombs set to explode at night. Pilots on surveillance were briefed to seek their own choke-points on roads, where a bomb blast would crater the roadway or bring down a landslide. . . . On the 2d Division front on 17 September, Fifth Air Force fighters dropped 210 x 110-gallon napalm tanks, killing an estimated 1,200 enemy troops as they attempted to retreat across the Naktong. Other fighters

saturated with napalm the 'Walled City' of Yongchon, the strong fortification resisting the Eighth Army advance eight miles north of Taegu, and left it ablaze.

From the <u>New York Herald Tribune</u>, September 17, 1950:

> Ever-increasing numbers of American war planes kept pace with the mounting United Nations offensive yesterday and rained fiery destruction on North Korean Communist front-line troops, supplies and rear bases.

At this time the "Communist front-line" was arrayed along a semicircle of South Korean cities, towns, villages and farms.

> *United States Far East Air Forces planes were loaded this morning with bombs, rockets, napalm and 50-caliber machine-gun ammunition for heavy strikes in South Korea in air support of United Nations ground forces. . . . United States Air Force planes concentrated along the battle line in the southeastern sector of Korea to keep the Communists pinned down. More than 400 sorties of all types were flown   (Official Release 445, September 16, 1950).*

> *"Light bombers picked up where they left off the night before and damaged or destroyed Communist vehicles, warehouses and other military targets in a thirty-mile circle around Taejon. . . . At Taejon a formation of B-29's dropped bombs on the marshalling yards, warehouses and storage area. Large explosions and fires*

followed direct hits. . . . Flying in close-support opera-tions . . . planes of the Fifth Air Force . . . attacked . . . buildings housing enemy forces all along the immediate battlefront. . . . Target areas included Tabu, Angang, Yosu, Chongyang, Pohang, Kumchon, Uiryong, Sachon, Hamchang and Sangju [all in South Korea]" (Official Releases 451 and 449, September 17, 1950).

On the northwest corner of the United Na-tions line, enemy strong points in the Walled City of Kasan and in the hills east of Waegwan impeded the progress of friendly troops (Release from Eighth Army Headquarters, September 17, 1950).

From the <u>New York Times</u> of September 18, 1950:

> The hardest fighting still prevailed along the front of the United States First Cavalry Division, in front of the Naktong River crossing at Waegwan, and along the road north from the advanced headquarters at Taegu to Tabu. At Waegwan, the main Taegu-Seoul high-way makes its river crossing, and this would be the most direct route for troops from the perim-eter to join hands with the invasion force to the north. . . . The enemy still held the Walled City on Mount Kasan – bastion of this region. . . .

Official Release 461 issued September 19, 1950:

> *United States Fifth Air Force fighters were off at first light this morning for Korea and another as-sault on retreating Communist troops as a follow-up[to] yesterday's banner results. . . . B-29 Superforts . . . car-*

ried out a special type of mission by saturating a two-square mile area west of the Naktong River. . . . [40] B-29's dropped 1,600 500-pound general purpose bombs that were fused to explode instantaneously.

Stratemeyer, Tuesday 19 September 1950:

Sent redline to Vandenberg:

Add the word '**beautiful**" to the several words already coined by ground forces in Korea to describe FEAF air efforts. Latest word — 'beautiful' was used by Major General Hobart Gay, First Cav. Commander, in describing B–29 tactical strike on Communist positions west of **Waegwan** on Monday, September 18, when 1600 bombs were dropped on a 2 square mile area just in front of U.N. positions.

"The United States Twenty-fourth Division recaptured burned-out **Waegwan**. . . ." (Washington Post, September 21, 1950).

On the 20th Stratemeyer wrote:

Partridge . . . had information that 3,800 dead were found by the ground forces in the walled city [Kasan] and that it is our opinion that our 60–tank napalm attack on 17 September did that job.

Official Release 457:

B-26 light bombers, F-80 jet fighter-bombers and F-81 fighters bombed, rocketed and strafed large concentrations of troops, causing a rout in at least one sector. Liberally bombing the area with napalm, scores of positions were made untenable and results for the day were reported as excellent by Air Force forward controllers all along the battle front.

Official Release 458:

> During a four-hour period yesterday morning the U.S.S. Missouri pounded more than 300 tons of high explosive into the **Pohang** [South Korea] area. . . . Making effective use of shore fire-control spotting, the Mighty Mo **pin-pointed** her targets, enabling ROK ground forces to cross a bridge over t he Hyongsan River standing up.

The Washington Post reported that the

> South Korean Third Division troops sent patrols **into Pohang,** the battered east coast port. The 16-inch guns of the U.S.S. Missouri, the mightiest warship in the world, **blasted the way** (September 20, 1950).

Just a few weeks earlier this unfortunate South Korean city had experienced Americans going the other way -- and burning up their rear. "Fallen Pohang was reported afire from American B-26 bomb raids. . . . Pilots reported Pohang was in flames. . . " (Washington Post, September 7, 1950). Now Pohang was **in front** of the advancing Americans, and we reduced it to pebbles.

Next page:
"Scene of Pohang, on the East Coast of Korea, after artillery duel and air strikes."   US Army 23 Aug 50   *Photo by Lt. Winslow*

LIBERATING KOREA?

CHAPTER IX

"BURN IT, IF YOU SO DESIRE"

The difference in destruction wrought by our bombs between the area south of the 38th parallel and that north of the 38th was primarily semantic. A town burned down south of the 38th was as much a heap of ashes as one burned north of it. But the one in the south was regrettably burned only incidentally or as "collateral damage" – the enemy was somehow using it so it had to be destroyed, or it was in the way for some other "military" reason. On the other hand, a town in the north was targeted to be burned down because it was above that line drawn by Dean Rusk late one night back in 1945.

The people in both towns may have looked the same, spoke the same language, might have been related and may have been part of the same culture for a thousand or more years. But the Dean Rusk Line nevertheless had designated those humans south of it as the ones we were saving, while those north of it were transformed into demons. Our propaganda made quite dramatic distinctions between the innocent"little brown people"we were saving and the demons we were destroying — though in fact we may have destroyed as many on one side of the line as on the other. To our diplomats and military planners, the killing of civilians in the south by our bombing was regrettable; but the killing of those north of the line was of "no concern." The G.I. on the ground or the pilot in the cockpit was at least being honest in reflecting real American policy when he referred to all Koreans as "gooks."

The destruction of the cities, towns, and villages north of the 38th parallel was intentional from the beginning. The killing of the civilians was a military goal to destroy the morale on the"other" side. Taken from them also were their means of livelihood — their factories, farms, vehicles, animals. Then every form of mechanism they may have had for modern life – electric power plants, sewers, telephone lines, dams, irrigation canals.

Those people who could not be killed directly with explosives, or burned to death with napalm or other incendiaries, were starved to death. Stratemeyer and Partridge struggled over the task of bursting the Hwachon Reservoir just north of the 38th parallel. Reservoirs of course not only provided water power for electricity, but controlled water for irrigation of the rice crops. Blowing up a dam not only cut off electricity, but it flooded the crops and villages.

Stratemeyer took a flight over the Hwachon Resevoir on January 16, 1951 and again realized the"uselessness of normal bombing"to destroy the dam and flood the fields. Stratemeyer had made a request to the Strategic Air Command in the US to make a special run with the heavier B-36 bombers from the US, carrying larger bombs than they had in Korea, to blow up the dams. General LeMay, however, reluctantly had to decline the request as they just could not afford to tie up the scarce B-36's in this way. The new heavy bombers were earmarked for Soviet targets in case of World War III. Partridge likewise was on the alert for any new war tools that would help blow up the dams. On March 1st he sent an excited memo to Stratemeyer asking for more information on the visiting General Vandenberg's casual remark, made to General Ridgeway, that there were new types of bombs being developed in the US that would be capable of destroying the Hwachon Dam.

The Far East Air Force had one B-29 Bomber Group when the Korean civil war started. Soon two other Groups from the already stretched Strategic Air Command were lent to the FEAF. Truman and the Joint Chiefs from 1945 had been shaping the military around the atomic bomb. With the Bomb, the theory was, one could reduce most of the rest of the military. But even the carriers of this weapon, structured to be able to deliver as great destruction on the Soviet Union as possible, were limited. So when the call came to General Curtis LeMay to divert two of his Bomber Groups to a tiny location in Asia, he considered it a nuisance and a distraction. But he applied the same strategic bombing philosophy to this small, remote and defenseless country as he had developed for the Soviet Union – immediate and massive destruction.

The North Korea air force, such as it was, had been obliterated in the early days of the war. Stratemeyer noted in his diary entry of July 10, 1950:"FEAF aircraft have held air superiority from the first and enemy activity has all but disappeared." For the first year at least, when most of the destruction was accomplished, the US Air Force had no significant opposition in the air. B-29's which would normally drop their loads from as high as 22,000 to 30,000 feet to avoid enemy ground fire or flak, in Korea were usually able to fly at 15,000 to 22,000 feet, select the angle best suited for their purposes and bomb at their leisure, generally without fear of serious flak from the ground or attacks from the air. The population of North Korea, designated by the Dean Rusk Line as the "enemy," was totally defenseless.

When he was called upon to assist in the Korean civil war, LeMay saw no reason why the US should not just continue where it had left off in World War Two, the massive firebombing of enemy cities. He had orchestrated the burning of Tokyo and numerous other Japanese cities. Now the cities, villages and towns in Korea, with their wooden and thatched homes and buildings, close together streets and lack of fire-fighting abilities, would make perfect targets. That the Koreans, unlike the Japanese and Germans, had not declared war against the US or killed any of our soldiers did not make any difference to LeMay. An enemy was an enemy. "We slipped a little idea under the door up there in the Pentagon. . . . Maybe if we turned SAC loose, not with atomic weapons but with some incendiaries, against four or five towns in North Korea, this will convince them we mean business and maybe it'll stop it" (Le May quoted in a 1972 interview as reported in Thomas Coffey's 1986 biography of Le May, Iron Eagle).

LeMay related to his interviewers how the cautious politicians at the time had rejected his idea of a fast, unannounced and devastating blow to knock out the North Koreans. Yet in the end, Le May observed, the same result had obtained. "So we go on and we don't do it, and [we] let the war go on. **Over a period of three and a half or four years . . . we did burn down every town in North Korea and every town in South Korea.** . . . And what? Killed off 20 percent of the Korean population." The total, north and south, Korean population in 1950 was 30,000,000. So by LeMay's estimate, we had killed off 6,000,000 Koreans.

LeMay's theory was that an early overkill would in the long run save lives on both sides as it would end the war quickly. His biographer, however, like many others, thought that such a strategy would have more likely brought China into the war earlier or even have set off World War III. However, neither the North Koreans nor, later in the war, the Chinese, were intimidated or stopped by the massive bombing ultimately employed by LeMay's B-29's.

General Stratemeyer understood from the beginning that any kind of bombing of industrial areas would result in civilian deaths. Initially he had struggled with the bombing in the cities. He even suggested to MacArthur that for public relations purposes before

the large scale strategic bombings commenced that some warning be given to the civilian population.

l/r: Generals Edward H. White, Emmett 'Rosie" O'Donnell, Jr., Raymond C. Maude and Francis L. Ankenbrandt. 24 Jul;y 1950 USAF

Stratemeyer, Tuesday, 4 July 1950:

Just received information, Vandenberg to Stratemeyer, that Major General Rosie O'Donnell as bomber commander, and the 22d and 92d Bomb Groups, were proceeding to Far East Command. . . . Vandenberg wishes . . . that all targets back of immediate battlefront within North Korea be taken out.

Stratemeyer, Tuesday, 11 July 1950:

1830 hours an appointment with CINCFE: following items are those I will discuss with him. . . . 7. I have issued direct orders to him (General O'Donnell) that no urban area targets will be attacked except on direct orders from you through me. 8. **Again, since our first strike targets are bound to kill and wound civilians,** I recommend that an announcement

be made by you urging them to vacate all urban
centers that are close to military targets; namely,
railroad centers, airfields, heavy industry locations,
harbors and sub bases, and POL [petroleum, oil, and
lubricants] storage facilities and refineries.

So the mass bombing of industrial sites commenced.
Strattemeyer's comment on issuing "direct orders" to O'Donnell
that he could bomb urban areas **only** if specifically authorized by
MacArthur and Strattemeyer suggests that Stratteneyer, at this
stage of the war, was wary of the flamboyant O'Donnell.

Major General Emmett"Rosie" O'Donnell, one of LeMay's
protégés and likewise a veteran of the firebombing of Japanese
cities, would later describe the recommendations he had made
when he went out to Korea in 1950. His testimony on June 25,
1951, during the hearings held by Congress to review Truman's
dismissal of MacArthur, would suggest that he wanted to use
atomic bombs on North Korea from the very beginning:

It was my intention and hope, not
having any instructions, that we would be able to
get out there and to cash in on our psychological
advantage in having gotten into the theater and
into the war so fast, by putting a very severe blow
on the North Koreans, with advanced warning,
perhaps, telling them that they had gone too far in
what we all recognized as being a case of aggression, and General MacArthur would go top side to
make a statement, and we now have at our command **a weapon** that can really dish out some
severe destruction, and let us go to work on **burning five major cities in North Korea to the
ground, and to destroy completely every 1 of
about 18 major strategic targets**.

The Congressional hearing record made public is full of "[Deleted.]" notations, so it is difficult to get the full picture of what these Generals at the MacArthur hearings were presenting to Congress at the time. But in the O'Donnell testimony that was not deleted, he spoke of using **"a weapon"** of great destruction. That would suggest that he wanted to drop an atomic bomb on each of the five major North Korean cities. At any rate, according to his testimony, a few months later when the Chinese entered the war, he was one of those advocating use of the atomic bombs.

LeMay and O'Donnell had suggested a massive strategic attack with B-29's as soon as O'Donnell and his B-29's were sent out to Korea in July 1950. However, as O'Donnell testified in 1951, General Stratemeyer, under whom he was working, "told us it would not be possible to carry out an attack such as that at that time, the reason being that our hard-pressed ground forces were in a very bad state, indeed, and that every weapon at the command of the theater commander must, and properly should be, used in support of the ground forces."

O'Donnell and his bombers encountered no significant enemy air action during the six months he was out in Korea . The casualty rate for the B-29 Bomber men and equipment, he testified, was minimal or equal to what they would have had during a training mission in the States.

Chairman Russell [Richard B. Russell, D., Georgia Senator, Chairman of the Senate Committee on Armed Services]:

> Now you stated that you could not burn the cities there, that you hoped to burn out all these cities. As I understood you intended to give them notice you had better get out of the war or we will burn your cities?"

General O'Donnell. "I thought that would take care of the humane aspects of the problem. . . ."

Chairman Russell. "What decision was made at that suggestion of yours?"

General O'Donnell. "We were not at that time permitted to do it."

Chairman Russell. "Was that for lack of adequate number of planes or was it some matter of policy?"

General O'Donnell. "I think it was an overriding political or diplomatic consideration, sir. I don't know. I am the bomber commander out there and I got the word from General Stratemeyer who said: 'No, not at this time.'"

Senator Bridges [Styles Bridges, R., N.H.]:"General O'Donnell, you spoke earlier in your testimony of cities or towns that you were prohibited from bombing or attacking. Were those towns and cities, some of them, within the area of North Korea?"

General O'Donnell: "All of them were, sir."

Senator Bridges: "About what period did that include; what time?"

General O'Donnell: "Well, this was initially when we first got out there we were instructed not to use incendiary bombs, not to burn down the cities, but there were no compunctions on the part of our commanders to bomb legitimate military targets within those cities with high explosives. . . ."

Senator Stennis [John C. Stennis, D. Ms]: "Early in your testimony this morning you said that the O'Donnell plan had 18 major strategic targets . . . and then you had five primary spots of some kind".

General O'Donnell: "The main cities were Pyongyang, first, the capital, Seishin, Rashin, Wonsan, and Chinnampo. . . . I could have done that in 10 days flat . . ."

Senator Stennis: "**Now, as a matter of fact, Northern Korea has been virtually** destroyed, hasn't it? Those cities have been virtually destroyed."

General O'Donnell:"**Oh, yes; we did it all later anyhow.**"

"Billowy columns of smoke and flames erupt violently from target following a bombing raid over CHINNAMPO, Korea, by B-29s of 92nd Bomb Group."
31 August 1950

While everything that could be destroyed in North Korea from airplanes was destroyed by the US by the end of the Korean War, there was much talk, especially in the beginning, about "pinpoint" and "precision" bombing intended to avoid civilian casualties. The US did in fact drop millions of leaflets in North Korea warning the citizens to get away from military targets as they were to be bombed.

But even an amateur analysis of the"military"targets in North Korea from the commencement of the war would suggest that massive civilian casualties were expected, and most probably intended. This, after all, was the heart and soul of "strategic" bombing -- to break the enemy's spirit. The various locations of the targets in each city were so spread out and the nature of bombing from 20,000 feet, often through clouds and guided by radar only, meant that a fairly good number of bombs would go beyond their targets, say, docks or warehouses, and hit residential areas. In fact, of course, that is what happened. Then later in the war even the pretenses of warnings and avoiding civilian casualties were dropped as entire cities and villages in North Korea were declared to be"military targets."

Futrell, the official USAF military historian, makes a valiant attempt to seem righteous on this issue, but his own scholarly honesty defeats his purpose. He makes pro-forma defensive state- ments in his study, such as:"To the end of the Korean war FEAF would be bound by a rule which was finally stated in this language: 'Every effort will be made to attack military targets only, and to avoid needless civilian casualties.'"And again he later writes:"The FEAF Bomber Command strategic air attacks destroyed none but legitimate military targets in North Korea, and the bombing was so accurate as to do little damage to civilian installations near the industrial plants."

Yet, as early as On October 14, 1950, when the following two photographs of Wonsan were taken by USAF reconnaissance, it would be difficult to tell whether there was"little damage to civilian installations near the industrial plants"– as there was very little standing, whether industrial or civilian.

This is still very early in the war, but "military targets"already included hotels, churches and banks. What buildings could be more civilian? The Air Force captions usually tried to give some excuse for what would otherwise seem like grim mass murder.

"BURN IT ... IF YOU SO DESIRE"

155

"Wreckage of hotel caused by bomb damage, Wonsan, Korea." USAF 23 Oct 1950

"This destruction of a hotel near marshalling yards in Wonsan, Korea, is the result of bombing by B-29 'Superforts' of the US Far East Air Force."   23 October 1950

"Fifth Air Force light bombers closed this No. Korean bank one Saturday afternoon. All that remained standing after the air strike were these three safes. . . ."

"Immediate explosion from a direct hit made by a B-26 Invader light bomber on a church containing high explosives for the Communists, is shown in this photo the second after the 452nd Light Bomb Wing's plane had dropped its bombs directly on target. Wonsan harbor. . . . ."   US Air Force Photo   March, 1951

By the time US photographers arrived to collect photographic evidence of the Air Force's work, it would have been easy to forget that perhaps these places had been filled with people when the bombs hit. There are, however, reminders of the humans this brick and motar had once served. In a closeup of a photo on the previous page (top, left), one could still see remnants of a bedroom in the headboad poking out of the hotel's debris. Also this same picture captured an image of two North Koreans -- perhaps searching for somone who was still missing.

Also, for a godless communist country there were certainly a lot of churches and temples the Air Force found threatening enough to try to destroy. These are some of the churches just in Wonsan in October and November, 1950.

Photos by
Navy
F. Kazukaitis

Army
Cpl. Hobert
Dangel

Air Force

Even with all that destruction, however, the Joint Chiefs of Staff still were not satisfied that enough damage was being done to the infrastructure of North Korea. They thought MacArthur was using the strategic bombing B-29's too much for tactical or troop support instead of what they were better suited for. They therefore "advised" him that "**mass** air operations against industrial targets in North Korea were 'highly desirable'" (Futrell).

This incident of nudging by the Joint Chiefs illustrates a point that General Rosie O'Donnell in his Congressional testimony did not make clear when he had whined to the Senators that he was not allowed to use incendiaries. While initially restrained from the use of incendiaries (which restraint was soon lifted in any event), most of the other elements of SAC's plan that he had taken with him to Korea were adopted. Specifically the concept of "area" or "mass" bombing of the industrial targets in the major North Korea cities.

Since the cities were not that large and the targeted industries in each city were close to each other, the number of raids required to destroy the targets could be reduced by bombing the whole "area," and not just the specific industrial site. This was the procedure adopted for strategic bombing. "Area" or "mass" bombing would seem by definition to exclude the concept of "precision" bombing. Nevertheless throughout the Korean War the US Government and Press repeatedly characterized the bombing as "precision" and "pin point."   *Release 188, August 2, 1950:*

> *United States Far East Air Forces medium bombers staged their second major strike against the North Korean industrial complex at the east coast city of Hamhung . . . [It] was hit with more than **400 tons of bombs.** Intense fires were seen and sharp explosions rocked the B-29's at an altitude of more than 15,000 feet. . . . Flames rising to an estimated 2000 feet and black smoke which mushroomed up to 12,000 feet **cut***

off any view of the target shortly after the beginning of the attack. The last Superfortresses to make their bomb runs found it necessary to **use radar** sighting.

The <u>Washington Post</u> reported: "*United States B-29 Superfortresses made their second* **mass attack** *in three days on the North Korean war production center of* **Hungnam** *today and preliminary reports indicated* **they almost blotted it out of existence**. . . . *Jubilant bomber crews said they believe it was the most successful aerial attack since the Korean war began. . . . Today's target area was two miles east of that bombed Sunday. The first crews over said that the area hit in the first strike* **looked pretty desolate and burned out**" (August 2, 1950).

Official Release 197, August 4, 1950:

The third major strike within five days against the North Korean chemical and munitions manufacturing complex [at **Hungnam**] *was made today when United States Far East Air Forces B-29 Superforts again dropped more than 400 tons of high explosive bombs. Today's target was . . . about three miles up the river from the explosives factory almost totally destroyed by B-29's on July 30. One-fourth of today's bombs was dropped visually and* **three-fourths by radar**. . . . *Bombing results were generally good, they reported, and fires were seen by some airmen through breaks in the clouds.*

A Stratemeyer statement quoted by the <u>Washington Post</u> on the 5th of August reported "the vital plant at Hungnam 'suffered such mortal damage in three large scale **precision** bombing attacks of the past five days that it can no longer be considered a major factor in the Korean war."

The Air Force, therefore, in early August 1950, seemed satisfied with the destruction already wrought on **Hamhung** and its port city, **Hungnam**. Nevertheless, the bombing continued mercilessly through the rest of August, September and most of October. Finally in late October the American troops under General Almond took physical possession of what was left of these cities.

"LIBERATION CEREMONIES AT HAMHUNG"

"Major General Edward M. Almond, CG X Corps., and his staff officers receive flowers from the civilian population of Hamhung in token of their appreciation of liberation. General Almond addressed the people during the liberation ceremonies."
26 October 1950   US Army Signal Corps   Cpl. Alex Klein

By September 3rd Stratemeyer could write in an official letter to O'Donnell that "practically all the Joint Chiefs of Staff targets have been destroyed." On September 27th he wrote MacArthur:

> "I consider the present status of the destruction of the enemy in Korea to be so much in our favor that I now consider it no longer necessary to retain all four (4) additional medium bomb groups in your command. The Joint Chiefs of Staff directive received [by] your headquarters direct cessation of all attacks on all strategic targets. . . ."

The Joint Chiefs by mid-September saw no point in continuing to bomb rubble. O'Donnell's bigger bombers, therefore, were grounded as there were no strategic targets of any worth left. The bombing crews spent their time doing practice runs while awaiting orders to return to the US.

Commentators in the United States were debating how the United States would deal with Korea after the war was finally over. For example, an article in the October 22, 1950 issue of the New York Herald Tribune started with the sentence:

> "The war in Korea drew to a close in spectacular fashion four months after it had begun. United Nations forces captured the Communist capital, Pyongyang, a city of 700,000 population, on Thursday."

General Stratemeyer was already drafting his "forwarding endorsements" to the anticipated final reports of his four major commands regarding the Korean Conflict (Monday, 2 October 1950). Even Stalin on October 12th had recommended to Kim Il Sung that he evacuate Korea and retreat with the forces he had left into Manchuria to fight another day (Richard C. Thornton, Odd Man Out).

"Lt. General Walton M. Walker, CG 8th Army; Col. Thomas Marnane, AG 8th Army; Lt. Col Sherry; Col. T.P. Finnegan, FEAF Chaplain; and Father Brian Geraghty, Superior of the Columban Mission followed By Bishop Paul Ro, Bishop of Seoul Diocese, enter the Catholic Cathedral at Seoul to celebrate a Solemn Pontifical Mass of Thanks for UN Victory in Korea."

20 Oct 50   US Army Photo by SGC. A. Guyette

Planners in the Defense and State Departments, without consultation with any other country contributing to the U.N. Forces and without input from Koreans, were devising schemes on how to govern all of Korea once the remnants of the North Korean forces were mopped up. A dispute even erupted with Sigmund Rhee who wanted to take authority over all of Korea. He had been sending in police agents behind the Army as it moved up North Korea. General Stratemeyer's and General Partridge's diaries disclose that discussions and plans were being formulated for the "post-war" structure of the Fifth Air Force. It was just about over.

But then Stratemeyer at this point, **October 17, 1950,** decided to indulge himself in some one-upmanship with his competitors in the Army and the Navy. With his bombers and fighters no longer so urgently needed or just with nothing to do, he tried to come up with some spectacular task for the FEAF. With no apparent necessity and while the US was on the verge of taking over all of Korea, he inexplicably recommended to MacArthur that they totally destroy the large North Korean city of Sinuiju **without warning**. This city of 180,000 (newspaper figures varied from 100,000 to 180,000, Strat thought it had 60,000) was in the extreme north, on the Yalu border with China.

> It is requested that I be authorized to conduct an air attack on the city of Sinuiju with all available air means at the earliest practicable date on which the attack can be launched under visual flying conditions. The types of attack recommended are listed in order of priority, as follows: (a) **An attack over the widest area of the city, without warning, by burning and high explosives.** . . .

Stratemeyer in his memo to MacArthur of October 17th gave various reasons for his proposal. His main reason was that he was concerned that Sinuiju was the last city in Korea that the retreating North Korean army would be going through. If it were destroyed it could not provide a foothold in Korea for the North Korean government to claim some legitimacy.

> This city, with considerable industrial activity and an estimated population of over 60,000 is a provincial capital and has the capability of becoming the capital of North Korea when Pyongyang is evacuated.

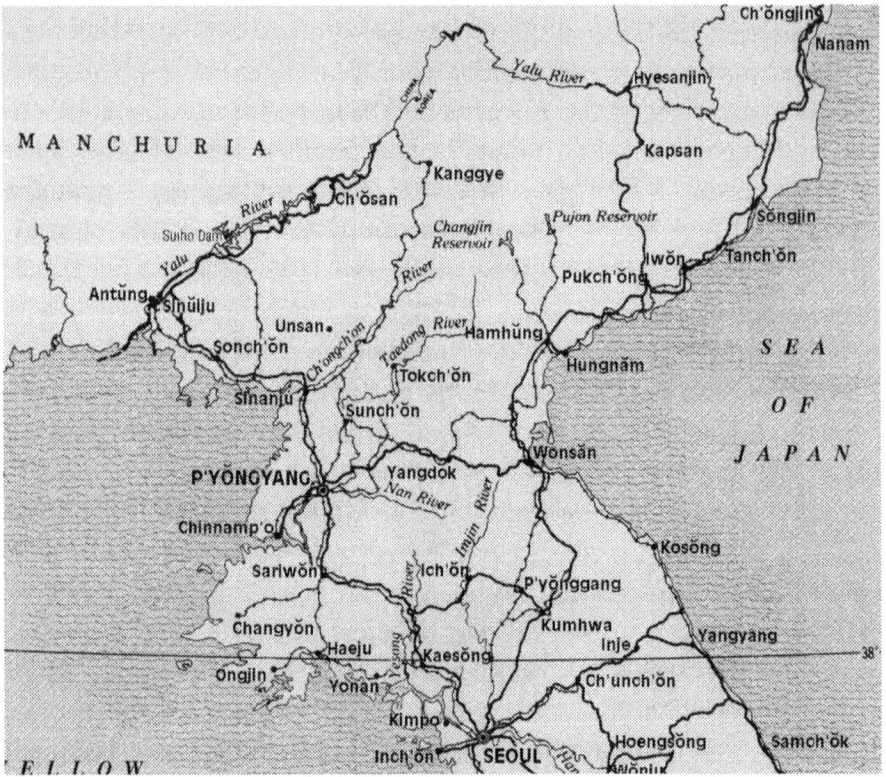

He also thought

> "that the psychological effect of a mass attack
> will be salutary to Chinese Communist observers
> **across the [Yalu] river** in Antung."

Another "lesson" to the Reds — consume tens of thousands of men, women and children in a firestorm. It appears that Stratemeyer, just a few months into the war and when it appeared to be over, had decided to kill as many people in as large a city as possible, primarily for political reasons – to scare the hell out of the Chinese and Russians. But his plans were put on hold.

Stratemeyer, Wednesday, 18 October 1950:

> GHQ [MacArthur's Headquarters] returned my
> memorandum of yesterday, subject: Destruction of
> Sinuiju .... 'The general policy enunciated from
> Wasington negates such an attack unless the military
> situation clearly requires it. Under present
> circumstnances this is not the case.'

Were the story to end here, I would say, "Thank God! There
was somebody around with a little common sense." But, unfortunately, the story does not end here.

Stratemeyer continued to press his case for the burning of
Sinuiju. It is not clear what was motivating him. Their diaries
indicate that he and Partridge met personally a number of times
in the next couple of weeks. One meeting was on October 25th
when they had a conference at Stratemeyer's office in Tokyo.

In any event Stratemeyer notes in his diary for November 3rd
that upon reaching his office that morning he fortuitously found a
radio message on his desk from Partridge. Partridge now "from the
field" was requesting "clearance to burn Sinuiju" because there
was "heavy antiaircraft fire from city."

Stratemeyer now had a "military necessity" reason for a
spectacular fire exhibition. The General immediately took this up
again with MacArthur late that morning. But to Stratemeyer's
continuing frustration, MacArthur again said no. However, this
time the reason given by MacArthur for the denial was somewhat
different. The Chief told Stratemeyer that he was thinking about
using the town himself when they got there. They were not far
from China's border now. MacArthur therefore "did not want to
burn it at this time. His intentions are to push the 24th Division to
the Yalu River, taking Sinuiju. . . ."

However, MacArthur was not going to let his airmen feel unwanted. "He [MacArthur] stated that he realized that there were not many targets left for the '29's but he wanted to get them back in the business." Therefore MacArthur, during the same meeting on November 3rd, did agree to let Stratemeyer show off his pyrotechnics on some other towns.

Stratemeyer suggested to MacArthur "that **as a lesson** we could burn some other towns in North Korea and I indicated **the town of Kanggye** which I believe is occupied by enemy troops and is a communications center — both rail and road.

"He [MacArthur] said, '**Burn it if you so desire**,' and then said, 'Not only that, Strat, but burn and destroy as a lesson **any other of those towns that you consider of military value** to the enemy."

Now the civilian populations of entire towns could be desginated as legitimate targets, provided only that Stratemeyer found a reason to consider them to be "of military value to the enemy." No lieutenant could have asked for a more generous delegation of power. Even without Sinuiju, Stratemeyer was now satisfied. He again had targets for his idle planes — whole cities and towns which he himself, with his own magic wand, could turn into legitimate "military targets."

These "lessons" being taught to the Chinese of course as we know only backfired. That is what Vito Marcantonio had predicted. The Chinese passion to protect their homeland was not going to be smothered by bombs or the threats of bombs, even atomic bombs. The Chinese had utterly no trust in American assurances that they did not intend to cross the Yalu into China proper. The US Air Force's unrelenting and seemingly senseless bombing raids on Korea, plus the previous American policy reversals on having no interest in Korea and then again the false assurances about stopping at the 38th Parallel, convinced the Chinese that the Americans intended to reignite the Chinese civil war and invade China proper.

As if to highlight the capricious nature of American policy, later that day on November 3rd MacArthur abruptly, without any explanation, changed his mind with respect to Sinuiju itself. Even though he had just hours before told Stratemeyer that he wanted to preserve Sinuiju for his own use, he now gave the OK to burn it to the ground.

> *"General Hickey [at that time MacArthur's Chief of Staff] called … that General MacArthur had approved the Partridge wire to burn Sinuiju. … Hickey asked that I drop in tomorrow morning and discuss other targets with him as the Boss had asked that this be done."*

On the 17th of October when Stratemeyer first raised the possibility of burning Sinuiju, the war was considered about over. MacArthur had just returned from Wake Island. There he had confirmed for the celebrating Truman that the Chinese would not enter the war and that the boys would be "home by Christmas."

"President Harry S. Truman waves his exuberant presidential greeting upon his arrival in Hawaii. The President and his party are enrout to Wake Island to meet General of the Army Douglas MacArthur, Commander-in-Chief, UN

Command, and stopped over for a day in Hawaii." US Army (Cordeiro) 13 October 1950

As of October 18, 1950 neither Stratemeyer nor MacArthur was aware that the Chinese were about to begin heavy infiltration into Korea across the Yalu, including through the city of Sinuiju. The Chinese, beginning on October 19th, according to Mao's letter to Stalin (Richard C. Thornton, <u>Odd Man Out</u>), moved skillfully by night and under heavy camouflage so that by the time of the incendiary attack on Sinuiju on November 8th there were already 260,000 to 300,000 Chinese soldiers in Korea.

The first time that MacArthur admitted that the Chinese were taking a serious interest in Korea had been on October 25 when Chinese troops suddenly appeared and decimated a ROK battalion near the Yalu. But when the Chinese as quickly disappeared, for their own tactical reasons, MacArthur and his intelligence chief, General Willoughby, immediately discounted them as a small number of "volunteers" and not to be taken seriously (Y'Blood Notes to November 3, 1950 Diary Entry). MacArthur was determined to get at least to the Yalu, then after that: Who Knows? So he did not want to see any Chinese soldiers. That may have given credence to his critics who were worried about his igniting World War III.

When the Generals talked about "burning" a city or town, they were speaking literally. The would "blow up" something with general purpose or high explosives bombs. But they would "burn" down a place with incendiary bombs.

The primary incendiary cluster bomb used by the US in burning down the Japanese cities at the end of World War II was the M-69. "The M-69 was a simple weapon, shaped like a long tin can and weighing just 2.3 kg (6.2 lb). Since dropping quantities of individual bombs from high altitude would be wildly inaccurate – it was designed to be incorporated into an 'aimable cluster,' a type of cluster bomb that contained 38 of the M-69 firebombs" (<u>Bombs Weapons Rockets Aircraft Ordnance</u>, July 15, 2003 <http://www.danhistory.com/ww2/bombs.shtml>). The cluster bomb would break apart at about 2,000 ft altitude and scatter the thin-skinned incendiary containers which would rupture on impact and ignite the disbursing highly combustible chemicals (e.g., magnesium, phosphorus or petroleum jelly).

The goal was to create a firestorm which would not only destroy property and people with flames at high temperatures but also would asphyxiate people by the resulting elimination of oxygen from the atmosphere.

This was not a pretty weapon. It obviously was by its nature "indiscriminate" in its destruction. The horrible purpose of using incendiaries on an entire defenseless city, to burn and suffocate civilians, could not be disguised. Naturally, therefore, Stratemeyer would be worried about the USAF's image when he later heard that there would be witnesses to this mission.

General Stratemeyer, 4 November 1950:

> I was a bit concerned this morning when I learned that ten (10) correspondents were accompanying the B–29's on their attack (burn) on Kanggye.... My statement will be generally, as follows: That wherever we find hostile troops and equipment that are being utilized to kill UN troops, we intend to use every means and weapon at our disposal to destroy them, that facility, or town. This will be the answer to the use of the incendiary–cluster type of bomb.

Stratemeyer need not had worried. The exponential jump from incinerating troops and equipment to flaming entire towns and cities, designating them as "military targets," was readily accepted by the American public as a regrettable event of war. There was no adverse reaction to his firebombing of Kanggye. Among other reasons, his attack coincided with the first news accounts of serious Chinese involvement in Korea.

Stratemeyer, Sunday, 5 November 1950:

Redline Vandenberg from Stratemeyer. FEAF Bomber Command this afternoon bombed **the military supply center of Kanggye** with about 170 tons of incendiary bombs with flash report indicating all bombing done is usually with excellent results. **Entire city of Kanggye** was virtual arsenal and tremendously important communications center, hence decision to employ incendiary.

Strat must have been surprised when nobody laughed at his calling an entire city of 120,000 people a "virtual arsenal." The USAF's characterization of this town a a military depot thus justified its oblieration -- with every soul in it, as this time the General decided to put the show on without any warning to the population.

Stratemeyer's public relations effort worked.

The New York Times , for example, most probably had a reporter among the host of correspondents Stratemeyer mentioned as having accompanied the B-29's. Yet the Times' November 6th report on the raid mentioned it only as one of an assortment of military activities that day and in fact gave it a Stratemeyer "spin:"

The largest United Nations effort in the air
[today] was made in a heavy attack on Kanggye

by Superforts of the Far East Air Forces Bomber Command yesterday after noon. Twenty B-29's plastered the Kanggye area with **incendiary** bombs. Observers said they saw large fires and columns of smoke rising from the **neighborhood of the city**.

Reconnaissance indicated, according to headquarters, that **the whole area** was being used as a supply base from which supplies and arms moved to Chinese divisions in the west coast area.   Somewhere in the area the Communist High Command is believed to have its headquar ters for the direction of the entire Korean cam paign.

Hence this firestorm raid, which had made the public rela-tions consious Stratemeyer somewhat uneasy, produced very little publicity.

It was different for the next attack. The incendiary raid on the larger city of Sinuiju three days later received more attention in the Western press. Perhaps because it was located just across the Yalu from China. Still, what would have been shocking news of a doomsday incendiary attack on such a large population had to share the headlines with some other alarming news. Suddenly, according to MacArthur, there were now approximately 70,000 Chinese soldiers in Korea. It was a new war, he declared. There were now "alien" forces who treacherously and without warning had attacked the UN forces. The cat was out of the bag. He no longer was able to hide the fact that China had finally reacted to his advance.

MacArthur did not mention that only days before he had officially reported facing only a **total force** of about 20,000 remain-ing enemy soldiers. In fact, to be painfully acknowledged weeks later, there were about 300,000 Chinese soldiers alone in Korea by this time. Nevertheless, because of the non-reaction to the incendiary attacks on Kanggye and Sinuiju, Stratemeyer's diary entry and public statements thereafter suggests less anxiety about public reaction to the burning down of a city and its population. All is well that ends well.

Stratemeyer, Wednesday, 8 November 1950:

> Reports on the bomb raid on the bridges and town of Sinuiju were made to me by General
>
> O'Donnell which I transmitted to General Hickey for General MacArthur. . . . The seventy (70) B–29's in squadron formations [each] loaded with **thirty–two (32) incendiary cluster bombs; all results — excellent. . . .**
>
> Each incendiary cluster is made up of 38 individual fire bombs; consequently, there were (32 x 38 x 70) 85,120 fire bombs on Sinuiju. **General O'Donnell indicates that the town was gone.**
>
> There were no hostile fighter interception of our bombers. . . .I reported to General Hickey that the missions forfor tmum efformum effort ndiary bombs, maximum effort of sixteen (16) B–29's would be over the towns of Sakchu and Puckchin. . .

There is no indication in the diary entries, the Official Releases or the related newspaper articles that the populations of Sinuiju, Sakchu or Puckchin were give any prior warnings so they could evacuate. Though as noted above, in any event escape to shelters or indoors would have been fruitless as either the fire, carbon monoxide or the elimination of oxygen would have been fatal to those in the shelters. The *Official Release (627)* described the target as "the key communications and supply center of Sinuiju" and detailed the various important military targets in the two and one-half square mile city.

There were **300 planes** in total involved in the strike and over **630 tons of bombs** were dropped. Ten of Maj. Gen. Emmett O'Donnell's B-29's in the "air armada" dropped 1,000 pound bombs on two bridges while the other **69 B-29's "rained 85,000 incendiary bombs** on the two and a half square miles of the built-up area on the southeast bank of the Yalu River." In plain language, they were obliterating the City proper itself, as the City consisted primarily of that two and a half square mile of "built-up area" – residences, schools, temples, stores, factories, etc. One notes the foreboding mention of an opening attack:

> *"Maj. Gen. Earle E. Partridge's Fifth Air Force F-80 jets and F-51 fighters raked the area prior to the attack with machine guns, rockets and napalm."*

If the entire place is about to be burned down with incendiaries, what would be the point of risking fighters "to rake the area prior to the attack?" It will be recalled that one of the methods of trapping the civilian population into self-made tombs was to chase them into shelters with preliminary attacks of regular explosives and strafing. Then the firestorms created by the subsequent incendiary bombs would generate carbon monoxide and also consume the oxygen in the shelters -- thus poisoning and suffocating everyone in them, however deep and however hidden -- they were all dead meat.

The Press stories published on the 9th of November could have been written by Stratemeyer's public relations officer as they followed the Party Line. There was no discernable objection to this form of warfare.

The first sentence of the New York Daily News read: "U.S. Superforts smashed the Chinese Communists' main border base in northwest Korea Wednesday with a massive attack of fire and demolition bombs." The headline on page one of the New York Herald Tribune announced: "MAIN CHINESE BASE IN KOREA RAZED BY RAID." The Herald article helpfully pointed out that "Sinuiju, a city of over 100,000 . . . is on the main west coast highway in North Korea, leading to the industrial center of Mukden in Communist China. It has been the chief base through which Chinese Communist convoys have been passing."

But notwithstanding the Official Release and the Summary's attempt to avoid saying it in so many words, the reporter for the Herald Tribune had no hesitancy in asserting that the "B-29 Superfortresses and B-26 bombers set out to flatten the town with explosives."

Describing Sinuiju as a "stronghold for supplies and communications to Chinese communist troops fighting in Korea," the Chicago Tribune quoted an Air Force spokesman as saying that early damage reports indicated "the town of 100,000 population was 'pretty well taken care of.'"

The headline in the Washington Post was : "80 B-29'S DESTROY 90 PERCENT OF CITY ON MANCHURIAN BORDER." The Post reporter related that "a jet pilot who watched the B-29s smash the city said that smoke pillars rose more than 50,000 feet after the attack and the entire city 'looked like it was on fire.'" The Times of London started its account of the attack by explaining that Sinuiju was "the chief ferrying point through which Chinese Communist troops are brought from Manchuria into Korea. . . ."

Fortune seemed to be smiling on General Stratemeyer, or at least on history's image of the USAF. When he first sent his memo to MacArthur on October 17,[th] entitled "Destruction of Sinuiju," and suggested the burning of the city, none of the five reasons he gave even mentioned that it was serving as a portal for Chinese troops and supplies, though he did think "that the psychological effect of a **mass** attack will be **salutary** to Chinese Communist observers across the river in Antung." The Dantean sight of 180,000 people roasting in the flames of Hell just across the river would put the Chinese in their place.

At the time he wrote his memo to MacArthur, General Stratemeyer had no idea that his Chinese observers would be viewing the annihilation of Sinuiju from the *same* side of the Yalu as he was. The Chinese began their movement into Korea on October 19th (Thornton), after finally giving up all hope that the Americans would stop their advance. So the main reason justifying the attack to the public *after* it actually occurred was not even on Stratemeyer's original laundry list of ostensible goals. But the facts by chance fell into place for Stratemeyer, thus avoiding whatever public criticism this extreme measure of warfare might have aroused.

As mentioned earlier, on November 3rd Stratemeyer's proposal to burn Sinuiju was at first denied by MacArthur because he was planning to use that town himself upon capturing it. Then MacArthur changed his mind that afternoon for reasons we do not know and gave the OK. However, MacArthur had already decided by then on an otherwise scorched earth policy.

"Strat," the Chief had told the General on November 3rd, **"burn and destroy as a lesson any other of those towns that you consider of military value to the enemy."** He had blessed the concept of a town or city itself now being desginated as a "military target."

The next day Stratemeyer, as instructed, met with MacArthur's Chief of Staff, General Hickey, to "discuss other targets." He found the conference "most satisfactory." General Hickey had

> *"confirmed the instructions that he had given me the night before that General MacArthur wanted an all–*

out air effort against communications and facilities with every weapon available to stop and destroy the enemy in North Korea. **He reiterated the burning of towns and emphasized the importance of taking out Sinuiju.**"

MacArthur on November 3rd had approved "as a lesson" the burning of Kanggye and Sinuiju to the ground, both recommendations of Stratemeyer. Then he escalated that "lesson" to include "other towns," presumably as recommended from time to time by Stratemeyer who would make the decision that the town could be "of military value to the enemy." Even that much appears to have something of a rational veneer to it.

But then just two days later, with no apparent change in any circumstances, MacArthur geometrically escalated whatever "lesson" they were going to teach. According to Stratemeyer's Nov. 5th diary, he gave the following instructions to Stratemeyer:

> **"Every installation, facility, and village in North Korea now becomes a military and tactical target."**

The Emperor-like CINCFE, by a simple nod of his head, had just christened everything in North Korea as "military." Exceptions were still being made for the major hydro-electric plants on the Manchurian border and the City of Rashin bordering Russia. **"General MacArthur reiterated his scorched earth policy to burn and destroy."**

General Stratemeyer immediately called his commanding Generals together and discussed with them the newly elevated scorched earth program. His adrenalin was running at a high level.

In discussing bridge crossings, one example that was shown to me indicated that **POW camp sites**

(reported), hospitals and prisons would be vulnerable to incendiary attack. **Whether vulnerable or not**, our target was to take out line of communications and towns.

So Stratemeyer was not only with the program, but with it enthusiastically. Eveybody gets flamed, even American POW's if necessary.

Stratemeyer's executing orders were issued Nov. 5th:

> *Except for Rashin, the Suiho Dam and other electric power plants in North Korea, **to destroy every** means of communications **and every** installation, factory, **city and village**. Under present circumstances all such have marked military potential and can only be regarded as military installations. . . .*

> *This destruction is to start at the Korean-Manchurian border and progress south. . . . FEAF Bomber Command [O'Donnell's B-29's] will destroy the cities and large towns. Aircraft under Fifth Air Force control [Partridge's fighters and B-26's] will destroy all other targets **including all buildings capable of affording shelter**.*

Ten million people driven into the snow.

Stratemeyer, Tuesday, 14 November 1950:

> *Went again to see MacArthur . . . . I told him . .*
> *. **I would continue to wash out all cities** and that 15*
> *Nov we were concentrating our entire bomber effort on*
> *Hoeryong.*

Cities great and villages small were burned to the ground.

O'Donnell knew what he was talking about when next June he testified before that Congressional Committee: "I would say that the entire, almost the entire Korean Peninsula, is just a terrible mess. Everything is destroyed. **There is nothing standing worthy of the name.**"

Yet the MacArthur "scorched earth" program did not work. The lesson to the Chinese Communists, who had been battling the Japanese for decades and at the same time engaged in a civil war with reactionaries, was not what MacArthur and Stratemeyer had intended.

No one cried "Uncle." Their resolve to defend their homeland was only strengthened.

The Chinese had warned in explicit and plain language, publicly and through diplomatic channels, that they would not tolerate an American Army on their border, no matter what excuses the Americans were giving for their march up the Peninsula.

On October 12, 1950 the Chinese publicly announced that the Peiping regime "cannot stand by idly" while the United States troops crossed the thirty-eighth Parallel. Ten days earlier Premier and Foreign Minister Chou En-lai had stated that while the Chinese people desperately wanted a "peaceful environment" so they could rehabilitate their country, the United States should not mistake this for weakness (New York Times, October 12, 1950).

MacArthur and the Truman Administration did just that. They brushed off these warnings as attempted "blackmail." (Reminiscent of the American reaction to the North Korean threats today.) The Americans assumed it would be foolish for the Chinese Communist, exhausted from their own civil war and admittedly so desperate for the time and resources to consolidate their administration of China, to engage in a battle with the most powerful nation on earth – a nation who had only five years earlier dropped atomic bombs on another enemy. Indeed, in the long internal debate among Mao and the other Chinese leaders about confronting the approaching Americans on their border, the damage that atomic bombs would do to China was discussed and the risk very reluctantly, but explicitly accepted.

Marcantonio in his June address to Congress in opposing the intervention, had warned that the Chinese would not shrink from protecting their country regardless of any threat of atomic bombing. It was obvious that we were threatening China by interfering in their neighbor's civil war. He pleaded with his colleagues to try to understand the power of the Korean passion for independence and revolutionary change. If the Americans in 1860 were ready to kill each other on a massive scale to keep a nation united that had been united for "four scores and seven years," imagine the passion for reunification of people who had been united for over a thousand years. At any rate, the Chinese soldiers, on foot and essentially armed only with their rifles, now drove the heavily armed Americans and South Koreans from their border.

The Chinese and North Korean foot soldiers, though grossly outgunned, kept marching down the peninsula. MacArthur had split his forces up and launched his "home for Christmas" offensive the day before the Chinese launched their own offensive, to the utter surprise of the Americans. Why MacArthur was again caught utterly by surprise is an issue that itself has produced books over the years. When the war began he had been looked upon by all political factions in the US as the one solid leader they all could count on. Editorials from the New York <u>Daily News</u> to the <u>New York Times</u> and the <u>Washington Post</u> joined in a sigh of relief that MacArthur was in charge. Suffice it to say that he might have been another wrong for the period, the wrong General for the wrong war.

General Walker with his Eighth Army in the west retreated pell-mell for the entire month of December. The Eighth Army hurried down the Peninsula, all the way to below the 38th parallel, abandoning Seoul again, while making little contact with the advancing Chinese.

Walker had been cautious and on the first appearance of the Chinese in late October, had slowed his advance to the Yalu and regrouped. When MacArthur ordered the general offensive on the 24th of November, the Chinese were ready with their own offensive. On Walker's line they concentrated their first attacks on the ROK troops holding the middle and quickly overran them. Walker thought it best to make an orderly retreat to a better defensive position without fighting in order to be able to preserve all his equipment and avoid being outflanked.

General Almond, on the other hand, with his X Corps in the

east, was under the more direct command of MacArthur and he had kept moving aggressively up to the border with China. His forces were met head on by the Chinese. The X Corps. fought fiercely in the bitter cold and took heavy casualties, but was battered and escaped annihilation only by an unopposed mass evacuation at the North Korean port of Hungnam.

Walker unfortunately did not live to see the end of the retreat. He was killed in a jeep accident on December 23, 1950. His replacement, General Matthew Ridgeway, found a demoralized, defeatist and retreat-oriented Army when he arrived a few days later, as well as a depressed General MacArthur. However it did not take him long to turn his men around, change their spirit and even go on the offensive. He soon recaptured what was left of Seoul and set up a rational line of defense across the Peninsula. That line, approximately along the 38th parallel where it had all started, essentially remained the same in a stalemate that did not end until July, 1953.

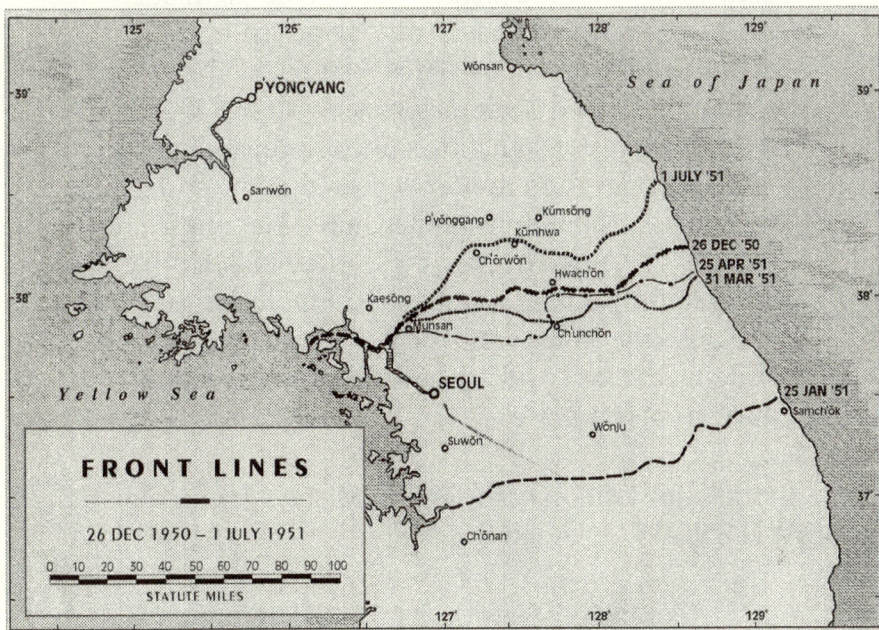

(Map from Y'Blood, *The Three Wars of General Stratemeyer*)

General MacArthur with his 8th Army Commanders;
General Walker and then General Ridgeway.

Richard J. H. Johnston's special report, entitled: "ABAN-
DONED PYONGYANG EERILY QUIET UNDER SMOKE PALL
FROM DEMOLITION" on December 5, 1950 in the New York
Times read:

> "This former North Korean Red capi-
> tal, eerily quiet under a pall of heavy black smoke,
> presented today the picture of desolation familiar
> to observers who had seen other cities being
> abandoned to an enemy. Fires were set by the
> retreating United Nations forces. . . . In bewil-
> dered, sullen and sometimes uncomprehending
> knots, Pyongyang's residents peered at the end-
> less retreating columns of the United Nations
> troops. . . . Fanned by freezing north winds, smoke
> sparks from flaming warehouses, supply dumps
> and gasoline stores whipped across the roads . . .
> stinging the eyes and nostrils of the troops riding
> away from this place. . . ."

In the same edition of the Times, Michael James reported
that "WITHDRAWAL A ROUT."

> "For the past few days installations at two of the
> landing fields in Pyongyang have been the scene of a
> 'scorched earth' policy. . . . Ammunition was not the only
> thing burning on the field. Large stocks of winter clothing

LIBERATING KOREA?

that had been flown in for friendly troops were giving off acid smoke."

The Chinese were reported to be 10 to 15 miles away. We further endeared ourselves to the local population by smoking up their town with burning winter clothing and a whole lot of other things that they could have used. At least these folks were north of the 38th parallel and, therefore, "of no conern."

The people of Pyongyang had good reason to be"sullen" while they watched the UN forces retreat. Those forces had brought only devastation to them. The Americans now had to move carefully as they retreated, since the locals were seething with anger against them.

"Little assistance from North Koreans could be expected by the United Nation forces. The retribution of the South Korean military authorities, and the frequent hangings of alleged Communists ordered by its summary courts, had alienated many people north of the 38th parallel. Aerial bombing had created a large homeless population, sullen and resentful. . . . With this terrain and in this political climate the United Nations mechanized columns, helpless off the roads and alien among the local population, were at a grave disadvantage. For the Chinese the hills were a friendly, if a choppy, sea, on which their troops would have the mobility of a fleet, a mobility which would enable them to outflank these road-bound columns"(Times (London), December 11, 1950).

The people of North Korea, unfortunately, had not seen the last of the destruction which the Americans could wreck. When Partridge and O'Donnell had begun systematically destroying North Korea's cities after MacArthur's "destroy everything"orders, the UN troops were still occupying some. So not everything in North Korea had been destroyed. There was more work to be done.

Stratemeyer, Tuesday, 28 November, 1950:

Dispatched the fol **REDLINE Top Secret** to Vandenberg:

.... Ground situation on right flank of Eighth Army bad. Partridge will concentrate great effort there today.

O'Donnell besides burning Taechon will burn ... other villages...."

Stratemeyer, Saturday, 30 December 1950:

Disptached the fol Stratline to CG Fifth Air Force ... **TOP SECRET PERSONAL PARTRIDGE** FROM STRATEMEYER: ... (TOP SECRET) We have authority **to destroy** the following towns: Pyongyang, Wonsan, **Hamhung**, and **Hungnam**. Attacks will be conducted **without** psychological warfare **warnings** or publcity. At first opportunity, inform Ridgway.

Stratemeyer, Monday, 1 January 1951:

Dispatched the fol ltr **to General O'Donnell** via courier: **Dear Rosie** — reference our authority **to burn and destroy** Pyongyang, Wonsan, **Hamhung**, and **Hungnam**, it is desired that **no publicity whatsoever** be given out as to these strikes. No reporters or personnel nor [not?] members of FEAF Bomber Command will be permitted to ride as observers on these strikes. Make sure that these instructions are strictly adhered to.

"BURN IT ... IF YOU SO DESIRE"

It would be easy just to say that MacArthur had gone mad and it was all his fault. Indeed it does seem that "the old general had lost his senses" as Thomas B. Buell observes in his <u>Naval Leadership in Korea</u> published in 2002 by the Department of the Navy, Naval Historical Center. Buell was referring to MacArthur's proposals during the low point of the war to pull out of Korea entirely and commence World War III by attacking China with atomic bombs. Likewise, Vandenberg's official biographer, Phillip Meilinger, writing under the auspices of the Air Force History Museums Program had this to say about MacArthur's, and incidentally, Stratemeyer's, sanity:

> The FEAF commander [Stratemeyer] was coming increasingly under MacArthur's spell and also moving for a widening of the war. . . . When MacArthur began to go over the edge in April 1951 Stratemeyer followed, waxing rapturous in his diary concerning the brilliance and patriotism of the old general.

But it was more than MacArthur. Or Stratemeyer. Or the Military Establishment. These were not rogue Generals or a military coup. LeMay and O'Donnell continued to collect roomfuls of medals and promotions. It was American policy executed by Harry Truman and enthusiastically supported by the country, at least until things went bad. And they may do it again – unless the North Koreans this time have a plausible deterrent.

CHAPTER X

"MR.MALIK'S LATEST LINE"

If the American bombing in Korea was so horrendous, why didn't the world react?

It did, but it made no difference. The United States was able to bottle up the opposition and do what it wanted, curiously similar to what it has so far been able to do with its 2003 invasion of Iraq. In 1950 the United States had complete control over the United Nations — most of its permanent members in the aftermath of WWII were either being fed or re-armed by the United States.

Soon after the creation of the UN, the US changed the nature of the UN. Instead of what Roosevelt and Stalin had planned it to be, a place for the real powers of the world to collaborate and settle what differences they might have, the Truman Administration reshaped it into a propaganda weapon to be used to bludgeon the Soviets.

In 2003 the UN was not as easy to manipulate, when even our allies were objecting to the Bush Administration's ignoring international law and going it alone against Iraq (with the British tagging along so as to get back into their old colonial stamping grounds). But no matter, even against the wishes of the United Nations and the world, the United States again did just what it wanted with the raw use of power.

Back in 1950 the world was indeed being told what the Americans were doing to the Koreans. For example, reporting from India, Robert Trumbull in the New York Times wrote on August 8, 1950:

> Accounts of repeated bombings of Seoul [at the time occupied by the North Koreans] by United States aircraft and reports of villages left in flames as United States troops withdraw arouse indignation here [India]. Consideration of military necessity is overshadowed by the fact that an Asia people is 'getting it in the neck again.'
>
> The Indians argue that killing Koreans and destroying property is not making friends for the United State in Korea, or in India.

Sounds extraordinarily familiar.

Trumbull dispatched his story from the capital of India, New Delhi, after trying to get a consensus of Indian opinion by talking to Indian legislators from all over the country gathered at the Capital. He told his readers that "with every day of the Korean war bringing more news of bombed cities and flaming villages, the unpopularity of the United States is growing." Indians thought it was pointless, according to what Trumbull could determine, for the United States to be killing and destroying in Korea. They did not see anything wrong with communism winning in Korea or in Indo-China "at this stage. They argue that if the United States system is better, it eventually will come to the top. . . ."

But in the United States in 1950 this type of common-sense thinking was close to treason. A person like Vito Marcantonio, who basically was beseeching his colleagues to adopt this philosophy, was branded as a "Communist Stooge."

This was a time of *feverish* anti-communism, where patient wisdom was not welcomed. There was no time to wait for the American Way of Life to win out over communism by simply being the better system. The newspapers were filled with belligerency, ranting and raving. They deamanded that we immediately "draw the line,"that we instantly "contain"the poison of communism. Soon it would be too late -- everything would be contaminated. The subversives among us would undermine our morale and spirit, would confuse the public. If peaceful means like economic pressure did not stop this venon from spreading, then we must knock the hell out of them with good, old American power. Certainly relunctantly, and with a heavy heart, since America is a land of peace and it is only peace that we seek with our armaments, but the communist enemy has left us no other option. . . . Such was the thiniking of those shaping public opinion.

Consequently, anyone who seemed to question this approach would be colored with red or pink and would lose his or her humanity. This applied to individuals as well as to whole masses of people alike. Those in our country who did raise their voices in objection to the brutality and wantonness of it all, were chased from their jobs, harassed and called fellow-travelers, communists or worse.

Even churchmen in the United State had caught this spirit. They called upon God to help them destroy the Devil, better know as the Communist. A good example of this is the purple and darkly threatening language used on the subject by Cardinal Francis Spellman, head of the New York Catholic Archdiocese. On July 20, 1950, a month after the war had begun and the day after Vito Marcantonio had been the only vote in Congress against a military armaments bill, the Cardinal had this to say:

This is a dire day for all America because **there are some counted among her sons**, who, by covert or overt acts of disloyalty, or **treacherous acts of apathy, stand guilty of the murder** of those American boys whose young, fear-frozen faces were filled with bullets as they surrendered, only to be slaughtered by **bestial Communist enemies**.

Entrusted with this peace [after World War II] and the future of our youth – we have once again failed ourselves and them – beguiled, deceived, betrayed, defeated by **Communists, fellow travelers, apathetic and guileful people and public servants. . . .**

No words can describe the **villainy of communistic acts**. Yet we who had time and warning enough, warnings even from the Soviets themselves, to build ourselves spiritually and materially strong, fell victim to their vices as we fell victim to our own"(New York Times, July 20, 1950; see also Daily Mirror [New York], July 20, 1950).

He does not sound quite like Christ and his Sermon on the Mount.

The Cardinal was condemning with equal and indiscriminate passion not only those Americans who were communists or fellow travelers, but also those who were just uninterested. He was also repeating a recurrent lament of a certain segment of our society when he bemoaned the fact that America had not used its monopolistic strength, i.e., the Atom Bomb, effectively after World War II. America had been the most powerful nation left standing after World War II, he was saying, and we should have used our atomic monopoly to impose our will on the rest of the world. God had entrusted America with a "Special Providence" [thank you Walter Russell Mead].

The good Cardinal saw no contracdiction between his constantly beseeching God to grant peace on earth to mankind and his equally constant belligerent instigations to hate, fear and violence. This man of peace had been one of the first to rush over to the White House on August 11, 1945 to lend his moral support to President Truman. Truman had just dropped atom bombs on Hiroshima and Nagasaki and some diffident voices were raising moral questions about it. The Cardinal wanted to smother those voices and bestow his blessings on the whole thing. "Archbishop Spellman praised Mr. Truman's leadership of the nation. . . ." (New York Herald Tribune, August 12, 1945).

Spellman just a few years later had the opportunity to inflict special pain on the family of one of the Church's sons "who, by covert or overt acts of disloyalty, or treacherous acts of apathy, stand guilty of the murder of those American boys. . . ." With seeming relish he petulantly prohibited Vito Marcantonio's widow and mother from burying Marcantonio in a Catholic cemetery. The legendary radical had died suddenly on a New York City street at the age of 52.

In 1950 the Soviets, on behalf of the Koreans, did indeed loudly complain about the bombing. Since most of Korea was in the hands of the Communists at that time, their protests were on behalf of most of the Koreans.

But the US Government treated these grievances with ridicule and contempt. The Press followed suit and the US public, encased in a cartoonish world when it came to the Soviets, was deaf to these cries of anguish.

One of the forums for the Soviet protests was in the United Nations. Jacob Malik, its UN Representative, introduced a Resolution to condemn the bombing. The US in the UN vigorouly defended itself by explaining that only "military targets" were being hit and that this was being done with "precision" bombing. In addition, the US was warning civilians to evacuate before the bombings. But the basic American answer to the protests was that:

"war is hell" and the aggressors were getting what they deserved. The "calamities" befalling the people of Korea were visited on them by the aggressors from the North who started the war. All the consequences, as regrettable as they may be, were the inevitable results of that aggression.

This was the response not just from the power elite in the United States, but from the Press, and, unfortunatley, it seemed from the people of America as well. The slaughter in Korea did not seem to bother us Americans. Only accounts of our own soldiers' deaths or some new atrocity supposedly committed by the North Koreans could move us.

Secretary of State Acheson, on September 6th, and in antici-pation of the Soviet's offering their resolution of condemnation in the UN on September 7th, issued a statement presenting the American side. Civilians regrettably were being killed, yes, but the fault was not that of the US. After repeating that only military targets were being bombed, he gave this explanation as to why civilians were being strafed in South Korea and why peasants in carts were being rocketed:

> It is well known that the Communist command has compelled helpless civilians to labor on these military sites. Peaceful villages are used to cover the tanks of the invading army. Civilian dress is used to disguise soldiers of aggression.

This Party Line was put into an official report to the UN in General MacArthur's name, as the UN Commander, and read at a Security Council meeting the next day by the American delegate, Ernest A. Gross:

> Since the enemy is apparently forcing civilian labor to his use, problems of identification have become difficult.... On land, civilians are car-rying supplies in **push-carts and donkey carts** which burn and explode when strafed. The enemy

hides vast quantities of military equipment in civilian dwellings, resulting in the **necessity to fire and destroy such dwellings** when such information is firm. However, **the problem of avoiding the killing of innocent civilians** and damages to the civilian economy **is continually present and given my [MacArthur] personal attention.**

At the UN Security Council meeting of September 7, 1950, the Soviet Representative, Jacob Malik, already an object of ridicule in the US Press, presented a resolution to condemn the "barbarous" American bombing on "undefended Korean towns" that were killing innocent civilians and leaving others without "a roof over their heads." From an August 22, 1950 cablegram sent to the UN by Pak Hen En, Minister for Foreign Affairs of North Korea, Malik put together some of the facts supporting his resolution:

The city of **Pyongyang** has been subjected to repeated bombings. . . . From 3 to 28 July, 18,203 dwelling houses in the city were completely destroyed. . . . More than 800 persons were killed and wounded. Ten plants and factories producing popular consumer goods, three hospitals . . .

"Bomb damage to military training area in center of city, Pyongyang, Korea."

USAF Photo
1 November 1950

Malik continued reading from the cablegram:

From 2 to 27 July the town of **Wonsan** suffered twelve attacks ... in which 4,028 houses were destroyed, 1,647 persons, including 739 women and 325 children -- were killed.

From 2 July to 3 August the town of **Hungnam** was subjected to eight attacks, in which 200 airplanes took part, dropping 2,000 bombs. As a result of these attacks, three schools, a theatre, two polyclinics, a library, and other buildings were destroyed, 297 persons were killed and 446 were wounded.

In a single air raid on the town of **Seoul** in the area of Yengsan on 16 July, fourteen hospitals, two educational institutions, a children's home and a Catholic church were destroyed. . . .

It should be added that the United States Command itself recognizes that its bombers meet with no resistance; this means that it subjects the undefended, peaceful towns and villages of Korea to barbarous terror attacks and thus commits its crimes against the peaceful population of that country with perfect impunity. . .

According to Mr. Boyle, a correspondent of the United States news agency, the Associated Press, another Korean town – Yongdong – was subjected to an equally barbarous bombing. He states: 'Yongdong, which only two weeks before had been the principal United States defence base in Korea, no longer exists. It looks like Nagasaki after the explosion of the atom bomb. It has suffered very heavily as a result of ceaseless attacks by United States army and navy planes. Only a thin wisp of smoke rises above the ruins of the town; the rest is a wilderness.'

The correspondent Robert Martin wrote in an Overseas News Agency report dated 7 August: 'A perpetual haze seems to hang **over South Korea** these days . . . from the **scores of little villages which each day are reduced to smoking ashes** by jet fighters and the F-51 Mustangs. . . .'

. . . .

Who [Malik asked] will believe that arms were hidden in 18,203 dwelling houses in Pyongyang or in 4,028 houses in Wonsan, hundreds of kilometers from the front . . .

The representative from India, Sir Benegal N. Rau, felt compelled to state: "I must confess that reports of large-scale bombings in Korea have been prevalent in India for some time and have greatly disturbed Indian public opinion. . . ." Yet the stranglehold of the US over the nations in the UN at that time was so complete that even the Indian delegate voted against the Soviet Resolution, ostensibly because "we cannot assume without investigation that all the allegations of bombing are true" **in the face of the adamant and detailed American denials** that were being made.

Malik also charged that the United States Army and Marines were putting the torch to villages in front of their lines and behind their lines in order to deny hiding places to the enemy. The inhabitants, according to Malik, were first asked to evacuate and retreat with the US forces, but those who refused to leave were executed. "Thus, in the burned down villages of Songjin and Nekwan over 3,000 Koreans have been shot; 600 have been shot in P'yongta'ek (Heitako) and about 1,000 in Taejon."

Later in the war, when the US and ROK forces recaptured these same towns, the ROK "discovered" thousands of murdered civilians and the world press was filled with headlines and pictures accusing the North Koreans of more atrocities. Could these have been the bodies of the same people allegedly killed in the US retreat?

Malik, in his UN presentation in September, 1950, also reported cablegrams from the North Koreans condemning the American employment of delayed-action bombs. The North Koreans claimed that these snake-in-the-grass explosives had been killing civilians after they came out of their shelters to repair a bombing raid's damage, to get food or to search for and bury their dead. Also reported by the North Koreans was repeated strafing of innocent people on the roads and peasants in their fields.

The response to Malik's charges was uniformly dismissive: "sorry, but that's what you get." For example, from the comments of the Norwegian Delegate, Mr. Sunde:

> I am not aware that the Soviet Union
> delegation has presented any semblance of proof

in support of its contention that the air force of the United Nations has carried out bombing in raids in Korea in violation of the accepted rules of international law.

War is always cruel and a naturally destructive business, and it is a matter of particular regret to all men of good will that it should be accompanied by such harrowing suffering by the defenceless civilian population; but such is war. The responsibility always rests on the aggressors who are willing to let loose the evil forces of war – in this case, the North Koreans.

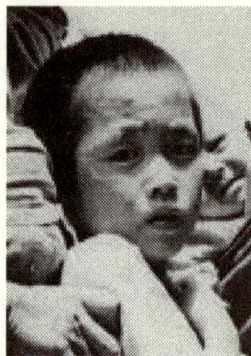

The New York Times, one of the more moderate American commentators on the Russian's charges, headlined its mocking editorial: MR. MALIK'S LATEST LINE. It too reiterated the American position that "the responsibility for the **unavoidable** horrors of war rests squarely on those who start it, and that, so far as the air force is concerned, it attacks **only military targets** of the invaders, though these often use churches, schools and civilians to disguise such targets."

Correspondents from the East, however, did not so casually find that the bombing damage was "unavoidable." Hsin Hua, an

Asian news agency correspondent reported from Korea on 11 August, as relayed by Malik:

> 'Taejon [South Korea] was a large modern city with a population of 200,000. Now practically nothing is left of it. There is nothing to bomb any more, but United States planes come here every day and bomb and strafe the city with unheard-of cruelty, trying to destroy every trace of its existence.'

The terrifying shocks from the delayed-fuse bombs dropped by the Americans received special mention in another cablegram of complaint from Pak Hen En. As read by Malik to the Security Council on September 18, 1950, it charged in part:

> 'In order to hinder relief work and increase the number of victims among the peaceful population, a considerable number of delayed-action bombs are dropped which explode just as the population are coming out of their shelters after a raid and beginning to look for the killed and wounded....'

Malik continued to quote from that cablegram:

> 'On 19 August over 60 United States bombers bombed the city [of Chongjin], dropping upon it 1,012 bombs; as a result of that bombardment, 2,626 houses were destroyed, 1,034 persons were killed and 2,347 were injured; and hospitals, the industrial technical college, the girls' high school and other schools, the people's theatre and many other cultural institutions ... were destroyed. Such bombardments take place repeatedly, as a result of which nine-tenths of the city of Chongjin, with a

population of 120,000, has been destroyed. . . . On 20 August in the counties of Taedong, Sunchon ... 68 United States dive-bombers carried out a raid and, flying low over the village, machine-gunned and dropped bombs on peasants working in the fields or gathered in market places; as a result 33 peasants were killed and 54 persons injured on that day. . . .'

The American Delegate on the 18th of September, Warren Austin, during his indignant defense of American bombing before

the Security Council, read from a MacArthur report to the UN covering the period August 16 to 31. MacArthur after the war would recall that even though he was the "UN" commander, he never had direct contact with the UN. He took orders from the US Joint Chiefs of Staff. MacArthur also recalled that his reports "to the UN" were actually sent first to the State and Defense Departments who censored them before going to the UN (Walter LaFeber, America, Russia and the Cold War).

The "MacArthur" report read by Austin therefore may have been written at least in part by someone in the State or Defense

Department or by Austin himself. This seems particularly so because a number of paragraphs appear to have been lawyerly crafted to counter charges that had been made by Malik back on September 7th. According to Austin's reading of the MacArthur report, MacArthur said:

> 'Our naval bombardment forces, both surface and air, are exercising **every precaution to avoid harming the civil population**, and are employing every possible means to identify and destroy military targets only. . . .

> '**Pin point** destruction of industrial and other military objectives in North Korea continues. Evaluation of photographs of these objectives after attacks shows **remarkable accuracy** has been obtained in striking the selected targets which in every instance have been of military significance. . . .'
> 'The North Korean populace has been warned by radio and by leaflets to vacate their areas that contain military targets. They have been urged **to leave these cities and go to the country or to the mountains.**'

"... go to the country or to the mountains."

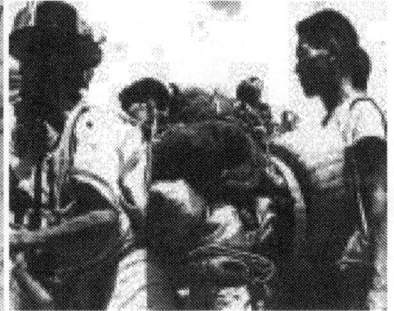

[[THANKS, FROM ALL THOSE OF US WHO DIED ON
THE ROAD TO THE COUNTRY AND TO THE MOUNTAINS.]]

The Russian UN Delegate also repeated the North Koreans' complaint that:

> "The United States interventionists are systematically de
> stroying the industry of Korea in an attempt to condemn
> the Korean people to unemployment, destitution and
> famine."

Indeed, that is exactly what the US was doing. Unwittingly, Malik had just given the standard American definition of "strategic" bombing.

Malik was also taken aback that no one seemed moved by the fact that most of the towns and cities on the long list that the North Korean Foreign Minister complained had been indiscriminately bombed by the US were located **below** the 38th parallel and supposedly friendly to the US. No one seemed disturbed that the American goal was admittedly the total destruction of a society.

This was the last time that the Koreans complained about the bombing. They now understood "strategic" bombing.

These are the memories which Kim Jong Il and the other North Korean leaders have today. This is part of what guides their negotiations with the coterie from the State Department and the White House.

CHAPTER XI

THE OCCUPATION: GENERALS HODGE, DEAN AND WARD

Fortuitously for the sake of history, the"forces that are"put a highly reliable witness"behind enemy lines"early in the war and for the duration. It was an American pair of eyes, trained in the military arts and familiar with Korea. As a POW General William Dean lived among the Koreans for three years, experienced the war to some extent from their side and thereafter had something to say, and was remarkably unhesitant to say it in plain English. I find in the frank yet casual and graceful comments that he gave us in his autobiography (William F. Dean as told to William L. Worden, General Dean's Story, 1954) an important evaluation of the main rationale Truman gave for the intervention; significant comments related to General MacArthur's claim of"pin point"bombing; and enlightening observations from the receiving end of the devastation wrought by American bombing on the cities of Korea.

Incidentally, I doubt very much that the lines in MacArthur's report to the UN about"pin-point"bombing or the regrettable necessity of killing South Korean men and women who had been forced to work for the Northerners were really written by MacArthur. He was in the process of nonchalantly ordering the burning down of entire cities and he would have thought it utterly foolish to be talking about"pin-point"bombing. He considered himself a heroic and invincible figure, such petty lying would be beneath him. Nor would he ever admit that he was allowing the indiscriminate strafing of civilians behind enemy lines. That was not in the image he had of himself – though someone in the State or Defense Department must have thought that this little admission would be a sympathetic explanation for the well-known strafing and napalming of civilians. Those lines were more probably written by a Paul Wolfowitz-type, who was attempting to deal with the outcry being made in the rest of the world, or at least in Asia, about the American bombing.

But before getting to the thoughts of the post-POW William Dean, we must take a closer look at the American Occupation of Korea from 1945 to the middle of 1948 when the government was turned over by the US to its choice as leader, Sigmund Rhee. This was after an ostentatious election below the 38th parallel supposedly supervised by and declared "free" by the UN.

There has been a decent amount written in English about the Occupation, with the acknowledged authority being Professor Bruce Cumings (The Origins of the Korean War, Volumes I and II). I have adopted for the most part his view of the Occupation. I have read extensively through what original documents General Hodge and his people allowed to survive of their papers in the National Archives and I have found nothing inconsistent with Professor Cumings' history and interpretations. Even with this narrow sampling in the National Archives of their activities, one can see why the Occupation was a sorry "mess," as one of the occupation Generals, Orlando Ward, routinely characterized it.

I will use the private diary of Major General Orlando Ward (1917 – 1978) to take a closer look and dwell somewhat over the role played by the other William Dean – the old Dean of an earlier life in Korea who presided as the Military Governor during some of the cruelest suppression of its people. I will also call from the grave the testimony of a Korean General, Kim Ik Ruhl. Kim was a Colonel at the time of the American Occupation, and he will testify about the way the old Dean as Military Governor handled the uprising by the people of Cheju-do. Unlike Dean's, the stories of Generals Ward and Kim remained secret during their lives. Thankfully they made arrangements to ensure that their eye-witness accounts ultimately would see the light of day.

Korea had been a colony of Japan for 40 years. The Japanese used it for their own purposes, structuring the economy, the education system, the food system, etc., for the benefit of the home country as all colonial powers have. Koreans were given very little authority in running their own country. Much of the school system and other such institutions were segregated between the Koreans and the large number of Japanese who emigrated to the important cities. While Korea was part of the Japanese empire, all the top civilian administrators of the Korean government as well as the administrators of the businesses and factories and hospitals, etc., in Korea were ethnic Japanese, either born in Korea or emigrated from Japan. At the end of WWII there were several hundred thousand Japanese in Korea, either as troops, or as managers of industry, the courts, the police system or just as ordinary citizens.

Stalin had promised FDR, Truman, Churchill and Atlee ("Yalta" and "Potsdam") that once Germany was defeated the Soviet Union would turn some of its forces to the East and help the Allies against Japan. He thought the turnaround time might be about three months. That is exactly what the Russians did. In early August, 1945, precisely three months after Germany's surrender, Russia, which had not been at war with Japan, declared war and moved its troops into Manchuria and Korea. But this happened to coincide with the US dropping atom bombs on Japan. Some in the Government were sorry now that they had asked the Russians to come in. They therefore immediately sought ways to keep the Soviets from taking advantage of Japan's imminent collapse.

When the commanders of the 375,000 Japanese troops in Korea saw the Russians advancing into Korea, they assumed that the surrender in Korea would be to the Russians. As a result the Japanese rushed to set up a native body of Koreans as a figurehead administration. It was hoped that this pliant body would help keep order and protect the lives and property of the hundreds of thousands of stranded Japanese civilians and soldiers.

The Governor-General, General Noboyuki Abe, also wanted a native body to inter-face with the Russians and help extricate the Japanese. The person finally selected by General Abe, after Abe was turned down by his first choices, Korean collaborators who now feared for their lives, was a long-time Korean nationalist who had respresented the Singer Sewing Machine in Korea but had no connection with the various Korean exile groups. He was Lyuh Woon Hong (Woon Kong Lyuh; Yo Wun Hyung). (Lyuh was assassinated on a street in Seoul two years later, his family accusing the by-then American favorite, Sigmund Rhee.)

To General Abe's surprise and discomfit, however, this figurehead body quickly took on its own life as it became swelled with the thousands of nationalists and political prisoners he had just released from the jails. Lyuh and his allies promptly set up a peninsula-wide administrative structure to govern Korea. The fast-moving group selected Seoul as their headquarters and declared themselves the"People's Republic"in early September, just days before the American occupiers arrived. The nationalists who had so quickly formed a functioning administration had been waiting and fighting for this day for 40 years — their time had arrived. The Lyuh organization was described in a United Press report as a "provisional Korean commission, representing all classes and all political parties" (PM, September 12, 1945).

American planners had been caught short by the sudden fall of Japan and they were unprepared for the Japanese surrender in Korea, much less for the task of occupying Korea. Nevertheless there were people in the US Government who wanted a presence in Korea as it would put US power right up into the face of Russia. Recall the banker-reparations chief Edwin Pauly's advice to Truman to grab as much of Manchuria and Korea as possible (above, pages 88- 89). So 45,000 war-weary men of the XXIVth Division were rushed from Okinawa for the surrender and occupation merely because they happened to be the closest. Their Commander, General John Hodge, one of the best combat Generals in the Pacific, accompanied them.

Hodge and his men finally arrived on September 8th, a month after the Russians had taken the Japanese surrender in the north of Korea. The Soviet troops, now totally unopposed, had dutifully halted at the 38th parallel in full compliance with the agreed General Order Number One issued by MacArthur as Allied Commander.

General John Hodge and his forces came into Korea with only an outline of instructions from the Allied Commander, General MacArthur. Hodge's primary dictate from MacArthur seemed to have been to keep the Soviets out. The Soviet Union was our ally, losing over 20,000,000 soldiers in the war with Germany, they entered the war against Japan at FDR's and Truman's entreaties to divert Japanese troops in Manchuria and Korea while we invaded the Japanese mainland. The newspapers were filled with pictures of the living and dead skeletons emerging from the horrow of Japanese POW camps. We were helping the British and French to take over again their abandoned old colonies. We were even transporting and arming the Nationalists Chinese in their civil war. Yet, we could only act with suspicion and barely disguised hostility to the Russians.

General Orlando Ward would later confide to a reporter that the US was in Korea only for its own purpose, which was to keep the Russians out. The reporter went on to quote Ward without attribution in an article (Ray Cromley, "Failure in Korea," Wall Street Journal, January 16, 1947). When Hodge read it he was furious and sent a heated letter around to his commanders reminding them to be cautious about what they said to reporters. Ward was amused and commented approvingly on Cromley's article.

Encounters between American and Russian troops at the 38th parallel produced many images of "what could have been."

This early friendliness was widespread, as American reporters who journeyed up to the Russian occupation headquarters would report (New York Times, September 15, 1945). But it was not to be.

Everything that could go wrong, went wrong from the very beginning of the American "liberation" of Korea. A curse of some sort that has come down to this very day.

The Koreans had expected Liberation! as promised repeatedly by the Allies since the Cairo Declaration of 1943. Instead two Koreans are killed by Japanese policemen as a crowd of workers attempt to greet the Americans landing in Jinsen. Then Hodge stupifies the Koreans by telling them not only that they are not capable of governing themselves just yet, but also by reinstating the hated colonial Japanese administration intact. The Governor, General Noboyuki Abe, and the Police Director, Tadao Nishihiro -- who had just killed the Koreans for trying to greet the Americans, were now working for Hodge. It was a colosal blunder and head-lined in the US as "flabbergasting" (PM, September 11, 1945).

Was this simply a blunder by a brave warrior inexperienced in the niceties of occupation? Or was it MacArthur's honest mistake, after all he had retained the Japanese administrators in Japan to enforce his orders -- though this was not Japan. It did not help the image of the Americans that the Russians were promptly expelling not only the Japanese from administration in their occupied area, but also the Korean collaborators who were just as hated by the population. The Russians were finding no shortage of native Kore-ans to run their area. Ironically, the collaborators and their allies would start their trek south and find a warm welcome in the American zone, gaining positions of prominence in Hodge's advisory committees. Their children would form the basis of Nazi-like youth groups, financed in large part by the US, who were to terror-ize the population in the south in the coming years as "anti-com-munist" shock troops.

But Hodge's subsequent behavior indicated more of a pattern that seems to exlude the"just a mistake"interpreation. Like the Russians, he found Lyuh's orgainzation operating somewhat efficiently, with administrators down to the village level. Unlike the Russians, however, who ably utilized these native committees, Hodge somehow convinced himself that they were not so much Korean nationalists but communists agents of the Russians. A bizarre conclusion that is hard to explain.

Someone in the US Government either fed him this line or he made it up out of wholecloth, but he did seriously testify to the UN Commission in 1948 that this body, the People's Republic, "dates back to many years of preparedness for the situation in which the Soviets were active." He seemed to have discovered that the year 1925 was important to communism in Korea. Every group from the US that visited the American Military Government in Korea in the coming years would receive the same lecture. Korea was crawling with communists, and they date back to 1925. Hodge browbeat his unit's historians until they produced an anti-communist diatribe which he passed off to visitors as a political history of Korea.

Thousands of protesters in the streets of Korea soon had Washington ordering MacArthur and Hodge to replace General Abe and the other Japanese. Still Hodge was for the most part on his own. He operated at first just under MacArthur's ad hoc general instructions and his own inclinations, since Washington as was noted had not expected to be occupying Korea and had no plans or instructions in place. Wherever he got it from, it was clear that from the very beginning Hodge was obsessed with the idea that his job was to keep the area under his occupation from moving politically or socially to the left – whether it be on the issue of land distribution, the opening up of government and education, the participation by peasants in the rice distribution, etc.. He shut down newspapers, arrested editors, fabricated excuses to constantly raid the offices and homes of leftists, refused to remove the most corrupt or tyrannical police chiefs.

He lumped everyone together and called them all "communists" if they showed interest in even a shadow of reform, much less radical change. On the other side, or anti-"commy" side, he put the missionary- educated Koreans who could speak English, who for the most part were the wealthy merchants and landlords who had collaborated with the Japanese. He added to them the wealthy merchants and landowners who were leaving the north which was now under reform minded left-wing and communist control.

Finally, saying that he could use them as figureheads, he brought back the ancient exiles, people like the missionary-educated Sigmund (Syngman) Rhee, who had set himself up in the US for the past 40 years as the representative of the Korean Provisional Government in exile; Kim Koo, the President of that Provisional Government in Shanghai who had been in China for 40 years, and Kim Kiusik(Kim Kusic), likewise an ancient exile from China. These men and their coteries had been living abroad so long that the ordinary Korean had a difficult time understanding them. Hodge would learn to his regret that these men were fierce independents with their own agendas and well beyond his ability to control.

MacArthur and Rhee, Oct. 1948

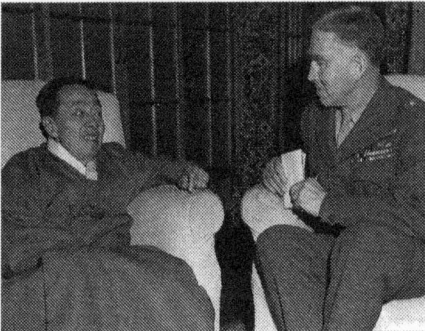

General Wilbur with (right) Kim Koo and (left) Kim Kusic. US Army XXIV Corps Photos March, 1947 (Bloomfield)

The resulting mix led to an extreme polarization of right and left -- with both sides angry at Hodge for impeding the unification of Korea, among other reasons. Hodge spent most of his time unsuccessfully trying to suppress the nationalists, the reformists who wanted a redistribution of land and the leftists, which he quickly branded as"commies."He used the police force and young goons recruited from the refugees as his main tools. There is no easy explanation for why he was not replaced even though observers in the US from 1945 were commenting on his failures.

The estimates of people who were killed for political reasons during the Occupation naturally vary widely, as the only ones with the ability to count, the American occupiers, were not counting. But undoubtedly many tens of thousands were killed. Just on Cheju-do the "pacification" claimed the lives of 60,000 Koreans, mostly villagers and peasants.

The lot of the Korean people did not get any better in August of 1948 after Hodge left the country because it was left in the hands of the autocratic Syngman Rhee. Even hawkish officials in the Defense and State Department who were pursuing the policy of using Korea to"contain"Russia or to"teach it a lesson,"thought that they may have made a mistake with Rhee. They found him often irrational and dictatorial, and that the widespread use of mass arrests and torture of both Left and Right opponents, together with the shutting down of any opposition newspaper and the arrests of even right wing members of the Assembly that opposed him — had all in effect created a police state. While the American ruling elite tried to keep this analysis away from the American public, the fact that Korea under Rhee in 1949 and 1950, well before the war, was not only non-democratic but was in fact a police state was widely known (e.g., article by Walter Sullivan with headlines: POLICE BRUTALITY IN KOREA ASSAILED: TORTURE, WHOLESALE EXECUTIONS OF REDS HELD DRIVING PEOPLE INTO ARMS OF COMMUNISTS, February 1, 1950, New York Times that was quoted by Vito Marcantonio during the February 7, 1950 House debate on aid to Korea.)

It is therefore no surprise that even after he left Korea and was stationed as the Commanding General of the Third Army at Fort McPherson, his "commy" obsession followed him. It must have been an occupational hazard, as so many Generals slipped into extreme anti-communist activities after their retirements, one is tempted to think of the word "paranoia." The most tragic example was James Forestall who fortunately was eased out as Secretary of the Navy before he did anything dangerous. Supposedly he killed himself in a Naval Hospital where he was put after an egregious hallucinatory episode involving communists trying to kill him. His brother always questioned the circumstances of his death.

General Albert E. Brown had served with General Hodge during the Korean occupation. In response to the now retired Brown's request for comments on the draft of General Brown's proposed memoirs, Hodge had this to say in a letter to him on January 24, 1951:

> There has never been any question but that the Communists had gone all out in establishing the People's Republic, in South as well as North Korea, in the month available to them after the Japanese had quit until we arrived 8 September for occupation. This was a long time, well planned operation, starting in the mid-twenties, with the Communists operating under the guise of patriots in the underground against the Japs. . . . **Flatly stated, one of our early missions was to break down this Communist government outside of any directives and without benefit of backing by the Joint Chiefs of Staff or the State Department**. (Albert E. Brown Papers, Box 3, U.S. Army Military Institute, Carlisle Barracks.)

This is an astonishing admission. Somehow he had decided that his main job was to dismantle a native governmental structure that was at least functioning and feeding the people and keeping law and order, because he suspected they were communists. Yet, as far as we know, whatever he knew of the local situation he had just learned from the Japanese Colonial Governor, General Able, whom he was supposedly uprooting or through his "interpreters." And he did this **without orders** and **without any "backing"** from State or Defense. One has to ask, from whom was he taking orders?

General Ward's diary was truly a personal diary. It is obvious that Ward was using it for his own reflection and as a discipline. It remained private until after his death and is now being lovingly preserved by the good people at the U.S. Army Military History Institute at the Carlisle Barracks, Carlisle, Pa. Ward's diary entries reflected his thinking as honestly as any writing could. We find in it his loves and his prejudices, both big and small. It rings with the sound of utter honesty, even where one may painfully disagree with his views.

Orlando Ward was born in Missouri, graduated from West Point, chased Pancho Villa in Mexico, fought in WWI and WWII, received his share of medals and could be said to have come from a military family – two uncles were Generals, among other relatives who served as officers in the Army. He was socially and politically what one may describe as conservative, with naturally a strong military and national security viewpoint on public affairs. He retired in 1953 and passed away in 1978.

The contribution that General Orlando Ward makes to history through his diary is contained in both his reflective as well as his off-the-cuff remarks about Korean society at the time, Korean politics, Korean and American personalities active during his stay of duty, the role of communism in Korea, what the Americans ought to have done about Korea and what the effect of the American occupation was having on Korea.

General Ward commanded the 6th Infantry Division during most of the American occupation of Korea, from October, 1946 to December, 1948. In May of 1948 MacArthur had recommended either Orlando Ward or John Coulter as a replacement for the departing Hodge. Coulter was eventually selected as he was senior to Ward and his tour of duty better coincided with Army plans (Memorandum, General Omar Bradley, Chief of Staff, US Army, FRUS, 1948 Vol.VI, p. 1194).

The US had two types of military in Korea during the Occupation. Some of the initial 45,000 troops served as a "tactical" army and some troops served as part of the "Military Government." The tactical troops were there more as a reserve for possible use to enforce the military government's orders. The Military Government troops, on the other hand, performed more of the political and intelligence functions of an occupying power. It was the Military Government's officers who acted in supervisory roles over Korean agencies and departments, including a fledging army ("constabulary") and, most importantly, a large, well-established and unpopular police force that had been trained by the Japanese and still controlled by the collaborators.

The unreformed and unrepentant police were deeply hated by the populace. General Hodge had kept the colonial police force intact except for the actual Japanese officers at the top. This decision to use them to control the Korean population was a watershed error. To most Koreans, therefore, it seemed that the Americans had just traded places with the Japanese.

As early as December, 1945, the US Counterintelligence Corps officers were sending in reports of Korean police mercilessly beating and even killing children holding peaceful demonstrations (unification with the north) while US Military Troops stood by and watched in apparent approval.

> "All the policemen as if at a given
> signal rushed in and began beating the students
> with sticks, clubs, rifle butts, or anything they had.
> Firing broke out . . . and the policemen kept after
> the students. . . small boys and girls were beaten
> just as mercilessly as were the older boys and
> girls. . . . A number of the Military Government
> troops were on the street during this whole

incident." (File No. 59-P-42, 19 Dec. 1945, RG 338, Box 26, Folder: "Historical Journal," N. A.).

Yet to Hodge, the police were a god-send. In 1948 he testified before a UN Commission sent to Korea to supervise the election:

> The charges against the police belong-
> ing to this or that political group cannot be sus-
> tained. . . . [On] the whole they have been loyal to
> the interim government [meaning, to him] and
> have followed through in the maintenance of law
> and order to the best of their ability. . . . **I hear
> from some sources that South Korea is a police
> state. I would like to point out that South
> Korea is an occupied area.** It is at present oper-
> ated under the direction of the military. The police
> force is charged with maintenance of law and
> order and, in addition, the observation for subver-
> sive activity aimed at upsetting the peace and
> security of the area.

This was news to the Koreans, who had been promised "lib-eration" by the Allies, not "occupation." No one, apparently, had told that to Hodge. The General's testimony before that Commission, incidentally, also revealed an attitude toward the Korean people, as a people, that was more "colonial" than anything else. Numerous times he referred to "these people" as if describing a different species. They were childlike and ignorant.

"When we came into South Korea, we found an exist-ence here of poverty, plus disease, plus communist-led people's committees in full sway and fairly well in control. . . . We found here a decadent nation without the slightest concept of polical life as the free nations of the world know it. These people had no concept of the responnsibilities inherent in the basic freedoms. . . ."

Again, this would have been news to the thousands who had died fighting the Japanese for independence, or to the thousands whom he had found "fairly well in control"when he arrived.

The tactical troops and the Military Government troops were each under a different command structure, though ultimately reporting to the Commanding General, John Hodge, and they would periodically conflict. As Ward noted once in his diary when he had a disagreement with the Military Government's officer in Pusan, it is difficult to manage with two heads. For purposes of the tactical troops, one Division covered the northerly area of the American zone and had its headquarters in Seoul, while the other Division, the one that Ward took command of, covered the southerly area. Orlando Ward's headquarters for the 6th Infantry was located in Pusan. At the same time Pusan had in effect a local military governor who had some troops of his own to enforce his orders.

In Orlando Ward's diary he would often mention something being done by the Military Government as if he were referring to a foreign entity. Some individual officers would at times be transferred from one unit to the other, as when Colonel Rothwell Brown, under the command of General Ward, was chosen by the Military Governor, who at the time happened to be General William Dean, to supervise the suppression of disturbances on Cheju-do in May, 1948. Generals Ward and Dean knew each other from World War II and from the comments of General Ward in his diary they seemed to have liked and respected each other.

The troops of Ward's 6th Infantry Division were scattered in small units at different strategic locations throughout the southern part of South Korea. An example of an outpost was the one on Cheju-do. Cheju is about 70 miles off the southwest coast of Korea. The tactical unit on the island, under Ward's ultimate command, consisted of a platoon situated in a few buildings on the outskirts of a town. Also on the island but at a different location and taking orders from a different command, was a small detachment of troops representing the Military Government. Ward would be constantly visiting his various outposts trying to maintain discipline and training among the bored occupation troops and keeping them out of conflict with the local population.

Ward's diary entries indicate much concern about living conditions for his wife and daughter for the time they were with him in Korea. He had set up a comfortable house for them with the usual servants within walking distance of his offices. He made a point of walking through the streets of Pusan and the surrounding countryside to get a better feel of the Korean people. He seems to have been an unusually open and friendly person for an occupying General. Various Koreans would just knock on his door and feel free to open political and social discussions with him and his family. In fact he had regular weekly visits by the same group of individuals, mostly teachers, who would have coffee or drinks with the Wards and exchange information.

Never, however, did he forget that he was representing an occupying power and he always took the necessary precautions. His compound was surrounded by a fence and guarded by MP's, who would periodically shot at moving shadows in the night, though he often remarked about finding the sentries asleep.

Ward was not a civil libertarian and one does not expect that he would be, given the nature of his occupation and training. He readily did things like run political groups which he thought were creating disturbances "out of town." But he was using a "light touch" compared to the mass arrests, the jailings based on "suspicions" and "associations" and the assassinations of assumed subversives being conducted by the Korean police under authority of the US Military Government at the time.

It took General Ward only a month after arriving in Korea to come to a dramatically different opinion from Hodge on the causes for the constant unrest in Korea. Even during his orientation meeting with General Hodge and MacArthur's staff in Tokyo he thought that the Americans were over-simplifying things. He was told that Korea was full of strikes by workers, riots and shootings against the hated police.

> *"Good briefing but gave impression that we had taught the Japs how to strike as well as the Koreans. And that we were blaming the communists for the results"* (October 17, 1946).

A month later he attended a meeting in Seoul called by General Hodge with various occupation officers and people from the State Department. With some sarcasm he noted in his diary: *"Hodge gave history of our **interference** and its **success**. . . ."*

Then Ward quite firmly and simply notes for posterity:

> **"Success here is impossible. To pull out gracefully is the best solution"** (November 19, 1946).

Rev. Monsignor Edward J. Flanaghan and Lt. Gen. John Hodge. 1947

The Occupation and how it was handled by the US can best be summarized in an examination of two events. One is the Independence Day Celebration of March 1, 1948 at which General Hodge, the Occupying General, spoke to 80,000 celebrants at Seoul Stadium. The other is the election held in May, 1948, from which Sigmund Rhee derived his legitimacy.

"Lt. General John H. Hodge, CG, USAFIK, reads an address to the estimated eighty thousand Koreans that Jammed Seoul Stadium this morning to commemorate the Korean Declaration of Independence from the Japanese in 1919. Gen Hodge informed the people of the US proposal to the UN for a free election in Korea this Spring." 1 March 1948 US Army Signal Corps(Cook)

Our General Orlando Ward immediately took a dislike to the way the Military Government was using the Japanese-trained and hated police for controlling the population.

"We are backing police in their strong arm policies...." (October 28, 1946).

Army photographers helpfully depicted exactly what General Ward had observed. Here are scenes from that March 1, 1948 Independence Day Celebration at which the Commanding General of the Military Government was the main speaker. One assumes the Americans were in control of this event.

"Another communist agitator is led from the crowd by Police after an attempt to break up the mass meeting of an estimated eighty thousand Rightists in Seoul Stadium. The small group of communists formed a football flying wedge scattering communist leaflets as they pushed their way through the crowd."
1 March 1948   *US Army Signal Corps (Cramer)*

[Previous Photo]
*"Korean Police break up a small group of young rioters during the celebration of the Korean Declaration of Independence from Japan in 1919. The day, normally one of violence, **was surprisingly quiet and orderly, due to the well disciplined Korean Police Force.**" 1 March 1948   US Army Signal Corps   (Cramer)*

The next picture was taken at the same celebration in which Hodge was speaking. Apparently the top US Military Government officials were tolerating, if not encouraging, handling peaceful demonstrators like this.

*"Korean Communists awaiting search after being forcibly removed from Seoul Stadium this morning. An estimated eighty thousand Rightists gathered to commemorate the Korean Declaration of Independence from Japan in 1919 when a small group of Communists started running through the crowd in a football wedge formation, **scattering Communist leaflets**. They were apprehended by Korean Police and taken off for further questioning."*
1 March 1950   US Army Signal Corps (Buerkle)

During General Ward's tour he also became uneasy with the heavy hand used by the Military Government and the various American and Korean intelligence agents it employed. Particularly poor was the handling by the Military Government of local disturbances and the blind support it gave to the brutal police. He tried to keep his tactical troops out of the way.

In a letter to his commanders on November 3, 1946 (The Orlando Ward Papers, Box 5, U.S. Army Military History Institute, Carlisle Barracks) he wrote:

> I feel that our [tactical] troops are a reserve and that they should not ordinarily be used singly or in pairs to lend an air of authority to the local police. By their presence in an area and by patrol visits to the police stations, they will lend sufficient authority to the local police. They do not take over the local police duties unless the situation demands.

> When on duty if they observe any act of cruelty, revenge or the unnecessary use of force on the part of local police, it is essential that they, at the appropriate time, (when the police will not lose face) remonstrate with the police. By so doing and by friendly talks with the local authorities they will gradually indoctrinate them with methods which will attain results without raising the ire of the populace through the misuse of their authority. Certainly our objective is to reach a time when local police can walk the streets singly at night with impunity.

This letter of instructions discloses the condition of Korean society at the time and the futility of our meddling. US troops were actually needed to **guard the local police** from the population – the local police who had been trained and utilized by the Japanese to keep the population suppressed. An impossible mission. A time-bomb.

On February 15, 1947 General Ward commented in his diary on some news reports he had been reading.

> "GCM [Secretary of Defense, General George Marshall] says cut in budget will cause withdrawal of troops from Korea. . . . – So what? **We are making a mess of** [Korea] and had better get out."

In September his attitude had not changed. He had gone up to Seoul at the request of General Hodge because touring Under Secretary of Defense Draper, whom Ward had known personally, wanted to speak with him. He reports in his diary what he had to say to Draper:

> "What a mess. . . . Had good talk with him. I think it is get out with as much face saving as possible. . . ." (September 23, 1947).

His conviction that it was a mistake to continue having the US military in Korea increased the longer he was there.

> To me KOREA is a STRATEGIC HAZARD rather than a STRATEGIC ASSET. We have not enough to save the people of the world and attempt to do so will so lower our potential as to make us subject to eventual debility – degeneration and disaster. There are too many in authority who do not analyze facts before acting – who do not measure the cloth with which they have to work. Our present policy is building southern Korea so as to be ripe for over running by the Soviet dominated North Korea. In other words, to no avail (May 9, 1947).

Ward also never could understand Hodge's insistence that every disturbance was communist inspired. He saw economics as moving the people in Korea, not ideology.

"More I see of . . . Koreans the more I think they are not much concerned about anything but their next meal. They are independent" (March 9, 1947).

After the 1948 US inspired elections in South Korea, which in effect split up the country permanently, the South Koreans established a constitution and other elements of government. Ward's dry but telling observation:

> *"Korean Constitution a dictatorship. What they want"* (July 15, 1948) and *"it will only end in Rich getting richer – Poor no better and [everybody] against us when we stop giving"* (November 7, 1948).

This time his predictions were right.

As Ward was preparing to leave Korea, he went to a ceremonial dinner in Seoul on November 16, 1948. He met the Rhees again and told himself in his diary that night that the Rhees were "dottering" old folks not up to the task; that Rhee

> *"continues his pressure to keep the US troops in Korea to see that his Government stays in office. . . [and Ward felt] that the US was making decisions based on giving individuals jobs, rather than in the interest of the US."*

The XXIV's G-2 (intelligence) file contains a record of an interview on December 4, 1948 with Chang, Taik-Sang, Minister of Foreign Affairs in the new Rhee government:

> Chang spoke very frankly as he is inclined to do with those Americans he knows well. . . . Chang [said] the Government of the Republic of Korea was getting farther removed from the people it governs every day. . . .[it] is floating around in the air like a fairy castle. . . The President [Rhee] has no respect whatsoever for rules and regulations and good governmental procedure. He will establish a rule today and forget he ever thought of it tomorrow. I hear about the decisions my office should be making

when I read the newspapers. The President flies
into an insane range every time I attempt to
obtain additional information on these decisions
he has made which pertain to [my] Ministry of
Foreign Affairs.

(Thomas Herren Papers, U.S. Army Military Institute, Carlisle
Barracks).

Ward summarized his feelings about the US Occupation of
Korea: *"We are on a stupid and fruitless endeavor which will cost much
and produce little or no good to us, to the Koreans and to the world"*
(October 19, 1948) .

Later, when the Korean War started and Truman decided to
intervene, General Ward, who had been put on the shelf by this
time and was heading the Army's Historical unit in Washington,
commented in his diary that it was probably the only thing Truman
could do. But by February, 1951 when everyone was calling Korea a
"disaster," he lamented Truman's sudden reversal of policy. In a
letter to Senator James Kem, a very conservative Republican Senator, he responded to a number of issues raised by the Senator.
Senator Kem had asked Ward to comment on the following observation of Kem's:

Any policy which forces us to fight the
Reds, as we are fighting them in Korea now –
across an ocean, within walking distance of their
masses of reserves, on terms of battle in which
they are forever superior – cannot be anything but
what it has turned out to be in Korea; a bloody
entanglement, to use Walter Lippmann's phrase.

Ward's response was: "There is an old saying to the effect 'do not get involved in the land mass of Asia.' It still holds. Korea, to me, is an example of where we had made a carefully thought out decision and then reversed it without careful consideration of the long-range outcome."

(Orlando Ward Papers, "Correspondence, Speeches," Box 6, U.S. Army Military Institute, Carlisle Barracks).

Ward remained a supporter, a "disciple," as he described himself, of General MacArthur and expressed annoyance in his diaries with the critical Congressional testimony of Generals Marshall and Bradley after MacArthur's removal. But unlike Stratemeyer, who adored MacArthur and followed him almost without question, Ward maintained a realistic view of the General.

Major General Orlando Ward

General Ward, Korea, 1948 with Col., later General, Chae.

Photos are Courtesy Orlando Ward Collection, US Army History Institute, Carlisle Barracks.

CHAPTER XII

CHEJU 4.3

Cheju is an island about 70 miles off the southwest coast of Korea. Near the end of the official occupation there began a bloody uprising which resulted during the next year in the wholesale slaughter of villagers and the burning down of their homes. The population of Cheju-do ("do" meaning "island") was approximately 300,000. The death toll for the islanders during the year-long suppression campaign, conducted at first directly by the Military Government and then by the Rhee Government with its army under the control of American advisors, was estimated at 30,000 to 60,000 – 10 to 20% of the population. An additional 40,000 people escaped to Japan. Seventy percent of the villages had been burned down and 100,000 people, one-third of the island, had been herded into guarded villages on the coast. Sixty-five thousand more people were homeless.

I think it is important that we grasp what happened on this remote island. Swept under the rug for 50 years, the story is important.

The uprising began on April 3, 1948 and the people of Korea remember it simply as "Cheju 4.3." Information on the massacres at Cheju (now called Jeju) was suppressed during the almost 50 years of subsequent dictatorship and junta governments in South Korea that were supported by successive American Administrations. In the past few years, however, survivors have begun to tell their story of an indigenous disturbance falsely labeled "communistic" and crushed with brutal force by the Korean national police and army from the mainland under American supervision (see New York Times, article by Howard W. French: "SOUTH KOREANS SEEK TRUTH ABOUT '48 MASSACRE," October 24, 2001; Paper presented by Professor Bruce Cumings at the 50th Anniversary Conference of the April 3, 1948 Chejudo Rebellion, Tokyo, March 14, 1998 as reprinted, November 15, 2002, http:www.kimsoft.com/1997/cheju98.htm).

Today those who want to recall the event comment on the re-invention of Cheju Island as a resort island with most of the best properties owned by the individuals and relatives of the police and youth groups who confiscated the land from the "communists."

Kim Ik Ruhl was the commander of the 9th Regiment of the Korean constabulary stationed on Cheju-do island in 1948 during the uprising. He was a Colonel at the time. The constabulary force was in its infancy and did not even have modern weapons. They carried for the most part old Japanese rifles, usually without ammunition, even though the US had given modern carbines to the police forces. Kim later served in the South Korean Army in the Korean War and ultimately retired as a Lieutenant General. He passed away in December, 1988. Among his papers was a manuscript with the title The Truth About Cheju 4.3. He asked his heirs to have it published after his death so that the truth about that massacre would be told. However, they could not get it published immediately because under the type of government Korea had until 1993, this controversial book would have brought danger to anyone connected with it.

This gentleman had lived for forty years with a secret he could not safely disclose. It was too dangerous in Korea during his lifetime to speak truthfully about what had happened. But his manuscript has finally seen the light of day and it is not flattering to the US authorities in charge at that time, including the Military Governor, William Dean.

I have used the translation of General Kim's manuscript as it appears on the Korean Web Weekly, http://www.kimsoft.com/1997/43kim11.htm. General Kim's manuscript is attached as an appendix to the five volume "4.3 Speaks" series by Chemin Ilbo, Volume 2, pp. 270-357, ISBN 89-7924-006-6, Seoul Publication Service, Seoul, Korea. The Library of Congress Control Number is 95473292 (Call No. DS917.55 .A14 1995 Korea).

I find some verification of General Kim's account in the diary entry of General Ward for April 29, 1948, relating his trip to Cheju-do with General Dean. That is around the time that Colonel Kim says Dean had come to the island with a group of Korean leaders and met with Colonel Kim and his American advisor, Colonel Mansfield. Further corroboration of Kim's story comes from the US Army itself. There is an Army Signal Corps silent black and white movie film called "May Day" which was filmed on Cheju-do from April 30th to May 5th 1948. The film features General Dean on a trip to Cheju-do around May 1, 1948 and actually depicts the cast of attendees later described by General Kim in his manuscript as meeting with Dean in early May ("May Day," NARA 023451, CR # 111 ADC 7114). This little gem of a film was located in the National Archives by Professor John Merrill who mentions it in his 1989 book: Korea: The Peninsular Origins of the War.

The following are pictures taken from "May Day" which show General Dean arriving on the island sometime between April 29 and May 5th, along with the individuals which Colonel Kim identifies in his manuscript. Professor Merrill describes the film as a propaganda film. It apparently is intended to demonstrate how the National Police and Korean Constabulary, under American guidance, rescue besieged islanders from the rebels. It also serves as proof, however unwittingly, that the Americans were in charge of the subsequent suppression campaign.

General Dean in Cheju do with:
Army Commander Gen. Song Ho Chang   *Civil Affairs Minister Ahn Jae Hong*

Col. Kim Ik Ruhl greeting Ahn Jae Hong   *Dean entering jeep on Cheju-do*

*Islanders who may or may have not made it during
the suppression of the next 12 months.*

According to General Kim, the islanders historically disliked the Koreans from the mainland, as he and nearly all of the constabulary were, and stayed away from them. The isolated people of the island spoke a dialect which mainlanders had a hard time understanding. The only thing approaching an ideology that Kim noticed among the islanders was that they considered the Americans merely to have replaced the Japanese as occupiers. Any Korean working with the Americans was as despised as those who had worked for the Japanese.

Kim knew from personal observation and information from some of his men who were natives of the island the basic cause of the uprising. The islanders had a long tradition of trading with Japan and China, skirting the regulations on all sides -- a free port, and resented any intrusion from the mainlanders. But some main-lander policemen and recently imported NorthwestYouth members were trying to muscle in on the smugglers. Some police were merely stealing, while others kidnapped smugglers and tortured them in jail until their families agreed to sharing the business.

CHEJU-DO MOUNTIES – "The Korean constabulary, either mounted or afoot, have proved their efficiency and reliability through working with the US Military Government. These mounted police are stationed at Cheju-do, Korea, as evidence by the Korean woman carrying her burden by shoulder straps."
   21 May 1948   USAF Office of Public Relations

General Kim's description, written in the '80's long after he retired, of the island's *de facto* "free-port" economy and the constant temp-tation to the police to rip off the unregulated traders is amazingly corroborated in every detail by a Confidential Memo dated 9 December 1946 from the Military Government's own Dept. of Public Information (Record Group 338, Box 26, Folder "Footnotes." N.A.). Ward's observations were also consistent with Kim's and the DPI's 9 December, 1946 Confidential Memo.

In addition, outraged officers, like a Lieutenant Colonel Lawrence A. Nelson, Special Investigator out of Occupation Headquarters, had been reporting about the friction between the mainland police and the islanders, the brutality of the police, the suppression of the leftists, the labeling of anyone opposing the Governor as "leftist," and the makings of an uprising if serious reforms were not made, including curtailing the police and removal of the dictatorial Rightest mainlander-governor imposed on the island by the Military Government. Nelson reported that "terrorism and beatings have been traced to the Govenor." In November, 1947 Nelson had warned that "the condition is becoming dangerous."

Colonel Nelson labored for months to try to avert what he was sure would be a catastrophe on Cheju-do. He first reported the results of his investigation of the situation on Cheju-do in a report dated November 22, 1947 to General John Hodge.

General Hodge, and the Military Governor, General Dean, at first asked the Colonel for more documentation. They gave as their reason for the delay that they could not just remove a governor appointed by the Korean advisory council – though they habitually did so.

This stalling went on for months into late 1947 and early 1948. Then when the final report was made by Colonel Nelson, still recommending drastic reforms on the island and the removal of the governor, Dean rejected the main recommendations. It was getting close to the showcase UN supervised elections and nobody wanted to rock the boat. Shortly thereafter the riots started. (R.G. 338, Box 83, Folder: "Cheju-do Political Situation." N.A.)

Clearly the real situation on Cheju-do had been widely understood within the Military Government from the beginning. There was a simmering economic and turf conflict between the islanders and the mainlanders that needed very little provocation to ignite. Finding the body of a police torture victim on April 3, 1948 was enough to set it off. Having known these fundamental facts, in my opinion, stamps the American Government's public description of the insurrection as "communist inspired" as a truly dastardly thing to have done to the people of Cheju-do.

When the uprising started on April 3, 1948, the Military Government, that is, General Hodge as Commanding General and his subordinate, General Dean as Military Governor, sent in massive police reinforcements from the mainland. It was a very sensitive time. Elaborate preparations were being made by the US Army for a showcase "free" election in this "test case" for democracy on the doorstep of Red Russia. Kim writes that "the US commanders and the police chiefs believed that once the suppression campaign started, 2-3 days would be enough to wipe out the rebels."

That did not happen, as the police tactics of indiscriminate arrests, killings and burnings only spread the rebellion until it encompassed most of the island. Colonel Kim, who was in charge of the small Constabulary force on the island but taking orders from the Military Government's officers, tried to work out a settlement between the islanders and the police, but to no avail. He ascribed the failure of negotiations primarily to sabotage by the mainlander police and their agents, members of the goon squads recruited from young northern refugees.

After the uprising had gone on for about a month, with things just getting worse, Kim was told by his American military advisor, Col. Mansfield, that General Dean would be coming down to review the situation himself. Kim was asked to help prepare a presentation for the General.

> *General Ward, April 29, 1948:*
> *Breakfast with Bill Dean. Off at 8:00 A.M. [to Cheju-do]. . . .* **Looks as if Police are reaping benefits of miss treatment of natives.** *6 police killed.* **60 islanders. No witnesses brought in alive. Thumbs wired together.** *Hung by heels. Shot sans trial. Resent mainlanders. Flew over island. Reminded me of Chasing Villa.* **Action they con-**

template will be fruitless. *Trouble should be cured at source. . . . Assistant G2 [intelligence] – hunted for and found communist backing.* **90% local and justified resentment.**

Some days before General Dean arrived for the conference, Kim received a mysterious order from Col. Mansfield. He was to go to the office of the Cheju branch of the US CIC, or counterintelligence, and meet with an unnamed American. Kim followed orders and went over to the CIC. This individual, according to Kim, refused to identify himself but said he was a political adviser to General Dean.

The unidentified American told Kim that the only way to stop the rebellion fast was to use the drastic methods that the Japanese had used in Korea and throughout their empire to deal with indigenous guerilla forces. This was called "scorched earth" tactics – basically burning down any village that the rebels might use for sanctuary or assistance and killing any villagers who resisted or who actually aided the rebels. Kim was asked to utilize these tactics and help the US during this high-publicity election time.

Kim was appalled by the idea. He told the American that there was just no way he would do that to his own people. The American offered various amounts of money, reached $100,00, which Kim refused, and then asked in exasperation how much it would take for Kim to do it. He also guaranteed safe passage for Kim, his family and relatives to the United States. He even showed Kim magazine pictures of the kind of life Kim and his family would have in comfortable suburban areas of the United States. Kim thought the whole thing was disgusting and he steadfastly refused.

General Dean came down to the island, according to Kim's account, on May 5th and had with him several people, including the Korean National Police Chief, Cho Byong Ok; Civil Affairs Minister Ahn Jae Hong; Army Commander Gen. Song Ho Chang; the local Police Commissioner; the local governor and some others. Dean was also accompanied by his interpreter, a Christian minister also with the name Kim.

At the meeting Colonel Kim explained that the insurrection had been caused by police greed and brutality and their attempt to strong-arm the smugglers. The police's brutal response had only enraged the islanders and spread the rebellion. Kim laid out a plan which would end the insurrection without further bloodshed.

The Police Chief, Cho Byong Ok, took violent exception to Kim's opinion. He and Colonel Kim Ik Ruhl thereupon got into a very heated argument, with the Police Chief accusing Kim of being a communist and with Kim punching the Police Chief. General Dean left in a hurry and seemed very upset.

Kim learned what General Dean had decided the very next day. Without any warning a Lt. Col Park Jin Gyon showed up at Colonel Kim's office the next morning. Kim knew Park and his reputation as an officer in the dreaded Japanese Kwantung Army. Park had spent 5 years with the Japanese Military in its Manchurian counter-guerilla operations and had also served with the Japanese on Cheju Island. Park brought an order from Kim's American advisor, Colonel Mansfield, which replaced Kim with Park. The order, however, did not remove Kim but made him an advisor or assistant to Col. Park.

Park promptly informed Kim that they were going to suppress the insurrection by a wide-scale use of the scorched earth method, burning down villages thought to be sympathetic to the rebels and herding the inhabitants to guarded settlements on the coast. Kim refused to do this to his own people and eventually had to be reassigned. Later on Kim would be arrested for investigation of involvement in a military mutiny at the city of Yosu, but he eluded his American and Korean enemies to go on to serve faithfully for many years in the Korean Army.

It was Kim's opinion that General Dean had issued secret "scorched earth" orders to Park because he knew that Park would carry them out, while Kim would not. "Washington told Gen. Dean to settle up the Cheju issue promptly and he urgently needed a Korean yes-man to command the 9th Regiment." Washington at that time was trying to showcase the little democracy it had created in the Far East right under the Soviets' nose. The "UN supervised elections" were only a month away and the Americans had been waging a vigorous campaign to make everything "look good."

From his grave Kim sent a curse:

> "Scorched earth tactics are not allowed even in war situations and any commander who uses them are deemed criminals and punishable as such. Ordering or condoning scorched earth tactics in peacetime in a territory under his command is a serious matter if the outside world discovered the truth. **Even if not convicted as a war criminal and punished, General Dean's conscience and humanity would punish him some day.**"

"Seated in the front row of the mass meeting held for the delegates of the United Nations Temporary Commission on Korea, in the Seoul Stadium, are, l. to r., Major General Albert E. Brown, Assistant CG, USAFIK; Major General W.F. Dean, US Military Governor of Korea; and Lieutenant General John R. Hodge, CG, USAFIK. They are among the 20,000 persons who have gathered there."
14 January 1948   US Army Signal Corps (Mootz)

An example of the brutality with which the uprising was handled is contained in one of the Army's Confidential G-2 (Intelligence) Periodic Reports (3 March 1949, Record Group 338, Box 32, Folder:"History of USAFIK." N.A.). G-2 related a Korean Army report on the continuing disturbances on Cheju-do.

> "On 20 February, 76 rebels from
> TODU-RI were executed by the MIN BO DAN
> (Peoples Protective Corps), who used spears in
> the performance of these executions. Five women
> and numerous children of middle school age were
> included in the group. National Police andKUNKI
> DAI (Korean Army Military Police) supervised the
> operation."

After relating this information from the Korean Army, G-2 then commented on it:

> *Four members of KMAG* [Officers in
> the United States Korea Military Advisory Group]
> *witnessed, by chance, the execution of 38 of the rebels
> and counted 38 already dead when they arrived.
> Previous reports have indicated that rebels were being
> executed by Armed Forces personnel, before a firing
> squad. This is the first report of a mass execution
> being conducted by the MIN BO DAN.*

What is one to make of this? We are at this time in complete control of the Korean Army and National Police. Our orders are usually conveyed by the officers of the KMAG. Are we to believe that these US officers just stumbled on this official "execution" by "chance;" that they could do nothing but meekly count 38 dead and then stand by to watch and count as the goons continued to slaughter 38 more men, women and"numerous children"? Imagine the time it took to kill 38 more people with spears. Imagine the screaming and crying that must have come from the children.Yet the Americans were just accidental innocent bystanders?

Or is it more likely that the Americans were the ones orchestrating this as part of their year-long pacificaation program during which 60,000 villagers were similarly slaughtered on Cheju-do? Subsequent G-2 Reports do not mention any reprimands or investigations or reviews of controls. That alone would seem to suggest that this event was in accordance with American wishes.

Conveniently the hawks now had a victory for Sigmund Rhee that they could show off to Congress. The violent quelching of the islanders was portrayed by the Military Government and Sigmund Rhee as a sound victory over a communist uprising which had been instigated and funded by the North. The bloody suppression was used as an example at later US Congressional hearings to prove that Sigmund Rhee's constabulary or army had reached a mature and trustworthy level.

General Ward, April 30, 1948:

> *"Dinner with IG [Inspector General] group at JRH [General Hodge]. . . . All 'commy' complex."*

General Ward, May 6, 1948:

> *"Chief [General Hodge] called from Seoul. . . . It is amazing how we were able to have . . . revolutions in SA and other places sans 'communist agitation.'"*

General Ward, May 9, 1948:

> *"The article in the <u>New Yorker</u> dated 1859 indicated that there could be strife at the Poles sans COMMUNISTIC instigation. We could years ago have revolutions in SA just for a revolution. I must remember that 'you can tell a general but you can't tell him much.' JRH [General Hodge] is a good example of that. He will not listen to anything not assumed to be communist in origin. He may be right to a certain extent. G2's [Intelligence unit] are prone to report fancies rather than fact. They are much like News Reporters who incidentally have in many cases confused*

liberty and license when they come to the truth."

General Ward, May 24, 1948:

> *"...JHR [Hodge] has 'communistic'*
>
> *[Red conspiracy complex] as has Rothwell Brown.*
>
> ...*"*

Ward had a feeling that General Dean would ask for Colonel Rothwell Brown who was serving under Ward, to deal with the uprisings in Cheju-do. *"McF and I bet Dean would ask for him. He did."*

Ward suggests that the reason Rothwell Brown had been hand-picked by Dean to supervise the campaign on Cheju was because Brown shared the Dean and Hodge viewpoint that all dissent in Korea was "communistic".

After Brown was chosen by Dean to take over the supervision of the United States tactical troops in Cheju-do, Ward saw Brown off at the Pusan airport. Part of Brown's orders in his new assign-ment was to report directly to Dean, thus taking Cheju-do, in Ward's bailiwick, out of Ward's jurisdiction, at least for the purpose of dealing with the uprising, and by-passing General Ward even with reports. General Ward did not seem to resent this, but he was worried that Dean and Brown were going down the wrong path. After seeing him off at the airport, Ward noted in his diary that Brown *"is creating situation in his mind on Cheju-do which he will fit into"* (May 18, 1948).

The next day, even though Cheju-do and Brown had just been removed from his jurisdiction, General Ward nevertheless wrote Brown a letter with a little gentle advice:

> I am sorry you are leaving the Divi-
> sion, and certainly wish you I am sorry you are
> leaving the Division, and certainly wish you the

best of luck in your new assignment. I am glad that they have assigned you in charge of Cheju Do, and I am sure that from here on out the place will quiet down considerably.

I have one caution, which may or may not be pertinent, but I cannot help but remember there have been times in the past when disturbances and revolutions of tremendous size were held in South America and other places without Communistic instigation. That doesn't mean there are not some on Cheju. On the other hand, **I do feel that the main trouble is that engendered by hatred of the police.** These disturbances will continue until this irritation has been removed by replacing those in whom the populace have no confidence, and by demonstrating the proper attitude.

However, Ward's efforts to point Brown and Dean in the right direction were fruitless. In a few weeks Brown supposedly had gotten to the bottom of it all and was able to make a report to General Hodge on the cause of the uprising. In his July 1, 1948 Report to Hodge and Dean, he relates that he had "approximately 5,000 inhabitants of Cheju-do" rounded up and "interrogated" by the South Korean police. These are the very police who were hated by the populace and which, according to Ward, was the cause of the uprisings. "Interrogation" by these Japanese-trained police routinely involved torture.

Sure enough, as Ward thought he would and as Hodge and Dean must have wanted, Rothwell Brown found that all the troubles had been instigated by **six** communist organizers "sent in from the mainland." He found that:

"at the height of the rioting, it is estimated that the People's Democratic Army [the rebels] had a **strength of approximately 4,000** officers and men. Less than **10% of this force was equipped with rifles, the balance** being armed with Japanese swords and **native made spears.** The Women's Auxiliary of the South Korean Labor Party was also established and very complete lists of membership have been uncovered."

Colonel Brown's torture interrogations also supposedly produced revelations that he compiled into a somewhat amusing report, at least reading it over 50 years later. According to the Colonel the Communists were Christ-like in their ability to multiply loaves and fishes:

> "It is estimated that not over **six** trained agitators and organizers were sent in from the outside . . . an additional five to **seven hundred** sympathizers . . . joined these six specialized organizers in the movement. It is estimated that between **sixty and seventy thousand** people on the Island actually joined the South Korean Labor Party. . . . **They were for the main part, ignorant, uneducated farmers and fishermen . . . .**"

Curiously, it was about 60,000 of these "ignorant, uneducated farmers and fishermen" and their families who died in the ensuing year at the hands of the Korean Government under control of the Americans.

Brown unconsciously damns himself and all the others who took part in this cruel scorched earth campaign when he gives one of the reasons for the difficulty of putting down the revolt: "Blood ties . . . link most of the families on the island and make it extremely difficult to obtain information."

Imagine what the hated police, the cause of the trouble, did to those poor prisoners to extract information from already recalcitrant and unwilling subjects that would endanger their relatives.

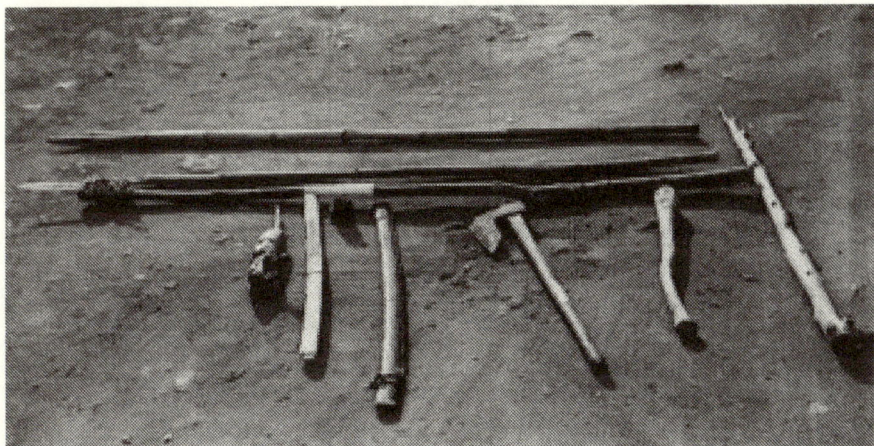

"Murder Weapons captured on Cheju Island during recent Communist raid included Bamboo Spears, Home Made Axes, knives and firearms. Weapon at left was made from breach of Japanese rifle, held between two blocks of wood. Samurai scabbord encased a home made sword." Army Signal Corps Mootz 1 May 1948

"TWO CONFESSED MURDERERS CAPTURED ON CHEJU ISLAND DURING THE REIGN OF TERROR CURRENTLY IN PROGRESS." Army Signal Corps Mootz 1 May 1948

The day after he wrote his Report, July 2nd, he finally responded to Ward's letter of May 19th:

> I am inclosing a copy of my report on the activities in Cheju-Do in the hope that it may be of interest to you. I realize that there have been many differences of opinion as to the causes of the rioting on the island. I hope that my report will give some clarity to the picture as it existed there. **One thing is absolutely certain – that the island was organized as a Communist base. The evidence was irrefutable once we really began to dig into the matter.** Police brutality and inefficient government were but incidental to the Communist designs on this island."

(Both letters and the Report are in Box 3, Rothwell Brown Papers, U.S. Army Military History Institute, Carlisle Barracks).

Photo of General Orlando Ward awarding a decoration to Colonel Rothwell Brown in the Spring of 1948 in Korea. This was before Brown was assigned by General Dean to supervise the suppression on Cheju-do.

Courtesy Orlando Ward Collection, US Army Military Institute. Carlisle Barracks.

The disturbances on Cheju were not completely put down for another year, and at a horrendous cost to the local population. Ward noted in his October 2, 1948 diary entry that the Military Government was using the toughs from the infamous extreme right wing North West Youth Group to act as a Korean counterintelligence unit on the island. *"Bad judgment by Col Voss and poor business."*

The US Ambassador to Korea in 1949, John Muccio, casually reported on the brutality with which the uprising was being put down. From a Confidential Memo he wrote on April 9, 1949 to Secretary of State Dean Acheson, he remarks:

> "Photographs of operations on Cheju indicate unusual sadistic propensities on the part of both Government and guerrilla forces. Signal atrocities have been reported, indicating mass massacre of village populations, including women and children, accompanied by widespread looting and arson. In some cases the Army has been guilty of revenge operations against guerrillas which have brought down vengeance on un-armed villagers."

Nevertheless, though the US still controlled the Korean Military, legally by secret treaty and in fact because every rifle and bullet was paid for by US taxpayers, nothing seems to have been done to stop the mass murders, lootings and burnings. Indeed the slaughter was offered by the Truman Administration as proof of the viability of Rhee's regime. Muccio continued:

> "Defense Minister Sihn Sung Mo is now on Cheju Island at express request of President Rhee, with orders to remain until guerrillas have been wiped out and order restored. . . . -   ..

"It is clear from the nature of the propaganda emanating from Soviet-controlled radio that Cheju Island has been chosen as the spot for a major Soviet effort to sow confusion and terror in southern Korea. . . . With such conditions deep in the rear area of the Republic, President Rhee has been forced to take the decision to stamp out unrest and insecurity. . . .It seems obvious that Soviet agents are being filtered into Cheju without great difficulty. . . . "

On June 20, 1949 the House Committee on Foreign Affairs was holding a hearing on the Administration's bill to provide $150,000,000 in economic aid to Korea. The question arose whether the money was being poured down a "rat hole," that is, whether Korea in any event had any chance of surviving as a nation. Congressman Fulton asked if the Korean Army was "dependable." The answer came from Dr. Edgar A. Johnson, Director, Korean Aid Program, Economic Cooperation Administration who had spent years in Korea and had just returned from there. Johnson described the year-long uprising in Cheju as a situation **"where a great number of misguided villagers had been persuaded to follow the Communist cause. . . ."**

"The test came . . . on the island of Cheju where the Communist forces had withdrawn into the interior. During the war the Japanese had six divisions on the island, and these troops had left considerable supplies in the caves in the mountainous center of the island. They were well supplied. . . . It was the first test of the Korean Army to overcome those forces. I was last on the island of Cheju in March of 1949 and the campaign was substantially finished. The Korean Army had drawn a tighter and tighter perimeter. . . . **The campaign took until the spring of 1949. However, that was successfully accomplished."**

CHAPTER XIII

DEAN WITNESSES

"Major General William F. Dean, Military Governor of Korea, addressing the estimated 30,000 that gathered at Seoul Stadium to commemorate May-Day. General Dean took advantage of the occasion to stress the importance of May 10, the date of the coming UN supervised elections."
     US Army Signal Corps   Porter   1 May 1948

General William F. Dean had a remarkable military life, filled with unusual contrasts and ironies. After serving with distinction in World War II, he was Military Governor of Korea during a period of great repression, when tens of thousands of Koreans south of the 38th parallel were killed by the South Korean police and constabulary under the direct supervision of the American occupying forces. Then he was one of the first Americans sent in from Japan to try to stop the North Korean troops after June 25, 1950. His extraordinary courage in the ensuing short battle earned him the Congressional Medal of Honor. The US Army museum building on the 38th Parallel bears his name. He soon, however, became a prisoner of war -- finding himself in the curious position of being held captive by the very people he had so recently governed. Once he was even housed in a prison he remembered as having inspected while Governor, but now the prison was actually being run by one of his former prisoners – who told Dean, cordially, that he also remembered the visit.

Dean barely survived the physical hardships of the next three years as a POW. But the experience seems to have created a new person, or finally revealed the real William Dean. His observations are contained in a biography written in 1954 with the assistance of a writer — just a year after his release from captivity. It does not have the same sense of private and unvarnished thinking that Ward's diary does – it often enough echoes American anti-communist rhetoric that was required of all public figures at that time – but it still contains frank observations that are sometimes startling, all set forth by General Dean casually and gracefully (William F. Dean. General Dean's Story, as told to William L Worden. New York: The Viking Press, 1954).

General Dean served as Military Governor in Korea under the Commanding General, John Hodge, from October, 1947 to the end of the official occupation, August, 1948. When the war broke out in June of 1950 he was the commanding general of the 24th Infantry Division, part of the 8th Army stationed as occupation troops in Japan. Presumably because of his recent familiarity with Korea he was hand-picked by MacArthur in early July, 1950, to head the American forces being rushed in from Japan piecemeal to stop the 200,000 advancing North Koreans, or at least to stop the South Korean retreat.

About 400 riflemen from the 24th Infantry Division in Japan were the first Americans sent in on July 1st under Lieutenant Colonel Charles B. Smith, forming the "Smith Task Force." Some speculated that the first show of American faces would freeze the invaders. Dean, the 24th Commanding Officer, followed the next day and was to make contact with Brigadier General John H. Church at Taejon after joining up with his men. Church had been sent in a couple days earlier on a fact finding mission that was changed mid-stream to a military mission when Truman ordered the troops in.

Taejon was familiar territory to Dean. Describing his attempt to identify Taejon from the air as he tried to land, he noted that "I had been over this area several times in 1948 and 1949." The first thing he noticed on landing, however, was that South Korean civilians were thronging the road heading south, and "unfortunately thousands and thousands of national police officers and some military also were marching south, apparently making no effort to stand and fight." The police force that had been under Dean's command while he was Military Governor and had so brutally suppressed all opposition to the Military Government and then to the succeeding right wing Rhee regime, now was running away from any real fight by the "thousands and thousands." The Dean who wrote this in 1954 wanted us to know that.

The South Korean headquarters was already operating under its third chief of staff, Lee Bum Suk, and was "torn by internal strife, with everyone shouting 'Communist' at one another. . . ." The first Chief of Staff had blown up a bridge over the Han River south of Seoul as soon as he got over it in the initial retreat, even though the bridge had still been packed with retreating South Korean soldiers and evacuating American and Korean civilians. The second Chief of Staff had gone over to the other side.

The first battles engaged in by the Americans were in the Osan, Chonan, Taejon area. With scorn Dean explains how his whole left flank, after he had retreated from P'yongta'ek, was

> "defended only by some dubious
> forces known as the Northwest Youth Group –
> five hundred or a thousand dissident, non-Com-
> munist North Koreans who had been armed by
> the South Korean government but were not part
> of the regular Army. Other people had consider-
> able confidence in them, but I did not share it –
> and the fact is, North Koreans harried our flank
> on that side from then on. There is no doubt that
> those Northwest Youths were blood-thirsty
> people who hated the Communists, but they did
> us very little good."

Dean certainly knew about how "blood-thirsty" these goons were. He had made his own use of them while he was Military Governor – for various tasks. Recall that General Ward thought it was a mistake for the Military Governmet to deputize the North-west Youths to help put down the uprisings on Cheju-do. But Dean and the authoritarian Rhee government that followed him wanted the services of Northwest Youths precisely because they were so "blood-thirsty" and cruel. They rampaged through Cheju-do for a year. They killed almost everyone opposing the Rhee government and then took their land, settled down and today it is said by some that they and their descendants own and run the prosperous resorts on Cheju-do.

In addition, Military Governor Dean on April 20, 1948, had recruited these youth groups to work as "volunteers" under the police and help maintain a "free atmosphere" for the 1948 UN supervised elections. These tough right-wing youths, standing "guard" at each of the polls, were probably redundant to the American efforts to elect Rhee and put on a good "election" show for the world. Though even the new post-POW Dean was very proud of having helped set up the "first free election" in Korea, it must be judged a sham by any standards – though it might have looked OK to an occupying power.

[Below]
"Korean students pass out election handbills to passersby at a busy intersection in Seoul in preparation for the coming elections on May 10."
US Army Lemire 4 May 1948

[Above]
"Korean population of a small village ... scramble for leaflets droped over their village by America L05's. The pamphlets giving the date of the elections and urging everyone to vote were droped by air from L-5's manned by American pilots in all small villages throughout South Korea." US Army Mootz 6 May 1948

The Military Government proudly announced that through its education efforts it had succeeded in getting 99% of eligible voters to register. Then after the election, it announced a similar percentage of registered voters had actually come out to vote. To close observers this would have been no surprise. Indeed, State Department second-guesses expressed some uneasiness as the fantastic numbers generated by the Army might create suspicions of manipulation.

The most important thing to Occupation Koreans was where they were going to get tomorrow's meal. The period of the American Occupation was marred by rice shortages in a rice-rich country.

The Millitary Government therefore had set up a rationing system and issued each Korean a rice ration card. The cards were issued from a local office, and often kept there, staffed by appointees of the Military Government with the advice of such Koreans as Rhee.

As it happened, one had to go to the same office to register to vote. Not surprisingly, almost 100 % of cardholders showed up to prove their loyalty and registered. Ditto for the election.

General Dean encouraged the police to deputize the ever-handy right wing youth groups as "volunteers" to run the election. Some UN observers initially thought that this presented an obvious infringement on voters' freedom, but that concern never surfaced in the UN's final report finding a "free and fair" election.

"Nae Chon . . . Small village of Cholla Nambo Province. . . . Koreans turned out en masse for the UN supervised elections and in many districts as high as eighty percent of the registered voters had cast their ballots before the polls had been open for two hours." US Army Signal Corps Porter 10 May 1948

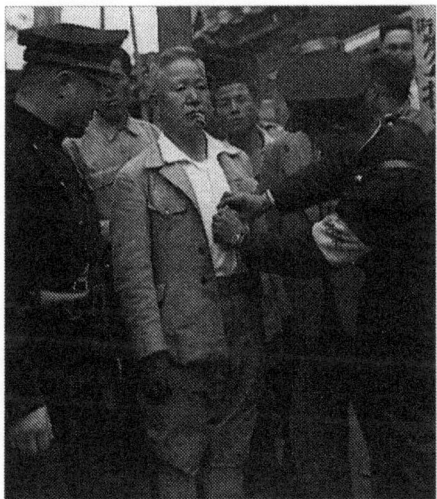

[Left] "Korean Police check superficial wounds suffered by election official when five Communists raiders attacked the polling place where he was working today. . . . Korean policemen closed in killing one of the Raiders and capturing the other four."

[Below] "Five Communist agitators captured in a surprise raid by Korean police this morning. This group, including two women, were apparently bent on destroying every police box in the city of Seoul. . . . "
US Army Signal Corps Evans
10 May 1948 (Both photographs)

"An important feature of the election itself was the employment of deputized civilians to stand near the polls. The . . . sight of five or six burly young men near each polling place, **wearing distinctive armbands and carry8ing clubs,** must have had a quiety effect. . . . " (G-2 Report, 12 May 1948, R.G. 338, Box 32, Folder: History of the USAFIK. N.A.)

The UN "observers" did indeed "observe", but that was about it (Press Statement by UN, 13 May 1948):

> "Some representatives have noted certain violations . . . we have observed the presence of members of National Defense Corps in and around some polling places. . . . Members of youth organizations, sometimes in uniform, were also in and around some voting offcies."

Aside from Sigmund Rhee, the most prominent Right wing leaders in Korea at the time were the other two patriarchs from the old Provisional Government in exile -- Kim Koo and Kim Kiusic. Both of these ancient gentlemen adamantly objected to the separate election in the south of Korea. They were more interested in the unification of Korea than in the ideologoical battle between the US and the Soviets. They foresaw, correctly as it turned out, that separate elections would result in the permanent split of Korea. If the US set up a government in South Korea, it was obvious, they argued, that the Soviets would feel compelled to set one up in the north. That would create yet another huge obstacle to their passionate goal of unification -- which is of course what transpired.

Generals Hodge and Dean carried out the farce, but it was not clear that they understood what US policymakers were contriving with this "free" election. In fact, Hodge was so annoyed at these right-wing "figureheads" whom he himself had imported into Korea from China, that he labeled them as "dupes" and "fellow-travellers" with the Communists. In a very short period of time these representatives of landlords, the wealthy classes and the other status quo elites, had moved from a "right-wing" designation to that of "fellow-travellers."

The other people on the political spectrum, from the moderate and the left, who could have been possible candidates also boycotted the election. Some were either in jail or had gone underground to avoid arrest or assasination. The most prominent leftist figure, Lyuh Woon Hong (Yo Wun Hyung), who had headed the short-lived People's Republic in 1945 which Hodge had dismantled, had been assassinated in 1947 (Rhee being a top suspect).

Consequently the much heralded 1948 "UN supervised" election that played such a large role in US propaganda, was a one-candidate election. Indeed, State Department officials in February, 1948, three months before the electtion, could confidently predict a grand showcase of an election with an almost 100% voter turnout and an almost 100% vote for Rhee's supporters.

During hearings in Congress in 1949 for economic aid to Korea, supporters frequently cited the"free"elections as proof that South Korea was a democratic country worthy of support. When asked if the US Military had taken any position with respect to candidates, the Administration's representatives, including Dr. Johnson who knew better, perhaps with tongue in cheek, answered "absolutely not, the US was neutral."

환영을받으시는 국-지장장 백아미장군 이대통령

There is in the National Archives a photograph which the Archivists frankly describe as a campaign poster for the party supported by the US Government in the 1948 election. Our having fixed this "free"election is not even a question today.The phtograph is a Sigmund Rhee poster with the picture and endorsement of General Douglas MacArthur, the Supreme Allied Commander.

But now, on the ground in 1950 and facing an armed opponent, Dean had no use for these "blood-thirsty" toughs who had helped him out on Cheju-do and during the 1948 elections. As regular soldiers he was let down by them.

It was outside of Taejon that Dean got separated from his men while fighting and began a month-long odyssey in trying to reach his lines again. The hills and villages he traveled through were all of course in South Korea and he had only recently been the Military Governor of this country. The people here were theoretically part of the South Korea which we had come to defend. They should certainly have been friendly to their ally and any soldier from the American side which was in trouble. Yet Dean found barely two people who would help him with food during that month. Quite the opposite, everyone seemed to be an enemy.

He soon was avoiding all the villages because groups of people, armed mostly with bamboo spears, from almost every village he came across began to chase him. Entire villages were organizing themselves to capture him. "I was afraid to go down to the villages." He became particularly angry at the little boys who seemed to be making a party of trying to capture him. He had to run from a number of these groups.

Aside from the risk of being captured, his biggest concern was getting food. Since he was avoiding villages he had to go up into the mountains. But there were other types of problems there.

"Up here in the mountain area I seldom found a house standing – the result of the South Korean government's prewar campaign against the guerrillas, which had consisted largely of burning the house of anyone the constabulary or police even suspected of harboring or cooperating with guerrillas." What Dean does not mention is that the police and constabulary had used the same methods for Dean while he was Military Governor.

He also had to avoid the South Korean men and women who were working on repairing roads and railroads that had been bombed by the Americans.

During the day I could see that the
Communists already had organized the whole
area. Labor had been impressed all over the place.
Men worked in big gangs, mostly on the roads;
and old Japanese or Russian rifles and burp guns
had been given to a few youths in each town.
These kids were swelled up with the importance
of their jobs as home guards and just itching for a
chance to fire those weapons. I couldn't take any
more risks.

He therefore early on learned to travel only at night. Nevertheless he was finally captured somewhere near Yongdam. He had
come across of group of women washing their clothes in the river.
He hid in some nearby bushes so as to avoid detection until they
finished. As they finally left to go back up to their village, he felt
safe again until he saw the woman. She apparently was a straggler
and was only now passing within a few feet of him. She showed
no emotion and her face remained entirely passive while she
passed and followed the rest of the woman up the hill.

He shortly realized that indeed she had noticed him and in
fact had allerted the villagers who were now down on him en
masse. They eventually had little difficulty in rounding him up as
by this time Dean was extremely weak from lack of sleep and lack
of food. After a charade of pretending to be helping him, they
disarmed the General and turned him over to the North Korean
Army, the "Inmun Gun."

If a US pilot went down in Britain during World War II,
anyone finding him would help him in any way possible. After all,
Britain was an ally and we had come to save her. Pilots shot down
in German-occupied France would also feel safe if they were
discovered by villagers. The French people were allies. Even though
under the gun of the Germans they would habitually take great
risks in hiding downed allied pilots. Even those pilots or soldiers

who found themselves stranded in Italy, theoretically an enemy country, could count on the many Italian partisans to assist them if they could.

So why was it that in South Korea, an American General could not find a friend? Could it say that the Koreans in the South had not been happy with the American Occupation? Could it also say that the Koreans in the South felt more of an affinity and a loyalty to their brother-Koreans coming in from the North? What does this make of the Truman claim that we had gone into Korea for the defense of the Koreans? Except for the ruling elite which depended on American support for the maintenance of their power, it seemed that few Koreans were happy to see the Americans.

Dean had come across many work gangs during his travels and he had referred to the"impressed labor." But these people whom Dean was walking among were the very civilians that the Americans were "regrettably" strafing and dropping napalm and delayed-action bombs upon. Recall the Wolfowitz-like explanation in the MacArthur UN Report – "sorry, but we have to do it as they are helping the enemy who are killing our boys."

On the first day of his captivity, he had been put by the local police in the back of a jail and sat there in the background as an observer to the goings-on.

Two North Korean Army paymasters . . . arrived shortly after I was brought in. They came with bundles of won notes and spent the whole night doling out piles of money to the local officials. Each gun-soo (corresponding to town or country officials) evidently had provided a hundred men for work on the roads, and this was the big pay-off. **The thing which struck me was that everybody was happy, and there was no resentment.** These officers were just **two Santa Clauses come to town, and nobody minded at all.** . . . I

never saw the Inmun Gun steal anything outright
. . . . When a soldier wanted a farmer's peach he
always paid for it. He went out and bought it. So
even when the currency turned out to be worth-
less, that individual soldier was not the target of
the farmer's wrath.

Neither the North Korean officials nor even the local officials
had paid the slightest attention to the bedraggled American prisoner sitting in the back of the jail. The next day he was to leave and
his escort on this march "consisted of one Korean youngster, in an
Inmun Gun uniform and armed with a long rifle, and a civilian
carrying a briefcase."

The one thing I noticed especially was
that **my guard was quite a hero to all the small
children we met on the way.** Whenever we
passed a group he would say a phrase to them
and the children would reply in chorus. It
sounded like "Chosen-all," which I assumed must
be some **Communist slogan about a united
Korea, because they all knew it and repeated it
with enthusiasm.** Often the children would start
singing a marching air, which I was to hear thousands of times – the Inmun Gun song.

He arrived with his escort in Chinan and taken to a house
which was being used by the military. In it he noticed that there
were two women in uniform and that the soldiers gathered were
being given what looked to Dean like a course in politics. The
course would be interrupted periodically by a series of rifle shots
and a bell which was used as an air raid signal. Everybody would
run for cover in doorways. "I was moved to a seat in a closet door-
way" for his safety.

Later in the same town he was put into another building and
had to sit in a corner for a long time. During his wait he heard
what sounded like endless military drilling and counting from

upstairs. It appeared that the local youths were being drilled all afternoon by instructors from the Inmun Gun in close order.

> Once again I was struck by the fact that if the people of South Korea resented the northern invaders, they certainly weren't showing it. To me, **the civilian attitude appeared to veer between enthusiasm and passive acceptance.** I saw no sign of resistance or any will to resist.

This was not Vito Marcantonio talking. It was a conservative General who had made every effort to suppress those South Koreans who had wanted radical change in their society. For saying much the same thing on the floor of Congress a month earlier, Marcantonio had been called a Communist Stooge.

The North Korean Army was now well into the south. There was an acceptance by the people. Could we have a more authentic survey than that of an American General given a front seat? There seemed to be no slaughtering or looting or raping. There was little death except what was being rained down indiscriminately on everybody by the American bombers and fighters.

What if we, as Vito Marcantonio and others had argued, had just left them alone? This passage from Dean's biography is the most eloquent and convincing argument against our intervention in Korea. By itself it eliminates the basic rationale which Truman gave for intervening, to save the people of South Korea from slavery, or some variation of that. On the day that the prisoner Dean came to the conclusion that the people of the south were accepting union with their relatives from the north, he must have wondered about the politicians in DC and their game plans that had led to his predicament.

General Dean's **capture** made clear that the people south of the 38th parallel preferred their own people to the Americans, or to the Rhee Government. Dean's **survival** as a POW, his treatment and then his release give the lie to the reputation that the Western

Press has given to the North Koreans. They did not try Dean for war crimes, as they might well have been justified to do merely on his "scorched earth" eradication program on Cheju-do. But they did not even make propaganda use of him, something that surprised Dean as he remembered how the Americans themselves had made propaganda use of captured German and Japanese high officials. If the North Koreans did not immediately kill Dean, whom nobody on our side at that time knew was in their hands, then how much less were they guilty of many of the "atrocities" ascribed to them by the ROK and the American Military? It is evidence of character, even more compelling than alleged eyewitness accounts.

If I stop there, I believe I have demonstrated that Truman had been in serious error and made an unfortunate mistake. But I am afraid that our history is much darker than that. Just think about it for a moment. General Dean could see **in a few days** on the ground in South Korea that the Koreans in the south were welcoming their northern brothers and were happy to be rid of the dictatorial Rhee and his American supporters. But during the previous years of the American Occupation and afterwards, we had an elaborate intelligence operation in Korea -- scores and scores of agents, spies and what not in North Korea, and hundreds of agents in South Korea. These agents were both Americans and Koreans. They were trained to pick up information, to determine the mood and desires of the people, to uncover any support the other side might have.

I am compelled to conclude, therefore, that the American policymakers **knew from before** June 25th what General Dean learned, the hard way, in August. So if we knew that the Koreans south of the 38th would prefer to be unified with the north Koreans, even by force of arms, then why did we interfere and make a wasteland of this small peninsula? If it were not for the stated reason, to defend democracy (as there was no democracy under the dictator Rhee in any event) or save the southerners from slavery, then what was the reason?

Running through the entire American experience with Korea, from before Colonel Dean Rusk drew his line across the heart of Korea, to Stratemeyer's and MacArthur's burning down of cities to "teach them a lesson," one sees variations of this type of motivation -- to terrorize the Soviets and the Chinese. As we saw, there was no military reason to have the Americans take the Japanese surrender in a territory like Korea, bordering Russia – we were just boxing them in ("containment") wherever we could, for our own policitcal reasons. The wasteland we made of Korea was intended to be our burning "line drawn in the sand"-- a meancing threat that consumed at least 4,000,000 Koreans and Chinese. Yet to our chagrin the other side would not succumb, would not heed our rule. It was all a waste in Korea -- and then we repeated it in Vietnam.

This brings us to what the Korean War means to Kim Jong Il and the North Koreans today. If the "liberal" Administration of Harry S. Truman was willing to kill 4,000,000 people for the sake of teaching the Soviets a "lesson," how many millions more would the likes of Bush, Rumsfeld, Cheney, Rice, Wolfowitz and Bolton be willing to sacrifice to advance their evangelical agenda? Would they nuke Korea, all of it? I am afraid the answer is — they certainly would. Thereafter the world would truly be at peace, an American-made peace as not a soul would question the will of the American people to fight for freedom, democracy and liberty.

Continuing on his journey under guard, the POW Dean arrived in the town of Chonju, "just as a flight of our bombers unloaded on one end of the town near the railroad tracks." He was rushed to the protection of an archway in a school in one of the mission compounds. Later when his guard brought him back they went "past a mission hospital, [where] we met townspeople carrying two litters with a woman and child on them. Both were bloody masses."

Why is General Dean reporting this in 1954? Why would an American General tell the world that American bombers killed women and children?

He continued his journey with his guard and "drove through the other end of town, passing a group of houses still smoking from the bombs while civilians poked through the wreckage, looking for other victims. I don't know what the objective of this bombing was, but the railroad, a spur line, was unhurt."

At one point early in his captivity he had been in Pyongyang when they quickly moved out to a village 16 miles north. Later one of his guards, Lee, told him that the reason they moved was "because of increased bombing of Pyongyang, including the use of anti-personnel, air-bursting bombs. . . . Lee told me . . . that the bombers were destroying the city. He was worried about his own family and friends, especially about his father, who was still living there."

Bill Dean in 1954, during the McCarthy high days of red-baiting and fear, wanted people to know certain things. He reports in his book a number of times how our bombers missed their targets, or apparently missed their targets, and hit and killed civilians. He was a witness, and his conscience would not allow him to be silent.

> "During the next three years I had a true worm's eye view of our air war. . . .[But] I could see only what was right in front of me. . . . So when I say that bombers missed or hit an apparent target, or that bombing increased the hatred which one of a thousand Kims had for the United States, no over-all criticism of aerial warfare is meant or implied. . . . The fact that a bomber did miss, or a man did lose his wife and children, must be told, however, in order to understand what happened to the people around me, and how they thought."

It was just a month later and after a lot more devastation, that our delegates in the UN were bragging about their "pin point" bombing which avoided damage to the civilian population.

On his way through the major south Korean town of Taejon, now in Communist hands, Bill Dean observed that "the whole town was full of adults, apparently in labor gangs, moving in the direction of the railroad. There were hundreds and hundreds of men, marching in organized groups but with no weapons except occasional shovels."

In the south Korean town of Suwon which had served as an American and South Korean headquarters for a time and was now occupied by the northerners, he found that it "was badly smashed by air attacks, and two more came while we were there. They both hit at the other end of town, and I was delighted to see air activity stepping up so much."

After the attack they continued north and ran into a long line of waiting vehicles loaded with women and children. "These looked like families, complete with all their household goods, going back to Seoul." These are the people who would be bombed by the Americans continuously until the "U.N. Forces, landing at Inchon, drove the Communists out of burning Seoul for the first time on September 26."

Time went by and two years later he had by then become a celebrity among the North Korean soldiers and was treated as a privileged guest – though still a prisoner. This, however, was after a period of repeated illnesses and a suicide attempt caused by ruthless questioning and privations imposed on the weakened Dean by one of his handlers in particular.

On a trip to Manchuria, the reason for which he could not figure out, they were near the city of Kanggye in February, 1953, when Dean made these observations:

> I had my first real chance to see what the bombers had done while I was listening to them during the last two years. . . . **most of the towns were just rubble or snowy open spaces, where buildings had been**. . . . **The little towns,**

once full of people, were unoccupied shells. The villagers lived in entirely new temporary villages, hidden in canyons or in such positions that only a major bombing effort could reach them.

These people had been hurt by bombing and still were being hurt by it, but it looked to me as if their countermeasures were improving faster than our measures of destruction. . . . .

The town of **Huichon** amazed me. The city I'd seen before – two-storied buildings, a prominent main street – **wasn't there any more**. . . . **What few people remained lived in dugouts**, and what had been a city was snow-covered fields.

This is an example of a "dugout." It was called a wummakjip. It is half-buried underground which afforded some protection against bombs and would have been difficult to see from the air.

Hanoak, Photo by Suh, Jai-Sik

This does not sound like a man who hated his captors or the people of Korea. It does not sound like someone who enjoyed seeing the damage done by his country's bombs. His book is interspersed with praise for the bombing and his joy at seeing aircraft coming over to do their destruction – but they read as pro-forma, obligatory sentences that had to be uttered in the America of 1954. One feels real emotion, however, when he tells of the guards who would quietly disclose to him the shocking news that they had lost their wives and children or parents in a bombing by the Americans of their village or town.

In the moments he had to wait for the final prisoner exchange he tells us about all the people who helped him while he was a prisoner, particularly the guards who both guarded him and took care of him. This is a different Dean than the Military Governor of the Occupation.

> "A good many things happened to me [during his captivity], but nothing more important than my opportunity to know these people as I never could have done in a lifetime as an uncaptured general. It may almost have been worth the three years."

When I hear the phrase "Proud to be An American," so often bantered about in these post-9/11 days, I think of these Generals, Orlando Ward and the post POW William Dean.

CHAPTER XIV

THE ATOMIC BOMB IN KOREA

Now we come to the Atomic Bomb. Kim Jong Il, the present leader of North Korea, has to ask himself whether the United States would drop the Bomb on his country. If the American destruction of Korea during the Korean War is any guideline, the answer would have to be yes – particularly with the "Strike First" crowd now in control of American policy.

The United States did not use the Atomic Bomb in Korea, though it had just dropped two on Japan at the end of the World War II. The horror pictures of devastated Hiroshima and Nagasaki were still fresh in people's minds. The Truman Administration tried to make the most of that during the first few Post WWII years

when it had an atomic monopoly. Much of the American diplo-
macy after Truman got into office was clumsily based on explicit or
implicit threats by the Americans of using the A-Bomb. We effectively rejected sharing of the bomb's secrets with our allies, except
for limited cooperation with Britain. But Russia, also an ally in
World War II, was deliberately frozen out – with the consequent
festering of paranoia on the part of Stalin. Another lost opportunity
for Truman, or for whatever power elite was running the country.

We were aware at that time not only of the immediate damage
that an atomic explosion could create, but we were also learning
about the long term effects of atomic radiation. Even before the
war in Korea started, there had been discussions about these
aftereffects, primarily what was unknown about them. Under the
caption: ATOMIC BLINDNESS, the Washington Post's editors, after
commenting on the higher percentage of cataracts among the
Japanese survivors, noted "the steadily growing fear that the
residual effects of atomic bombardment may be even more terrible
than the immediate effects. One of the great anxieties is the possible hereditary consequences of radioactivity . . . ." (June 22, 1950).

In 1949 the Truman Administration learned that it no longer
held a monopoly, that Russia had exploded an atomic bomb. Its
response was to take destruction to the next level, development of
the hydrogen bomb – a vastly more destructive weapon.

During the Korean War, Truman had explored every option of
using the Bomb, and publicly threatened the Koreans and the
Chinese with its use. In the month after the Chinese came into the
war and started to drive, it seemed almost effortlessly, the Americans down the peninsula, the American Press began openly discussing the pros and cons of totally evacuating the American
troops from Korea.

Stratemeyer was participating in preparing plans for an evacuation by air and sea (Stratemeyer, Monday, December 4 and 5,
1950). General Partridge was convinced that they would have to

retreat back down to Pusan and then *"evacuation through Pusan will be forced upon us"* (Stratemeyer, Saturday, January 6, 1951).

Senator Harry F. Byrd stated that "it had been 'clearly obvious' for two weeks that American troops should be withdrawn from Korea because no reinforcements were available from any source. . . . 'In simple language we are outnumbered and defeated in Korea. . . . the military reverses . . . have brought about national peril in a degree which we have never faced before in our history'" (New York Times, December 17, 1950). A Washington Post article by John G. Norris on the issue was headlined "EVACUATION SEEN AS DIFFICULT; FEW SUITABLE PORTS AVAILABLE" (December 5, 1950). The Post's editors also commented that "the situation is desperate . . . the cream of our Army is in Korea. We, and the non-Communist world, could ill afford to lose it or see it hacked to pieces" (December 5, 1950). In somewhat the same vein but a even more dramatical was the New York Times military expert Hanson W. Baldwin with one of his articles captioned : **"Western Civilization Faces Destruction if Threat From East is Not Met Boldly"** (December 1, 1950).

In this atmosphere Truman indeed responded "boldly" to a

question at a press conference about using the ultimate weapon, the atomic bomb, with language that was quickly interpreted to mean that he had already given MacArthur authority to decide when to use the atomic bomb. As worldwide panic immediately erupted, the White House rushed out a clarification statement -- that it would be the President who will decide on using the bomb, and only as a final measure. The Daily News [New York] "TRUMAN PUTS BOMB USE AS 'LAST RESORT' " reported: "President Truman today confirmed reports that use of the atom bomb in Korea has been considered but in a special statement made it clear that he would authorize its delivery only as a last resort."

Even with that qualification, however, world leaders reacted sharply. As the editors of the New York Times remarked: "the very mention of the atom bomb sent an electric shock around the world. . . [T]he world went through a veritable convulsion on Thursday at the mention of the possible use of the atomic bomb, and that is why Mr. Atlee [British Prime Minister] is coming here" (December 2, 1950).

Reporting on the reaction in India, a dispatch stated: "Certainly the revulsion of feeling in this country [India] against any suggestion of using the atom bomb in Asia is great, and has caused an intensification of the latent anti-American sentiment among politically conscious people" (Times [London], December 4, 1950). Even our allies in Europe were startled and quickly unified behind British Prime Minister Atlee's race to urge caution on Truman. Atlee rushed the next day to Washington. The Australian Foreign Minister, Spencer, thought that since it was United Nations' forces fighting in Korea, including Australian troops, that any resort to the atomic bomb should be a United Nations decision and not just a unilateral American decision (Times [London], December 1, 1950).

That Truman intended his comments to be a serious threat, and that he would carry it out at any time by himself, became clear during his talks with Atlee during the next few days. Truman steadfastly refused to promise in any way that he would first obtain European concurrence before using atomic bombs in Korea or

China. Nor would he agree even to consult with his allies before-hand. He did hope, he told Atlee, however, that he would not have to use the bomb and promised the British Prime Minister that he would do his best to keep his allies informed. The British were not happy with this, but they tried to put the best face on it (Times [London], December 12 and 13, 1950)

Two days after Truman's public threat to use the A-Bomb, Army Chief of Staff, General J. Lawton Collins, took off on a much publicized trip to speak to MacArthur in the Far East. The Press speculated that discussions would include possible evacuation of American troops from Korea and the use of the atomic bomb. With Collins, significantly, traveled Major General Charles P. Cabell, director of Intelligence for the Air Force and Vice Admiral F. S. Lowe, the Deputy Chief of Naval Operation for logistics. General Stratemeyer's cryptic diary entries around this time give tantalizing clues, but no full explanation, as to American plans to use atomic bombs, and indeed biological and chemical weapons as well.

On December 1st Air Force Chief of Staff Vandenberg sent an "EYES ONLY" to Stratemeyer which quoted a news release from Washington about President Truman's threat to use the atomic bomb. Immediately upon receipt of this news both MacArthur and Stratemeyer jumped into action.

Stratemeyer, Friday, 1 December, 1950:

> General MacArthur at 1400 hours today, in his office, stated that in a war with Communist China and if he was given the use of the atomic weapon, his targets in order of priority would be: ANTUNG, MUKDEN, PEIPING, TIENTSIN, SHANGHAI AND NANKING. [Capitalization in the original] That if we get in the big one [war with Russia], his targets would be VLADIVOSTOK, KHABAROVSK, KIRIN, and a

fourth one which I believe was KUYVYSHIEVKA.

Later that day Stratemeyer send a TOP SECRET radio to Air Force General Twining, Chief of Operations:

> Dr. Ellis A. Johnson, Director ORO, DA [Operations Research Office, Department of the Army] has proposed to provide GHQ [MacArthur] within next week a critical evaluation of the possible use and effectiveness of atomic bombs in close support of ground forces in Korea. . . . It is understood that ORO analysts have been working on this project since September. . . .

Stratemeyer, Saturday, 2 December, 1950:

> Reached the office this AM and was handed Twining's reply: — **"the matter raised in your [message] will be discussed with you by Gen. Cabell** who will arrive your hqs in the next 2 or 3 days for a visit."

Twining obviously did not want to put in writing any discussion of the a-bomb. The messages will be oral and delivered by the head of Air Force Intelligence, General Cabell.

Stratemeyer, Monday, 4 December, 1950:

> General Cabell with General Collins and Admiral F.S. Lowe arrived this AM . . . Was called to General MacArthur's office with Cabell to hear a discussion. . . . **There were other subject matters discussed that**

were of such a high classification that I dare not even put them in this document.

Stratemeyer, Thursday, 7 December, 1950:

Attended conference in General MacArthur's conference room; present beside himself were Generals Collins, Hickey, Wright, Whitney, Willoughby, Cabell and myself; Admirals Joy and Lowe. . . . General Collins then posed this question — with the use of your present force, and the potential that might be made available, and **a possible recommended use of the A bomb** — what would you do? . . .

The British military staff that was assigned to MacArthur's headquarters must have picked up the American excitement about the possible use of the A-Bomb. Stratemeyer gives us their views in his diary. *Saturday, 9 December 1950:*

1500 hours, [British] Air Vice Marshal Bouchier gave me the following information . . . . British Chiefs of Staff view is that if the atom bomb was used in Korea it would not be effective in holding up Chinese advance — but make the situation more desperate by inevitably bringing the Soviet Air Force into the war. The 'A' bomb is our ultimate weapon and we should surely keep it in reserve as a deterrent, or for use in event of Russia launching a third world war. . . .

The General ended his comments for that Saturday: "This was a tough day."

Over a month later, utilization of the A-Bomb in Korea and China seemed still to be under serious consideration.

Stratemeyer, Tuesday, 30 January, 1951:

> "At 0800 hours I was briefed by General Banfill and Colonel Gould on the study that was sent to the Director of Intelligence, Washington, D.C., **on the A bomb targets in the Far East.** Every target selected by CINCFE and those selected by us were reviewed and complete data on each was submitted with our recommended list of targets."

The Chinese brushed off Truman's A-Bomb announcement as "saber rattling threats" that would not affect Chinese actions. The Russians, on the other hand, began warning their people about the possibility of a general war with the United States.

The fears about the long-term effects on mankind, while known, however, do not seem to have played any role in American strategic thinking during the Korean War. The snatches of comments one catches among the Generals during the War give no hint of that concern – the central question was whether the A-Bomb would help "win" the war. There certainly had been no hesitancy about mass killing of the civilian population. As LeMay and O'Donnell readily acknowledged, they killed as many people using conventional explosives as they would have by using anything else. The answer as to why the A-Bomb itself was not used in Korea or China during the Korean war is contained in the desperate arguments between the Joint Chiefs of Staff and MacArthur on this issue and their testimony in Congress.

From this testimony, certain of the minutes of the Joint Chiefs of Staff where the matter was discussed and the diary of General Stratemeyer, it is evident that there was no moral compunction about its use. The only issues were: 1) Would it be effective in winning the war? 2) Would Russia retaliate and 3) Could we win this World War III?

As much as they studied the subject, and the records indicate that it was being considered from the very beginning, the conclusion always was that the A-Bomb in Korea would not be an effective weapon. In 1950 the 300 atomic bombs held by the United States were blockbusters with a great deal of radioactive fallout. Their use in the confined area of Korea would endanger as many American soldiers as enemy soldiers. This simple mathematical fact-on-the-ground, however, did not keep some of the rambunctious Generals and politicians from constantly suggesting its use.

But even of greater concern to serious US policymakers, was whether its use in Korea or in China might trigger a retaliatory attack by Russia. Were Russia to decide that American use of the Atomic Bomb in Korea or China meant World War III and that it had to retaliate before being extinguished, it had options which no power in the West could prevent. First, and most easily, it could overrun our Allies in Western Europe with its vast armies stationed in East Europe. But more ominously for our side, our Generals could not guarantee that the Sovietw could not deliver an Atomic Bomb to the United States from their relatively small stockpile, estimated at about 30 at the time. Finally, the US simply did not have enough atomic bombs and airplanes to eliminate <u>both</u> China and Russia at the same time, so one of them might be able to survive the United States. In order words, the Joint Chiefs of Staff in 1951 were concerned that in any all-out World War III with China and Russia, that we might lose.

Hoyt S. Vandenberg, the Air Force Chief of Staff, testified as much before Congress during the hearings in 1951 on MacArthur's ouster:

> The fact is that the United State is
> operating a shoestring air force in view of its
> global responsibilities . . . we cannot afford to
> peck at the periphery. . . . **While we can lay the**

countryside waste, as well as the principal cities of China, we cannot do both. . . .

"Gen. Hoyt S. Vandenberg, US Air Force Chief of Staff, toured advanced air bases [in Korea]. . . . [l. to r.] Jim Becker, AP war correspondent, Major Thomas D. Robertson, Lt. Col. Jack Dale, 35tn Fighter Intercepter Group Commander, Gen Vandenberg, Richard Cresswell, CO of a Royal Australian squadron and Lt. James F. Kirkendall, CO of a 35th squadron. January, 1951 USAF

Vandenberg's biographer, Phillip S. Meilinger (Hoyt S. Vandenberg: The Life of a General, Air Force History and Museums Program), tells us that the portion of Vandenberg's testimony deleted by the censors stated that **80** percent of the USAF's tactical strength and **25** percent of her strategic forces were already tied up in Korea. An expansion of the war, in view of the known enormous Soviet air strength in the Far East which as yet had not stirred, would make the Air Force "extremely hard pressed." In other words, while we had more A-Bombs, the Soviets had enough air power to eventually get around our defenses and into the US. The realization that we might lose a war with Russia and China began to sink into even the densest heads on Capital Hill. Thereafter the outrage over MacArthur's firing began to be muted and then faded entirely, except for fringe elements for whom neither reason nor common sense played any role.

This testimony may have been given in secret, but it was widely understood that we could not win a war against both China and Russia. General Omar Bradley, Chief of the Joint Chiefs of Staff, in arguing for extraordinary sums to rearm the United States and its allies, had "bluntly emphasized the 'bruising and shocking fact' that as a result of our commitment in the Korean conflict this country is now without an adequate margin of military strength to meet a general enemy attack, much less defend our allies" (Editorial, Mr. TRUMAN AND THE CRISIS, New York Times, December 15, 1950).

However, by 1953, again according to Vandenberg's biographer, Meilinger, the Chiefs seem to have changed their minds. President Eisenhower, pressing for an end to the armistice stalemate, asked the Joint Chiefs to revisit the subject of the Atomic bomb's use. While reluctant, they now recommended that an attack could be successful if "undertaken so as to obtain maximum surprise and maximum impact on the enemy."

Fortunately, shortly thereafter there was movement by the Chinese at the conference table and an Armistice was signed. Some historians attribute the movement at the negotiations by the Chinese as resulting from the threat to use the A-Bomb that the Eisenhower Administration had delivered in 1953. That is difficult to buy since Truman had made the same threat, even more aggressively, in December of 1950 without any effect on the Chinese. The Chinese had factored in American employment of the A-Bomb and still had determined that the defense of their homeland against the invaders warranted the risk, and even the damage, that American atomic bombs could inflict.

As for the use of chemical and biological weapons in Korea, I cannot find anything definitive among the diaries, though I would not expect to find anything there. The Chinese and North Koreans at the time had accused the US of employing chemical and biological weapons, but nothing definitive has turned up in the Archives. And no veteran has suggested that such was used. After 50 years, this absence of evidence should be enough to exclude the probability of their having been employed. That they were considered is clear from the diaries, but whether they were used is another issue.

Stratemeyer, Thursday 22 March 1951:

> "In Colonel Zimmerman's [Don Z. Zimmerman, Director, Plans and Policy, FEAF] report as a result of his trip to Washington . . . two items disturbed me: . . . and (2) **they (USAF) desired a request** from FEAF for the use of **chemicals and biologicals** in the Korean war."

General Stratemeyer seems here to be saying that the Air Force planners in the US wanted the Far East Commanders to request chemical and biological weapons. The weapons apparently were already in stockpiles. Washington wanted the FEAF Command to ask that they be delivered for application. Stratemeyer is not happy with this, but does not explain why. No mention again of this subject appears in Stratemeyer's diary.

George Stratemeyer

Earle Partridge

General Partridge's diary does not refer to employing chemical and biological weapons, except for napalm and other incendiaries. Partridge, however, was a lot more circumspect about what he put into his diary. Though there is one interesting discussion he relates about trying to destroy the Korean rice corps.

Partridge, Saturday 3 March 1951:

> This morning, Doctor Cohen came in response to my request for an Operations Analyst. While he is a statistician, and on his way up to Kimpo to analyze the bomber damage there, I took advantage of his presence to pitch him a problem regarding the destruction of rice supplies. We currently locating rice in piles which are stacked in light straw bags without any cover from the elements other than the bags themselves. It seems to me that there should be some **way of insuring that this can be made inedible.** Presently, we are attacking it with Napalm in an effort to burn up the stacks themselves. We are not sure that this method is effective and I asked that the Operational Analysis study the problem.
>
> In passing, I mentioned that there are now available in the States **many chemicals which might be utilized for spraying rice crops** to discourage the growth of the rice while still in the paddies. He mentioned the use of 24D weed killer as an example of the type chemical now coming available. We have no idea how much would be required per square mile nor would be strictly exploratory.

Partridge does not mention this subject again in his diary.

A FINAL WORD

I believe the lesson which the US has given the nations of the world is that if you do not want this bully to beat you up, you had better have a stick you could poke in its eye.

At the present time the North Koreans are seeking assurances from the US that the US would not attack it. The US, in response, has taken the position -- dismantle first.

This disingenuous response may have been credible at one time. But not after Iraq. Iraq dismantled, then we attacked. First there were ten years of US-led sanctions and peripheral bombing that crippled its economy and eroded its infrastructure; then there was the UN supervised destruction of its "Weapons of Mass Destruction" and, once disarmed, invasion by the US. Understandably, North Korea does not wish to play the role of Little Red Riding Hood to the US's Big Bad Wolf.

Marcantonio represented East Harlem from 1935 to 1950, except for the years 1937 and 1938. He always ran as the candidate of the American Labor Party, a number of times also as the Republican or Fusion candidate, and twice (1942 and 1944) he was the candidate for the three major parties in his district: ALP, Republican and Democratic. The original base of his support was the Italian immigrant voters in East Harlem, then they were joined by Puerto Ricans and Blacks. He represented the poor and the oppressed from the beginning to the end of his career.

His politics were always radical. During the Depression he did not want just minimum wage jobs, he wanted universal employment with decent living wages. In 1935 he did not just want Washington DC desegregated, he wanted the government and all US industry to hire people without discrimination as to race, creed or national origin. He did not just want autonomy for the Puerto Ricans, he wanted the island to be an independent nation. He did not just want the Communist Party to be legal, but he wanted it to have every right and privilege that any other party has in our political system. He was not a moderate. He was not a liberal. It was not his kind that Martin Luther King, Jr. was berating from his Birmingham jail cell in 1963 when he wrote:

> I have almost reached the regrettable
> conclusion that the Negro's great stumbling block
> in his stride toward freedom is not the White
> Citizen's Councilor or the Ku Klux Klanner, but
> the white moderate.

Marcantonio's opponents tried everything to get rid of him. In 1944 they gerrymanded his district to include more well-to-do and a large number of conservative German and Irish voters down the East Side to 59th Street, only to have him enter into and win the primaries of all the three parties. Then they passed a law in Albany directed just against him, prohibiting a person from running in the primary of a party without that party leadership's prior approval. But he kept winning anyway, as his devotion to his constituents and his endless hours of work for them were repaid at the ballot box each election day.

In 1950, just before the start of the Korean War, the Republican and Democratic leaders agreed to join forces and field only one candidate against him. Meanwhile the more conservative labor leaders had broken away from the American Labor Party and established the "Liberal" party. That break-away "anti-communist" labor party also agreed to support the one candidate being fielded by the Republicans and Democrats. The numbers in his district now were against him. But he ran anyway.

It did not help that he was the lone *vocal* dissenter that summer on the Korean War, nor that he took to the streets to oppose the war. Nor did it help that just before the November election some Puerto Rican extremists tried to shoot Truman in an outlandishly hopeless assassination attempt. Marcantonio had been closely linked in the public mind with the Nationalists and their cause of Puerto Rican independence. His enemies made the most of the guilt-by-association smear. The local papers promptly reprinted photos from 15 years earlier when he had gone to Puerto Rico to help defend the nationalist leader, Dr. Pedro Albizu Campos. Campos, the President of the Nationalist Party, had been convicted essentially for advocating the independence of Puerto Rico and subsequently served seven years in jail for his beliefs.

Every mainstream paper in New York, and in fact papers across the country, including the Washington Post, was calling for Marcantonio's head. The New York Times, I believe for the first and last time in its history, even went so far as to limit its congressional ballot recommendations that November to just one race, Marcantonio's. The Times strongly advocated the candidacy of the nonentity fielded by the three other parties in his District, whoever he was. The only common thread in all of this was the passion to defeat Marcantonio.

Volumes could be written about why this was so. I think I have some clues as to why this could have happened in 1950. Marcantonio was born at the beginning of the Twentieth Century, as were my mother and father. I heard stories from them that Marcantonio must also have experienced. He was more likely to have read something like Pietro di Donato's Christ in Concrete, than Harry Potter. An immigrant Italian family, a fierce struggle just to live in a world of unfettered capitalism, dangerous working conditions that sometimes killed or crippled the family breadwinner, bigotry and discrimination against immigrants, no help from the government, massive and sudden layoffs, no safety net for the worker, endless hours and meager wages, the pointlessness of World War I that only enriched bankers and armament makers while it killed a generation of men in Europe, the Palmer raids,

Sacco and Vanzetti, the lynchings, the Depression. . . .

But what to me seems extraordinary,however, is that Marcantonio's perspective or worldview, for a man who was born, lived and died within the same few blocks in East Harlem, became universal early in his life. His passion for what was fair and just embraced every person that he came across. His vision for what could be done in America for the masses of people was remarkably ambitious -- yet he always remembered that a family needed first to eat.

I raise all this here only to highlight how wrong public opinion could be, at least the dominant public opinion as expressed in the media and by political leaders. He never felt that the **real** people were against him. He knew that the causes that he undertook so relentlessly were supported and sustained by millions in America who did not have a voice. He was their voice. Reading the correspondence among his papers in the New York Public Library discloses that even in some of the darkest days, like the beginning of the Korean War and his fierce public opposition to it, people across the nation beseeched him to continue to speak out for them.

And speak out he did until literally the last minute of that Congressional Session in which he was a lame duck. We can catch a glimpse of the extraordinary measure of the man in two incidents during his last days in Congress. Both struck chords he had been sounding since his arrival in Washington in the mid-thirties.

On December 15, 1950 he moved to amend a Korean War military appropriations bill to add the following provision:

THAT NONE OF THE FUNDS APPROPRIATED IN THIS ACT SHALL BE PAID TO ANY PERSON, PARTNERSHIP, FIRM, OR CORPORATION WHICH DENIES EQUALITY IN EMPLOYMENT BECAUSE OF RACE, COLOR, OR CREED.

This was his famous "Harlem Rider" that he and, later upon his arrival in Congress, Adam Clayton Powell, for a number of years would attempt to attach to various bills. It was a slow educational process, not a Don Quixote gesture. He had been trying from his first day in office in 1935 to generate support for a national policy of non-discrimination in employment. He actually had some success during the extraordinary days of World War II with the Fair Employment Practices Commission and Executive Orders of FDR covering the defense industry. But things had gone backwards with the end of the War. By this motion he was telling his colleagues: "You talk about rescuing the 'little brown people' in the Orient when you are still sending segregated military forces to Korea and you won't give decent jobs to whole segments of our population just because of who they are." His motion, as expected,was defeated, 219 to 1. He had agreed with the leadership not to use the procedural weapons he had long since mastered to delay the bill, provided they agreed to take a recorded vote. To the final countout, he insisted that posterity be able to read the names of these people who were doing the wrong thing.

The Marcantonio "Harlem Amendment" thereafter went into eclipse as its supporters were silenced during the ensuing days of McCarthism. Indeed, some "liberals" like Arthur Schlessinger, Jr., unwilling to admit that they had abandoned the oppressed, gave themselves cover during those difficult days by attacking people like Marcantonio. These "liberals" were the one-careful-step-at-a time type that King later berated from his jail cell. Schlessinger even made a profession of writing eloquent books sporting new philosophies to rationalize what was essentially the cowardice of these anti-communist liberals.

The second incident I wanted to highlight occurred on the very last day of that Congress, itself a rare New Year's day session on January 1, 1951. It was during the most grim period of the Korean War. The leadership of the departing Congress was trying to get unanimous approval for a number of items to clean up its business. The most important was an amendment to the War Powers Act which would allow for the renegotiation of government contracts for the purchase of armaments and the like for the Korean War. Many companies had been complaining that the price of raw goods had gone up since they signed contracts with the government to produce the military clothing, the airplanes, the tanks, the armaments, and all the other products necessary for the war effort. Many now threatened bankruptcy and the consequent disruption of war production if they were not allowed to renegotiate the contracts and increase the prices. Industry's friends in Congress quickly got an emergency renegotiation bill, that is, a bill to raise the cost of the contracts, and Congress was ready to pass it unanimously.

But Marcantonio got up and objected.

He did not want to thwart the will of the Congress, he said, nor delay the production of goods necessary for the war, as much as he opposed the war. But he was not going to sit still while some people took advantage of the war to gouge on indecent profits.

> "I believe this bill is in the interest of
> increasing war profiteering and the men in Korea
> are being used as an excuse for war profiteering."

He moved to amend the bill so that all requests for renegotiation of prices had to be reviewed by the Comptroller General, an independent and trusted accounting arm of the Government, and not just by an official in the Defense Department's procuring office. This fundamental review procedure, which was a basic safeguard to all government contracts, should not be skipped by merely calling the situation an "emergency." The Comptroller had the resources and the know-how, Marcantonio argued, so the renegotiation process would not be delayed.

> "I think every Member of this House,
> will agree that the best guaranty against mulcting
> the Government and the people of these United
> States in using this emergency for war profiteer-
> ing in this connection would be simply to add

these words: 'Subject to the approval of the Comptroller General.'"

Marcantonio's request was too simple and overwhelmingly compelling. No one could get up and argue against it.

Emanuel Celler, the Brooklyn Congressman who was an old friend of Marcantonio's and who, until that year, had always run on Marcantonio's American Labor Party line in addition to the Democratic line, was handling the bill on the House floor. But Celler had to be wary, as his friend was now radioactive. He only reluctantly agreed to add Marcantonio's words to the Bill, since even the Virginian sponsor of the Bill himself was not objecting. But just as the House was about to approve Marcantonio's amendment requiring Comptroller General review of all renegotiations, the Speaker, Sam Rayburn, intervened and put the Bill aside, saying he would take it up tomorrow – with the new Congress, that is, without Marcantonio.

And so it went.

"I tell you that the issue in China, in Asia, in Korea and in Vietnam is the right of these peoples to self-determination, to a government of their own, to independence and national unity."

Congressman Vito Marcantonio, June 27, 1950

"I'll never forget the sight . . . when an old Korean man carried in on his back a very old Korean woman whose right hand had been completely blown off. They were quiet, no fear was on their faces, and the fortitude of these people, to me, is amazing."

General George Stratemeyer, March 24, 1951

"The little towns, once full of people, were unoccupied shells. The villagers lived in entirely new temporary villages, hidden in canyons . . . .

"These people had been hurt by bombing and still were being hurt by it, but it looked to me as if their countermeasures were improving faster than our measures of destruction."

General William Dean, 1954

Wonsan, North Korea
November 2, 1950
US Navy Photo
F. Kazukaitis

LIBERATING KOREA ?

Index

Symbols

LIBERATING KOREA?

L

Lardner, Ring 59
Lawrence, H. W. 104
LeMay, Curtis 147 - 148, 280
Lee Bum Suk 255
Lemke, William 33
"Liberation" vi, 50, 54, 92
Lodge, John 12 - 13, 17
Lodge, Jr., Henry Cabot 52
Lowe 277
Lyuh Woon Hong 27, 260

M

MacArthur 2–3, 4, 41, 45, 95, 124, 150, 168, 203, 208, 211, 261, 281
MacNamara v
Madison Square Garden 59

Malik, Jacob 193–195, 205
Manchuria 90, 92, 176
Mansfield 240
Mao 23, 29, 31
Marcantonio, Vito 8, 11, 25, 35, 51, 52–54, 58, 94, 168, 191, 266, 288
Martin 197
"Mass Bombing" 160, 177
McCarthism 291
McCarthy, Joseph R. 50, 269
Merrill, John 235
MIG ALLEY 85, 112
MIG-15 85
MIN BO DAN 244
Mirim-ni 95
MOKPO 73
Mokpo 103, 113
Muccio 30, 251
Muccio, John 108
Mukden 277
Mustang 103

N

Nagasaki 193, 197
Naktong 138
Naktong River 105, 107, 138
Namwon 102
Nanking 277

www.ingramcontent.com/pod-product-compliance
Lightning Source LLC
Chambersburg PA
CBHW021043090426
42738CB00006B/166